MW01517673

CHALLENGING MODERNISM

250101
#109.00

Challenging Modernism
New readings in literature and culture, 1914–45

Edited by
STELLA DEEN
State University of New York, New Paltz

ASHGATE

Published by
Ashgate Publishing Limited
Gower House
Croft Road
Aldershot
Hampshire GU11 3HR
England

Ashgate Publishing Company
131 Main Street
Burlington, VT 05401-5600, USA

Ashgate website: http//www.ashgate.com

British Library Cataloguing in Publication Data
Challenging modernism : new readings in literature and
    culture, 1914-45
    1.English literature - 20th century - history and criticism
    2.Modernism (Literature)
    I.Deen, Stella
    820.9'112'09041

Library of Congress Cataloging in Publication Data
Challenging modernism : new readings in literature and culture, 1914-45 / edited by Stella Deen
    p. cm.
    Includes bibliographical references and index.
    ISBN 0-7546-0670-8
    1. English literature--20th century--History and criticism. 2. Modernism (Literature)--Great Britain. 3. Feminism and literature--Great Britain--History--20th century. 4. Women and literature--Great Britain--History--20th century. 5. Great Britain--Civilization--20th century. 6. Sex role in literature. I. Deen, Stella 1960-
PR478.M6 C465 2002
820.9'00912--dc21

2002022347

ISBN 0 7546 0670 8

Printed and bound in Great Britain by MPG Books Ltd, Bodmin, Cornwall

Contents

Acknowledgments   vii
List of Contributors   ix

INTRODUCTION

Rereading the Space Between
Stella Deen   3

PART I—CROSSING THE BORDERS OF SELF AND OTHER

1   Lilied Tongues and Yellow Claws: The Invention of
    London's Chinatown, 1915-45
    Shannon Case   17

2   *Over the Frontier* and into the Darkness with Stevie Smith:
    War, Gender, and Identity
    Diana Austin   35

3   Citizenship in the Salon: The Public Private War of
    Violet Hunt
    Debra Rae Cohen   55

PART II—THERE *IS* A STORY THERE: LITERARY FORMS
OF PROTEST

4   A Feminine Conspiracy: Contraception, the New Woman, and
    Empire in Rosamond Lehmann's *The Weather in the Streets*
    Andrea Lewis   81

5   "There is No Ordinary Life": Privacy and Domesticity in E.H.
    Young's *Celia* and Elizabeth Bowen's *The Death of the Heart*
    Stella Deen   97

6   *There's No Story There*: Inez Holden's Lost War Literature
     Kristin Bluemel   115

PART III—REVISITING MODERNISTS

7   The Politics of Modernism in Kay Boyle's *Death of a Man*
     Phoebe Stein Davis   137

8   Eating the Maid: Leonora Carrington's "The Debutante"
     Natalya Lusty   163

9   T.S. Eliot in the "Journalistic Struggle"
     Patrick Collier   187

     Index   213

Acknowledgments

I am grateful to the following publishers and copyright holders for their permission to reproduce material from their publications in this volume: Fort Hays State University, for permission to reprint "Lilied Tongues and Yellow Claws: The Invention of London's Chinatown, 1915-1945," which first appeared in *Precursors and Aftermaths: Literature in English 1914-1945* 1:1 (2000); the James MacGibbon Estate, for material from *Over the Frontier*, by Stevie Smith (London: Virago, 1980, 1989); New Directions Publishing Corporation, for material from *Death of a Man*, by Kay Boyle, copyright © 1936, 1989.

I would also like to thank Jason Taylor for preparation of the camera-ready copy of the volume.

List of Contributors

Diana Austin is Professor of twentieth-century British literature at the University of New Brunswick in Fredericton, Canada. Her research and teaching focus on World War I and gender/genre issues.

Kristin Bluemel is Associate Professor of English at Monmouth University in New Jersey. She is the author of *Experimenting on the Borders of Modernism: Dorothy Richardson's Pilgrimage*. Her current research is on the wartime writing and politics of George Orwell, Stevie Smith, Inez Holden, and Mulk Raj Anand.

Shannon Case is a Ph.D. candidate in English at the University of Virginia. She is finishing a dissertation called *Tramping Writers, Writing Tramps: Literary Vagrancy in England, 1860-1940*.

Debra Rae Cohen is Visiting Assistant Professor of English at the University of Arkansas. She has published on women's home front fiction of the Great War and the literature of the interwar period. Her book *Remapping the Home Front: Locating Citizenship in British Women's Great War Fiction* is forthcoming from Northeastern University Press.

Patrick Collier is an Assistant Professor at Ball State University, where he teaches nineteenth- and twentieth-century British literature and culture. He is working on a book about the relationship between modernist literature and the popular press, and has published several articles on literature and journalism.

Phoebe Stein Davis received her Ph.D. in American Literature from Loyola University in Chicago. She works as the Communications Coordinator for the Illinois Humanities Council and teaches at the Newberry Library. She has published on Gertrude Stein's World War II writings and on *The Autobiography of Alice B. Toklas*. She is currently working on a book about Gertrude Stein and American culture.

Stella Deen is Associate Professor of English at the State University of New York, New Paltz. She has published on Enid Bagnold and on E.H. Young, and is currently writing a book on E.H. Young and domestic modernity.

Andrea Lewis is Instructor of Writing at the University of Colorado at Boulder. Her research examines gender and imperialism in twentieth-century British and Commonwealth literatures.

Natalya Lusty is completing her dissertation on surrealism, feminism and psychoanalysis in the Department of Gender Studies at the University of Sydney.

Introduction

Rereading the Space Between
Stella Deen

Early twentieth-century studies are enjoying an enormous resurgence of scholarly interest; interest that can be gauged by a glance at three organizations recently formed to study the period: *The International Review of Modernism*, whose first issue appeared in the autumn of 1997; *The Space Between*, a society for the study of literature and culture between the wars; and the *Modernist Studies Association*, convening nearly 450 scholars at its first conference in the Fall of 1999. As Scott Heller noted in *The Chronicle of Higher Education* after this inaugural conference, "it [is] clear that many scholars are less interested in analyzing modernism as a literary movement than in conducting a cultural study of modernity writ large" (A22).

With the title of her 1944 novel, *There's No Story There*, Inez Holden captured and critiqued contemporary assumptions that there were only a few appropriate novelistic subjects and protagonists. An apt subtitle for *Challenging Modernism* might be "There *Is* a Story There": more than fifty years later, these essays grow out of a literary-critical atmosphere characterized by renovation of twentieth-century studies. In this more open climate there is gathering consensus that only a fuller spectrum of early twentieth-century literature can claim to illuminate its time and that judgment of what constitutes important or interesting literature ought to include analysis of the cultural and political dimensions of imaginative literature.

The essays gathered in *Challenging Modernism* focus on the space between and enfolding the two world wars, a period that has yet to be fully charted. Europe during this complex period saw the upheavals of technological change, continued political tension, economic depression, urbanization, and both the growing power and the repression of organized labor. In the aftermath of the Great War, European populations reeled from an enormous sense of loss and struggled to regain normalcy even while signs of new or ongoing political tensions manifested themselves on the continent.

In Britain and the United States, some patterns of change arguably had a special impact on the production of literature and culture during this period: an expanding, unsettled middle class, the development of mass forms of reading material and cinema, and debates about sexuality and gender roles. Thus the reception and meaning of a new creative work was bound up with, for example, the way it encoded feminine or masculine values, its invocation of and divergence from contemporary voices on this matter. But its reception and meaning also derived from such extra-literary circumstances as whether it met the requirements of a market for a new popular genre,

3

whether it was published by a Little Magazine or by the Northcliffe Press, and whether its author also claimed authority as a critic or journalist.

Intellectual cross-fertilization compounded this societal, political, and cultural complexity. The most ambitious artists and writers of the day were eager to communicate across disciplines: to engage with the newly emerged theories and practices of anthropology, psychoanalysis, and "sexology"; to draw on the insights of physics and philosophy; and to transpose the methods of visual and musical culture into verbal language. The openness of literature to other disciplinary practices and other art forms was by no means unique during these years, but in the period between the wars it was underpinned by a widely shared urgency to reassess the world in the wake of the European war: to grapple with loss on an unprecedented scale, to craft art forms appropriate to a world that was felt to be vastly changed, and to identify the global patterns that would expose hitherto unperceived social and human realities, including those that had produced the war.

In addition to its inherent complexity, the space between the wars eludes us because our literary histories have been slanted by the academic domination of modernism. For decades, scholars have debated how to define modernism, how to date it, and how to measure its significance. However variously described, modernism has been the password for admittance to a highly exclusive literary canon. Thus Lyn Pykett defines the moment of modernism as "a prolonged one in which a hegemonic version of literary history and value is first produced and then reproduced by a literary academy committed to working constantly over the same relatively small group of texts" (10-11).

Some scholars have challenged the "limited canon of unquestionably great authors." Such a canon is best resisted, argues Bernard Bergonzi, "by discovering, reading, discussing and making available other texts which may be excellent and interesting without necessarily bearing the numbing accolade of 'great'" (xiv). In his study of American poetry, Cary Nelson adds that for much of the twentieth century—until the early 1980s—"the literary and social history we promulgated as sufficient in fact suppressed an immense amount of writing of great interest, vitality, subtlety, and complexity" (5).

While critics such as Bergonzi and Nelson have directed us to a wealth of interesting literature that has not been called modernist, other scholars, especially feminists, have exposed the ideological engines behind the establishment and entrenchment of the modernist canon and questioned the value and the valorization of modernist texts themselves. Suzanne Clark and Andreas Huyssen in particular have described the self-fashioning of modernists in opposition to a mass culture they characterized and devalued as feminine. More generally, recent scholarship has questioned the validity of both contemporaneous and retrospective claims to modernism's subversive role in early twentieth-century culture. Among others, Rita Felski, Shari

Benstock, Celeste Schenck, Ann Ardis and Lyn Pykett have challenged the extent to which modernist literature can be described as innovative or radical.[1] Clearly influenced by the methods of cultural analysis, these critiques of modernism have refused the opposition between "a 'high' literature assumed to be inherently ambiguous and self-critical and a mass culture equated with the reproduction of a monolithic ideological standpoint" (Felski, *GM* 29).

The high/low divide has also been troubled by postmodern reassessments of the relationship between modernism and mass culture. Among others, Ellen E. Berry, David Trotter and Thomas Crow have interrogated high modernists' apparent hostility to mass culture. Berry argues that unlike many high modernists, Gertrude Stein "attempted to merge high art with certain forms and genres of mass culture and the culture of everyday life" (168). David Trotter examines the similar strategies of modernism and popular fiction. Trotter challenges the notions that modernist texts subvert orthodoxies whereas popular texts merely imitate existing literary forms: both "rework the literary and ideological conventions elaborated by a previous generation of writers" (193). Writing about the visual arts, Thomas Crow offers a detailed history of the traffic between modernism and commodity culture, a history that helps to theorize their symbiosis. Arguing that the survival of "high" art depends on its renewal with the aesthetic discoveries of non-élite groups, Crow describes a cycle through which an avant-garde selects and packages for an élite audience aspects of mass culture that "retain some vivid life in an increasingly administered and rationalized society." Once legitimated within the province of high art, modernism is repackaged as chic and kitsch commodities for consumption by the masses (253).

If the prevailing histories of twentieth-century literature have too readily associated modernism with an experimental aesthetic and often credited it with a radical politics, these recent developments within twentieth-century studies call for consideration of the range of cultural phenomena within which modern literature takes its place. Thus Deborah Jacobs urges "radically re-visioning 'modernism'" by "reading texts from other newly forming/firming 'disciplines' alongside the literary (and literary-critical texts)" (289). This is the explicit project of Lisa Rado's two edited volumes, *Rereading Modernism* and *Modernism, Gender and Culture*. The first of these, pointing out that during the era of literary modernism "science, art, psychology, technology, sociology, anthropology, and philosophy were simultaneously undergoing a period of revolutionary change in which each discipline borrowed liberally from the experiments and innovations of the other," urges feminist scholars to bring "a more culturally based criticism, a more historical and interdisciplinary approach" (12) to the study of modernism. The essays in *Modernism, Gender and Culture* explore the connections between gender and cultural discourses of the period 1890-1945, in order "to generate a greater cross-disciplinary understanding of women's contributions to modernist culture" and to suggest the many ways in which modernist culture was inflected by gender issues (9).

When literary texts are read within the context of dialogues stretching across disciplines and cultural formations—dialogues about the meanings of race, gender, nation, class and culture, to name a few locuses of important debates in the period—they reveal themselves to be far from disengaged, but strenuous participants. Classic texts take on new meanings; previously unremarkable works become noteworthy or even critical within our new visionary framework. And questions arise about the particular functions of *literary* contributions to these debates.

Such questions and perspectives underlie the essays in *Challenging Modernism*. Plans for the collection began at "Border Crossings," the second annual conference for *The Space Between*, held at the State University of New York at New Paltz. After its first meeting in the autumn of 1997, at the University of Nevada at Reno, some of the conference participants decided to come together as a society for the study of literature and culture between the wars. They were frustrated by the absence of a forum for interdisciplinary and international discussion of this rich cultural period. Many wanted to study and teach texts that the academy had not canonized and that in some cases were not in print. Interest in the *The Space Between* has grown, and the Spring of 2000 saw the first issue of its journal: *Precursors and Aftermaths: Literatures in English, 1914-1945.*

The scope of the essays in this collection is narrower than the interests of *The Space Between* society. First, the essays concentrate on English and American responses to the interwar European terrain. Second, they treat without exception the connections between literature and its cultural and material contexts. The volume's focus enables a number of the essays' overlapping concerns to emerge, including the construction of the "literary" in the period; women writers' innovative or strategic use of language to negotiate avenues of power or explore its attractions; and the narrative modes affording access to the forbidden or unknown spaces of Others in the culture.

The articles in *Challenging Modernism* demonstrate that when literature is no longer viewed as an enclave in isolation either from history or the institutions and discourses of its time, new and meaningful portions of the cultural dialogue in which it is engaged can be heard. And that dialogue, judging from the essayists included here, is characterized by contention rather than consensus. The essays illuminate particular instances in which the meanings of femininity, class and race were being actively fought over; and they show that distinctions between high and low culture, public and private spheres, or self and Other—far from being settled—were continually contested and renegotiated in the period.

This view of unsettled borders may be threatening to our literary taxonomies. With due attention to the conventions informing literary genres, the contributors to *Challenging Modernism* none the less envision continuity between genres, audiences, and periods that our literary histories have construed as distinctly separate. They consider that the illumination of forgotten writers as well as the unearthing of "new" modernist moments are worthwhile enterprises. But more broadly, the essays collectively ask how representations of the character and borders of early twentieth-century literature—designations such as "modernism" and "the Auden Generation"—will shift when we take into account, say, war literature in which women or working-class characters take center stage, or popular and "middlebrow" novels whose messages about urgent topical issues often reached large audiences. And how will those chronicles change when we have reconsidered prominent modernists in light of newly examined material and political, rhetorical and aesthetic contexts?

The contention that our literary histories can fruitfully be re-envisioned aligns the articles in this volume with such important revisionist accounts of the era as Andy Croft's *Red Letter Days: British Fiction in the 1930s*; Alison Light's *Forever England: Femininity, Literature and Conservatism Between the Wars*, and Rita Felski's *The Gender of Modernity*. Croft and Light both work across the divide dialectically drawn between "high" and "low" fiction. Croft's study of Thirties' writing reveals that the concerns of the Left were neither restricted to an intellectual minority nor doomed to expire at the end of the decade; these causes enjoyed broad consensus and infused the literature of the next decade. In her study of British women's fiction, Light points to gaps in standard accounts of interwar literature, variously centered around radical Thirties' poets, social documentary, or late high modernism. Light maintains that British culture between the wars was marked by the new national and public significance of private life. Felski's study is not restricted to imaginative literature and documents somewhat earlier formulations of and responses to modernity. Uncovering a masculine norm behind many theories of the modern, Felski considers the cultural landscape that emerges when one considers distinctively feminine encounters with modernity:

> Those dimensions of culture either ignored, trivialized, or seen as regressive rather than authentically modern—feelings, romantic novels, shopping, motherhood, fashion—gain dramatically in importance, whereas themes previously considered central to the sociocultural analysis of modernity become less significant or recede into the background. (22)

Challenging Modernism joins an ongoing dialogue about who and what was modernity. Some of the essays take up previously denigrated—or merely overlooked—modern texts and reveal their strident or subtle contributions to the vital debates of their day; others discuss writers who have never fallen from our view but whose engagement with a contemporary topography of shifting material, political and psychosexual features has not yet been fully illuminated.

Crossing the Borders of Self and Other

This study is organized into three sections. The first, "Crossing the Borders of Self and Other," explores writers' strategic deployment of contemporary political, imperialist, and nationalist discourses to establish—or to erode—the distinctive anatomies of self and Other. In "Lilied Tongues and Yellow Claws: The Invention of London's Chinatown, 1915-45," Shannon Case studies two fiction writers who gave London's Limehouse district a newly Orientalized discursive presence in the British imagination. Popular fiction writers Sax Rohmer and Thomas Burke joined a tradition of urban exploration under the pressures of an increasingly complex, heterogeneous, and for some chaotic, city space. Drawing in addition on Orientalist discourses, each writer reified imaginative distinctions between East and West even as his fiction insisted that a remote, exotic China—its threats and its mysteries—could be found within the heart of London itself. The two writers fashioned opposed sets of tropes for the Orient, construing its nefarious darkness or its inscrutable Otherness *vis-à-vis* the West. Not only did the writers give to London's Chinatown an imaginative presence it had not previously enjoyed, as Case shows, their different configurations of the Oriental Other are central to the construction of their own Western, male, bourgeois identities.

Writing about Stevie Smith and Violet Hunt, respectively, Diana Austin and Debra Rae Cohen consider how these war writers renegotiated female identity in relation to public and national discourses. "*Over the Frontier* and into the Darkness with Stevie Smith: War, Gender, and Identity" participates in the current resurgence of interest in women's war literature. Feminists in particular have countered the dominant critical tradition of androcentric literary treatments of war, drawing on a Foucauldian notion of discourse to argue that, as the manifestation of a network of social conditions and power structures, war cannot be limited to the experience of men fighting a series of discrete battles, just as the home front cannot be readily distinguished from the war zone. As Lynne Hanley puts it, war is "a continuous and ongoing condition of twentieth-century life" (33). Like Kay Boyle, also under discussion in this volume, Smith questioned the established dichotomies of her time and refused to draw a sharp line between fascist and antifascist thought; the protagonist of *Over the Frontier* embarks on a journey of self-exploration that leads her to confront "the darkness of her own power hunger." Pompey also contests "the restrictive gender boundaries of her time." Despite her accession to military power, she never loses the advantage of her insider/outsider duality, and continually questions her own complicity in the war discourse. Pompey's journey over the multi-faceted frontier thus offers one model for unsettling and challenging the power imbalances behind war.

Like Austin's discussion of *Over the Frontier*, Debra Rae Cohen's analysis of *Zeppelin Nights: A London Entertainment* centers on wartime self-fashioning. Collaboratively written by Ford Madox Ford and Violet Hunt, *Zeppelin Nights* in fact showcased Hunt's considerable literary authority and rhetorical shrewdness, as Hunt wove together the historical vignettes already published by Ford with the commentary of a "fictional" literary coterie. In Cohen's reading, grounded in biography and in political and cultural history, *Zeppelin Nights* unfolds Hunt's strategic manipulation of "the power politics of authorship, nationality, and gender." "Citizenship in the Salon: The Public Private War of Violet Hunt" shows that through these intertwined discourses, Hunt could variously promote herself *vis-à-vis* Ford, re-establish the respectability threatened by her relationship with him, and test models of female citizenship. Invoking the model of the *salonnière*, for example, Hunt destabilized the distinctions between male and female spheres so essential to War Office propaganda and assumed an art-centered and "anti-maternalist" form of power. Like *Over the Frontier*, *Zeppelin Nights* undermines public-private distinctions, reminding us that women writers of the two world wars were not merely constructed by propaganda discourses but could harness those discourses for their own purposes.

There *Is* a Story There: Literary Forms of Protest

The writers discussed in this section crafted novelistic forms to communicate urgent topical issues to middle-class readers. Andrea Lewis and Stella Deen each examine novelists' contributions to public debates about private matters. Female sexuality and reproduction are at issue in Lewis's "A Feminine Conspiracy: Contraception, the New Woman, and Empire in Rosamond Lehmann's *The Weather in the Streets*." Lewis makes a compelling case for the importance for feminist studies of Rosamond Lehmann's 1936 novel, arguing that it treats middle-class abortion practices in greater social, economic and psychological depth than any other novel of the period. While the protagonist's abortion defies state calls for middle-class women to breed sons and daughters for the race, it is also motivated by an internalized belief in the class distinctions that imperialist and eugenicist programs relied on to make their appeal. Lehmann's novel is thus ultimately ambivalent, "shifting between an indictment of and complicity with hegemonic social and political modes of thinking." Lewis situates Lehmann within a tradition of writing that assessed women's existence in the early twentieth century as a "personal and political wasteland." Lehmann's novel astutely demonstrates that convention and transgression were not necessarily the two poles of women's response to this existence, but were two deviously entangled strands of thread.

While *The Weather in the Streets* concentrates on middle-class women, the novelists discussed in "'There is No Ordinary Life': Privacy and Domesticity in E.H. Young's *Celia* and Elizabeth Bowen's *The Death of the Heart*" broaden their focus to scrutinize middle-class marriages and families. Does the domestic subject matter of Elizabeth Bowen's *The Death of the Heart* and E.H. Young's *Celia* disqualify them from attaining the status of "important" literature? Stella Deen's analysis calls into question the categories that have traditionally been used to demarcate the "major" from the "minor" literature of the era. Both novels in fact participate in a national debate about how to reconceptualize the relation between private and public experience. Both novelists find family life to be the most visible arena in which to analyze widespread, postwar trends, including disillusion, inertia, and a willful refusal of the past. Both novels, finally, articulate a ground on which domestic life might legitimately renew a national social and political life.

In "*There's No Story There*: Inez Holden's Lost War Literature," Kristin Bluemel recovers the novels and short fiction of a middle-class writer who convincingly and compassionately portrayed workers on the British World War II home front. Bluemel traces the development of Holden's commitment to a fictional form that could win middle-class readers' support for her working-class characters. But she looks beyond Holden's specific contributions to ask how consideration of such fiction forces us to reconsider both the character of our designated literary periods and the logic of our periodization. Addressing the strengths and blind spots of several recent histories of Thirties' literature, Bluemel argues that the war did not bring an end to the political fiction of the Thirties, and that women workers and women writers are essential to our literary revision of this era. Pointing out that "consideration of the sex of the writer can influence understanding of even gross patterns in literary production," Bluemel lobbies for "the importance of seeking and valuing 'Thirties' novels' written in the 1940s, of looking to women's writing for our war literature."

Revisiting Modernists

The essays in this section expose new facets of the political, cultural and sexual struggles behind modernism. In "The Politics of Modernism in Kay Boyle's *Death of a Man*," Phoebe Stein Davis makes a strong case for the political value of experimentation with language in Kay Boyle's 1936 novel.

Davis contributes to recent work in modernism questioning one of the dominant legacies of American New Criticism: the belief that a literary work is a self-sufficient verbal entity and therefore has no political consequences. On the contrary, Boyle insisted that "language can never be a matter of merely literary concern because language and content, form and subject matter ... cannot be separated. They are one and the same thing" (quoted in Davis). Davis reviews the reception history of *Death of a Man* to demonstrate the ways in which Boyle's representation of fascism has been misconstrued. Early reviewers decreed that Boyle's experimental narrative mode could not adequately represent the realities of fascism. Yet, argues Davis, Boyle's melding of memory, imagination and reality was not a way to foreground her experimental aesthetic but was essential to the representation of the trauma experienced by individuals under fascist regimes. More recent readings of the novel have also missed Boyle's shrewd analysis of the inextricable bonds between language and fascism. Drawing on Erin G. Carlston's recent work on women writers and fascism, Davis argues first that "the rise of the Nazi movement and the production of its fascist subjects" were accomplished through language; and second, that *Death of a Man* necessarily reproduces the fascist thought it depicts.

Davis invites us to reread *Death of a Man* with some awareness of its reception history. Similarly, Natalya Lusty urges us to consider how contemporary perception of female surrealists was influenced by their subjection to a system of male introduction and patronage. Lusty's "Eating the Maid: Leonora Carrington's 'The Debutante'" reads surrealist women's writing as a potent critique of the culture's oppression of women. Focusing on Leonora Carrington's macabre "The Debutante," Lusty argues that it satirizes not merely the rituals of a narrow social class but the wider cultural and aesthetic exchange of women in 1930s' British society. Lusty reveals a pattern of complicity and resistance that links the "reluctant debutante" of Carrington's story to the practice of surrealist women and to the tactics of women intellectuals during this era. But the significance of Lusty's work extends beyond this newly illuminated set of cultural and social practices, for in the pattern of complicity and resistance Lusty finds a parallel between 1930s' and contemporary feminism. Perhaps the most provocative dimension of Lusty's analysis, however, is her situation of Carrington's surrealism *vis-à-vis* that of her male counterparts. Despite André Breton's eager endorsement of Carrington and her fiction as emblems of surrealism's transgressive poetics, Lusty shows that canonical male surrealism itself erected a set of disciplinary boundaries hostile to the complexity of female surrealists' experience. Lusty's reconsideration of female surrealists such as Carrington challenges the "revolutionary" rhetoric of the male canonical surrealist aesthetic, suggesting that male surrealism, though it championed female rebellion, did so by endorsing a dichotomous economy of woman as idealized and debased. And in contrast to Carrington's fiction, male surrealism failed to address the racist and classist dimensions of the bourgeois culture against which it claimed to protest.

Concluding the volume is a re-examination of T.S. Eliot's criticism in light of publicizing and commercial imperatives. In "T.S. Eliot in the 'Journalistic Struggle,'" Patrick Collier complicates the commonly accepted view of Eliot as purveyor and guardian of high culture by exploring "overlooked conflicts" in Eliot's relationship to journalism. While Collier concedes that by 1940, when Eliot's reputation and financial success as poet and editor were ensured, he energetically affirmed a divide between high and low culture, the track record of Eliot's utterances on the subject of culture and journalism was far more mixed. Examining Eliot's essays and letters, Collier uncovers the many ambiguities, shifts and contradictions in Eliot's stance on the matter. Exploiting the historically unstable distinction between "literature" and "journalism," Eliot redefined or qualified the meaning of these terms to justify his own journalistic practices. And although Eliot blamed the press for the decay of culture, he used it both to earn money and to build his reputation as a cultural authority. Collier's essay contributes to the important new work exploring the entanglement of modernism with popular culture and marketplace forces.

Virginia Woolf provides a commentary on the potential meanings of the voices collected in this volume. In "The Russian Point of View," Woolf praises Russian writers first by addressing their apparent deficiencies, their oddity to the English ear. The English reader of Chekhov is bewildered: "What is the point of it, and why does he make a story out of this?" (175). Characteristically, Woolf then suggests the way those judgments grow out of habits of mind produced—or at least reinforced—by the shapes of our own stories, especially their built-in imperative for a conclusion. But if we can suppress the promptings of our cultural bias, then Chekhov reveals to us "a new panorama of the human mind," characterized by the melting of our cherished divisions between categories and classes of people. Woolf uses Chekhov to call for a more honest literature, especially one that does not force conclusions when it is more truthful to admit the mixed nature of the subject—the human soul. "There may be no answer to these questions, but at the same time let us never manipulate the evidence so as to produce something fitting, decorous, agreeable to our vanity" (177). I hope that the essays in *Challenging Modernism*, introducing new texts and discursive contexts into the academic discussion of interwar literature and culture, will prompt readers to discard habits of mind built up by the story of modernism, to melt old divisions between categories and classes of literature.

Challenging Modernism offers readers an opportunity to reexamine the period between and encompassing the two world wars, a period in Europe marked by unprecedented domestic and international pressures. The essays newly illuminate many of these pressures, addressing such issues as authorship and citizenship during wartime; the writerly construction of urban space; and the challenge of war to traditional notions of female pacifism and male aggression. Where they address modernism, the essays demonstrate unequivocally individual writers' manipulation of or engagement with, not their aesthetic distance from, contemporary social and political phenomena. Finally, the collection demonstrates forcibly the importance of women writers to the meaning of modernity and its periodization: The featured female writers bring us new insights into eugenics, imperialism, citizenship, domesticity and its relationship to national and international concerns, the working class and World War II.

Challenging Modernism will undoubtedly fill in some blank spaces but also raise new questions and open new avenues of inquiry. Since new materials will continue to suggest themselves for our investigation and since disciplinary methods of investigation will continue to change, we should not expect the space between the two world wars ever to be "fully charted." Yet the essays in *Challenging Modernism* collectively testify that as "modernism" and "postmodernism" loosen their hegemony, something new can be constructed: a story of unique historical and literary relations in the period encompassing the two world wars.

Notes

1. Schenck, for example, argues: "if ... the radical poetics of Modernism often masks a deeply conservative politics, might it also possibly be true that the seemingly genteel, conservative poetics of women poets whose obscurity even feminists have overlooked might pitch a more radical politics than we had considered possible? I wish, in short, to question the equation both conservative Modernists and radical theorists have made between radical form and radical politics" (230-1). See also Benstock 21; Pykett 13; and Ardis 263-4. Ann Ardis, in her essay on the fiction of Netta Syrett, and f, in his study of modern American poetry, argue that work undertaken in traditional literary forms often advances a significant challenge to political orthodoxies. Felski's argument in "Modernism and Modernity" is similar (194), but in *The Gender of Modernity* she avoids any correlative argument about the radical politics of supposedly conservative texts. Emphasizing the complex and often contradictory ways in which modernity was experienced and has been construed, she refutes the notion of any single text "embodying the truth of the modern Zeitgeist in a uniquely representative way" (26).

References

Ardis, Ann. "Toward a Redefinition of 'Experimental Writing': Netta Syrett's Realism, 1908-12." *Famous Last Words: Changes in Gender and Narrative Closure.* Ed. Alison Booth. Charlottesville, Virginia: University Press of Virginia, 1993. 259-79.
Benstock, Shari. "Expatriate Modernism." Broe and Ingram 20-40.

Bergonzi, Bernard. *The Myth of Modernism and Twentieth-Century Literature*. New York: St. Martin's, 1986.

Berry, Ellen E. "Modernism/Mass Culture/Postmodernism: The Case of Gertrude Stein." *Rereading the New: A Backward Glance at Modernism*. Ed. Kevin J.H. Dettmar. Ann Arbor: University of Michigan Press, 1992. 167-89.

Broe, Mary Lynn, and Angela Ingram, eds. *Women's Writing in Exile*. Chapel Hill: University of North Carolina Press, 1989.

Clark, Suzanne. *Sentimental Modernism: Women Writers and the Revolution of the Word*. Bloomington, Indiana University Press, 1991.

Croft, Andy. *Red Letter Days: British Fiction in the 1930s*. London: Lawrence and Wishart, 1990.

Crow, Thomas. "Modernism and Mass Culture in the Visual Arts." *Modernism and Modernity*. The Vancouver Conference Papers. Ed. Benjamin H.D. Buchloh, Serge Guilbaut, and David Solkin. Halifax: Press of The Nova Scotia College of Art and Design, 1983. 215-64.

Felski, Rita. *The Gender of Modernity*. Cambridge: Harvard University Press, 1995.

——. "Modernism and Modernity: Engendering Literary History." Rado, *Rereading Modernism* 191-208.

Hanley, Lynne. *Writing War: Fiction, Gender, Memory*. Amherst, Mass.: University of Massachusetts Press, 1991.

Heller, Scott. "New Life for Modernism." *The Chronicle of Higher Education*. 5 November 1999: A21-2.

Huyssen, Andreas. *After the Great Divide: Modernism, Mass Culture, Postmodernism*. Bloomington: Indiana University Press, 1986.

Jacobs, Deborah. "Feminist Criticism/Cultural Studies/Modernist Texts: A Manifesto for the 90s." Rado, *Rereading Modernism* 273-95.

Light, Alison. *Forever England: Femininity, Literature and Conservatism Between the Wars*. London: Routledge, 1991.

Nelson, Cary. *Repression and Recovery: Modern American Poetry and the Politics of Cultural Memory, 1910-1945*. Madison: University of Wisconsin Press, 1989.

Pykett, Lyn. *Engendering Fictions: The English Novel in the Early Twentieth Century*. London: Edward Arnold, 1995.

Rado, Lisa. "The Case for Cultural/Gender/Modernist Studies." Rado, *Modernism, Gender, and Culture* 3-14.

——. "Lost and Found: Remembering Modernism, Rethinking Feminism." Rado, *Rereading Modernism* 3-19.

——, ed. *Modernism, Gender, and Culture: A Cultural Studies Approach*. New York and London: Garland, 1997.

——, ed. *Rereading Modernism: New Directions in Feminist Criticism*. New York: Garland, 1994.

Schenck, Celeste M. "Exiled by Genre: Modernism, Canonicity and the Politics of Exclusion." Broe and Ingram 226-50.

Trotter, David. "A Horse is Being Beaten: Modernism and Popular Fiction." *Rereading the New: A Backward Glance at Modernism*. Ed. Kevin J.H. Dettmar. Ann Arbor: University of Michigan Press, 1992. 191-219.

Woolf, Virginia. "The Russian Point of View." *The Common Reader*. First Series. 1925. Ed. and introd. Andrew McNeillie. San Diego: Harvest-Harcourt, 1984.

Part I—Crossing the Borders of Self and Other

1 Lilied Tongues and Yellow Claws: The Invention of London's Chinatown, 1915-45

Shannon Case

From roughly 1915 to 1945, the Limehouse district of East London was home to a small community of resident and alien Chinese. Named for Limehouse Causeway, near the East India Docks, Limehouse had been inhabited since the sixteenth century by successive groups of ethnic immigrants as well as working-class English people. Chinese seamen had sojourned there sporadically since the mid-eighteenth century, but it was not until after the Great War that Chinese men, women, and children began to form a visible community. From 1901 to 1931, the number of China-born residents of London rose steadily, from 120 to 1,194. (These figures do not account for their London-born children or grandchildren.) There were approximately 2,000 Chinese immigrants in London by World War II, at which time they abandoned Limehouse and dispersed into other areas of the city (Choo 6). Limehouse sustained extensive damage during the blitz, and in 1963 the city demolished most of the remaining buildings in the area; it then suffered a "dead" period until gentrification began in the 1970s (Choo 20).

Apart from census data and one sociological study conducted in 1962 (when many of the early immigrants were still alive), we know very little about the Chinese of Limehouse, whose community appeared and then vanished so quickly in the brief space between the wars. We know that in the 1910s and 1920s, most of the immigrants were young men employed as seamen or dockworkers; the rest were laundrymen, shopkeepers, or restaurateurs, a few of whom also ran or worked in gambling houses or opium dens. Once they had established themselves, the men would send for their wives and other family members; however, it was not uncommon for Chinese men to marry working-class English women. We know that for recreation the immigrants partook of small-scale gambling and, less commonly, opium smoking; they also gathered socially to share the news and newspapers they received from home (there was no Chinese paper published in London during this period). There were trade clubs, too, as well as a Chinese Masonic Hall, whose members supported the 1911 revolution in China to overthrow the Manchus and end the Ch'ing dynasty. About the immigrants' children little is known. A philanthropic society set up a Chinese school for them in 1935, and its one teacher taught in Cantonese. Just before the war, however, the teacher was accused of communist activities and

17

deported; the school closed and never reopened (Choo 10-20).

Since the Chinese of Limehouse were a small, orderly community who rarely competed with English people for jobs, they remained to a certain extent invisible and thus, it seems, escaped much of the systematic violence with which Anglo-Londoners greeted other immigrant groups, such as Germans and Russian Jews. The only recorded instance of sustained, organized hostility was that of British seamen opposed to the British merchant marine's employment of the Chinese, who worked for low wages and sometimes served as strikebreakers. This hostility came to a head during the 1911 seamen's strike, when strikers destroyed about thirty Chinese homes and laundries in Cardiff (May 116). But this seems to have been an isolated incident, and there was no such violence—none reported, at least—against the Chinese of Limehouse.

In fact, before World War I, the community was still too tiny to attract much notice at all. In his chapter on "The Alien" in *East London* (1901), Walter Besant states dismissively that "Compared with the Chinese colony of New York ... that of London is a small thing and of no importance" (204). In a study of pre-war attitudes toward the Chinese in London, Liverpool, and Cardiff, one researcher has concluded that "[al]though occasional notes of disquiet were expressed with respect to the Chinese presence" at this time, other evidence points to "attitudes of indifference and even acceptance" (May 111). Records show that although the public occasionally raised objections to the two "Chinese vices" of gambling and opium smoking, the police considered these activities harmless and generally looked the other way (May 117-20). Nor did Chinese-Anglo marriages arouse public concern. Police did once respond to a British headmistress's accusation that two Chinese men were corrupting teenage girls, but the inspector in charge of the case concluded that "the Chinaman if he becomes intimate with an English girl does not lead her to prostitution but prefers to marry her and treat her well" (quoted in May 119). In *A Wanderer in London* (1907), E.V. Lucas reports that the "silent discreet Chinese who have married English women and settled down in London ... are, I am told, among the best citizens of the East End and the kindest husbands" (157).

If before the Great War the Chinese of Limehouse were, as one researcher puts it, "of little concern to the majority of Britons amongst whom they lived and worked and created no significant problems for the ... authorities" (May 122), during the space between the two world wars their situation changed. Though the community was still small compared with those of other immigrants in London, suddenly it was *seen*: in the space of a few years the all-but-invisible Chinese quarter became "Chinatown," a mapped territory and a densely signifying space.

The change was wrought primarily by two popular fiction writers whose works suddenly gave Limehouse-as-Chinatown a discursive presence it had not had before. For both Sax Rohmer, author of the best-selling Fu Manchu series of thrillers as well as other "tales of Chinatown"; and Thomas Burke, a less successful, but still popular writer of the same period who, like Rohmer, set many of his stories in Limehouse, the Limehouse district was London's true Orient: a local urban territory that was an integral part of their city's "dark underworld" of native and immigrant slum-dwellers, but also different—more or differently suggestive—because of what they saw or imagined to be its specifically Chinese character. Limehouse became, in fact, an obsession for both writers (though with strikingly different results) and the fictions they produced and reproduced about it helped situate it within what was already a complex and polysemous imaginative cityscape.

Rohmer and Burke make a compelling pair because their narrative encryptions of Limehouse intersect and compete in ways that render it what Judith Walkowitz would call a "contested terrain"—a public space that becomes a site of "conflicting and overlapping representations" (5). Whereas Rohmer's Limehouse is strictly a den of (oriental) thieves, a place where the humdrum conceals the outré, where white men and women fall into foreign hands, where nondescript warehouses are fronts for the "Yellow syndicate," an exotic and sinister underworld bent on ending Western civilization, Burke's Limehouse is a tense, complex, diverse community of the working poor, with a motley crew of underclass characters and types— music-hall "artistes," copper's narcs, smugglers, peddlers, boxers, drunks, religious fanatics, as well as a few "beautiful souls" who find love or loveliness in unlikely places. In Burke's Limehouse, in stark contrast to Rohmer's, English people and Chinese mix socially and even fall in love, albeit always ill-fatedly.

These different visions of Limehouse can both be placed within the larger context of urban exploration and the crisis of representation with which its literature was fraught at the time. In her chapter on urban spectatorship in *City of Dreadful Delight: Narratives of Sexual Danger in Late-Victorian London* (1992), Judith Walkowitz shows that in the nineteenth century, "the fact and fantasy of urban exploration [was] an informing feature of ... bourgeois male subjectivity" (16). Whether guided by a rationalist sense of self-possession and "scientific" distance (as in Henry Mayhew), or by the consumerist and "subjective" sensibility of the flâneur (as in Henry James), the urban explorer's gaze was a steady, privileged, and proprietary one that presumed and secured a "right to the city" for the writer and his readers (16). By the 1880s and 1890s, however, the public urban landscape was increasingly the site and object of contests among other, emergent social actors, such as women and workers. Their claims and methods would register many of the crises that characterized the period: "religious self-doubt, social unrest, challenges to liberalism and science, anxiety over imperial and national decline, as well as an imaginative confrontation with the defamiliarized world of consumer culture" (17). As a result, says Walkowitz, the public space traversed by the urban spectator became "an unstable construct," and social explorers' narratives lost the more secure, unified perspective they once had:

> Some [writers] rigidified the hierarchical divisions of London into a geographic separation, organized around the opposition of East and West. Others stressed the growing complexity and differentiation of the world of London, moving beyond the opposition of rich and poor, palace and hovels, to investigate the many class cultures in between. Still others repudiated a fixed, totalistic interpretive image altogether, and emphasized instead a fragmented, disunified, atomistic social universe that was not easily decipherable. (16-17)

These competing perspectives amounted to a crisis in representation for the urban spectator, whose defining object of consumption—public space—had become a battleground, a landscape "threatened internally by contradictions and tensions and constantly challenged from without by social forces that pressed [the] dominant representations to be reworked, shorn up, reconstructed" (17-18). In so far as they see and write as urban explorers, Rohmer and Burke find themselves in a similarly embattled landscape: the psychosocial disturbances of the 1880s and 1890s had not abated by 1910; if anything, they had intensified. Faced with the "unstable construct" of modern London, then, Rohmer and Burke follow two of the lines of response that Walkowitz describes: one vehemently reasserts a rigid hierarchical map, and the other just as strongly rejects it, elaborating instead a "fragmented, disunified ... social universe that was not easily decipherable."

If the social explorers' tradition and its late-Victorian ruptures form one context for Rohmer and Burke's Limehouse fiction, a second, more important context is Orientalism. Indeed, the two traditions are continuous, as Peter Stallybrass and Allon White note in *The Politics and Poetics of Transgression* (1986). When the social explorer ventures into the East End and other "underworld" territories marked by scenes of suffering and degradation, he confronts the low-Other with a mixture of "repugnance and fascination," seeing an upside-down, or carnivalesque, image of the bourgeois self to which he aspires. As in Orientalism, this repugnance and fascination are "the twin poles of the process in which a *political* imperative to reject and eliminate the debasing 'low' conflicts powerfully and unpredictably with a desire for this Other" (4-5). Though finally not reducible to each other, both Orientalism and social exploration involve a mode of relating to the low-Other that has been central to Western, bourgeois, male identity-formation. In both cases, the subject "*uses* the whole world as its theatre in a particularly instrumental fashion, the very subjects which it politically excludes becoming exotic costumes which it assumes in order to play out the disorders of its own identity" (200). The main disorder of that identity,

Stallybrass and White maintain, is the fact of its being empty, a negation. As such, it is voracious, forever needing new territories in which to expand, new or recycled sources of Otherness to consume—that is, to reject in disgust and then study, imitate, and gaze upon with a mixture of fear and desire.

The voraciousness of Western bourgeois identity was one factor that caused Limehouse finally to be seen—and seen as Chinatown. One important circumstance that distinguished Rohmer and Burke from the earlier generation of social explorers was that by 1910, there was little "virgin" East End territory left to discover. That previous generation—journalists such as Henry Mayhew and James Greenwood, as well as countless sociologists, Poor Law reformers, parliamentary investigators, and the like—had so "discovered" and "exposed" the East End, had so mercilessly inspected, analyzed, and "gone into" it, as to have effectively consumed its inhabitants, the once-alien urban poor. Finding new sources of Otherness would entail either remystifying those territories, re-covering what had been laid bare (as, for instance, T.S. Eliot would do, using myth, in *The Waste Land*) or finding and embellishing a secret heart more secret than the slums and sweatshops had been. As it happened, Rohmer and Burke, by different routes, stumbled upon Limehouse and recognized—quite deliberately, in Rohmer's case—its potential as a secret heart.

This potential lay in its being an East End neighborhood that was both overlooked and palpably Chinese. That it was Chinese would have conferred an aura of mystery upon it automatically, given the West's centuries-old idea, central to Orientalist thought, that the Orient and Orientals are essentially inscrutable. The supposed inscrutability of China in particular was enhanced by its relative remoteness. Although generalizations about the Orient implicitly included the Far East, until the early nineteenth century British Orientalism—as an academic discipline, literary tradition, and network of political-military institutions—principally focused on the Bible Lands and India (Said 16-17).

Yet China was becoming—or was forced into being—an increasingly important British interest, and recent troubles there, including the Second Opium War, the Boxer Uprising of 1900, and the republican revolution of 1911, had been very much in the news. If recent history warranted an expansion of the space allotted to China in the cultural memory, Rohmer, as we will see, was designedly aware of it. Thus it is doubly suggestive that he reportedly said, "I made my name on Fu Manchu because I know nothing about the Chinese! *I know something about Chinatown, but that is a different matter*" (quoted in Van Ash 72; my emphasis). China and Chinatown were two different matters: Rohmer understood that the cultural work of placing China in the British imagination required not useful information about the Chinese as an ethnic, racial, cultural, or socio-economic reality, but rather a strong image, and an idea of place. The image, an unreality concocted from Orientalist stereotypes, needed Chinatown to bring it home; Limehouse would serve to twin the image and express it locally, so that what had been remote was now inwrought and memorable, the Orient's signature found in the very blueprint of a London neighborhood, in its architecture and arrangement, streets and alleys, attics and sewers, and all its hidden rooms.

As we will see, Burke too finds the Orient's "signature" in Limehouse, but his tracing and retracing of it causes confusion more than division—a confusion of inks, as it were, a commingling of the Orient's with his own, so that China seems to "occupy" him, his own body and memory, as much as it occupies London. The essential premise, in both Rohmer and Burke's fiction, is that "The Orient is Here," and it functions as a kind of mnemonic geography, as a device for placing and remembering an idea of China and, in turn, an idea of England, Englishness, and the West.

Orientalism makes the Orient mobile, a portable rather than fixed spatial field. As an ideology, Orientalism depended on and benefited from its geographic "obviousness," the seemingly natural geographic division between East and West elaborated as a kind of racial, cultural, and historical determinism. "Geography," observes Edward Said, "was the essential material underpinning for knowledge about the Orient. All the latent and unchanging characteristics of the Orient stood upon, were rooted in, its geography" (216). In the Limehouse fiction, however, the Orient gets loosed from its traditional geographic moorings, translated across Western borders, and reconstructed on British soil, as the secret heart of London, the city that already represented the heart of Western civilization. In Rohmer's version, that secret heart is corrupt: Limehouse is the source and being of corruption, the site and expression of an Oriental plot. In Burke's version, the secret heart is, instead, uncanny: as the site of initiation into an Oriental secret that gets transmitted imperfectly across a cultural divide, Limehouse is the "strange familiar" that both occasions and characterizes Western self-knowledge. In Rohmer, the Orient is literally Here, as a cancer against which England and Englishness must strive; in Burke, the Orient is Here no less literally, but its meaning lies in its transformative and figurative power.

Despite and even because of their differences, the maps that emerge from the Limehouse fiction of Rohmer and Burke remind us that place can be invented and made to signify. Their imaginative border crossings yield narratives that—though often shallow art—are deep representations, their two versions of Limehouse being also two versions of the modern urban experience and two articulated possibilities for a British urbanite self. These maps, experiences, and selves draw upon, and signify within, other texts and contexts that were part of the cultural geography of London at the time. In this chapter I will focus on urban spectatorship and Orientalism, but it bears noting that there are other discourses and signifying practices—melodrama, spiritualism, occultism, a popularized bohemianism, silent film, and slum fiction—that could help us read Rohmer and Burke's Chinatown as an encrypted text, one fashioned from cultural currents—and a writing opportunity—that the space between the wars provided.

From early youth until he died, fittingly, of the Asiatic flu, Sax Rohmer pursued the East as an amateur Orientalist. His imagination was fired by the Orientalist fiction, the vocabulary, images, tropes and symbols with which his nineteenth-century predecessors had invented, disciplined, and made a discipline of the "Orient." He consumed Orientalist texts both scholarly and spurious, from Lane's *Modern Egyptians* to books on Eastern magic, medicines, poisons, and insects; and he was a collector—of Eastern lore at first, and later, when he could afford to travel, of Eastern "experiences" and artifacts. As a young man, of course, he had dreamed of a career in the East, but failing the civil-service exam cut his dream short. Unabashed, and otherwise unemployable, he turned to writing fiction, and through his fiction managed to make the East a career anyway, by bringing the Orient home to London. His early stories, which had Eastern settings and themes, proved popular and tagged him as a writer with "Oriental enthusiasms." So when, in 1911, a magazine editor familiar with his work asked him to write an article on "Mr. King," a reputed Chinese drug trafficker operating out of Limehouse, Rohmer found himself in a privileged position, poised to deploy the symbology he'd absorbed in staking out an as-yet unrepresented "Oriental" territory—one conveniently right in his own backyard. Having seized his opportunity, Rohmer would proceed to Orientalize Limehouse just as Orientalists throughout the tradition had Orientalized the Orient. And just as that Orient was, as Said demonstrates, the stage on which Europe played out the East-West drama it had invented to help define itself, Rohmer's Limehouse would become the local Oriental stage on which he would fashion a persona and a career. It was both the site and opportunity for the series of performances that composed his life and work.

Many years later, long after Fu Manchu had made him famous, Rohmer claimed (in a conversation with his biographer) that at the time he went in search of Mr King, it was an "established fact" that almost all of the Chinese in Limehouse were our "enemies." They were cunning criminals, he said, outlaws who confounded the police because they "did nothing in the expected way," "thought differently," and spoke an alien tongue. Moreover, they were not independent (since, he explains, "To the Asiatic mind, our conception of humanity in terms of individuals is an absurdity") but instead were organized into guilds, powerful syndicates controlled by their "parent societies" in China and "holding monopolies on every kind of profitable activity—political, religious, commercial, and criminal" (quoted in Van Ash 73-4). Rohmer cites no source for these "facts," nor, as we have seen, is there evidence of their being, before Fu Manchu came along, commonly-held beliefs about Limehouse. They are Rohmer's fantasy, and the assumptions and stereotypes on which they are based—the Chinese are insidious and wholly alien; the "Asiatic mind" is herd-driven and unassimilable—are orthodox Orientalism. They are also conspiracist. Said characterizes Orientalism as a kind of paranoia (72). And evidence of paranoid-conspiracist tendencies can be deduced from Rohmer's other pursuits, too: as a committed, practicing spiritualist and a member of at least one secret society, the Hermetic Order of the Golden Dawn, Rohmer clearly had an affinity for the language of Secrets, Plots, and Keys and for the style of thought that delights in the idea of mysterious, occult forces—supernatural and/or malign and human—causing events.

Rohmer's fantasy of a Limehouse controlled by a Chinese criminal network quickly grew into an idea for fiction: once he realized that "what was happening in Limehouse was happening likewise in the Chinese communities of foreign cities throughout the world," he "fell to dreaming":

> Suppose, I asked myself, a number of those sinister organizations—perhaps, even all of them—were in turn responsible to the direction of some super-society? Such a society would hold the power to upset governments, perhaps change the very course of civilization .... (quoted in Van Ash 74)

In this paranoid, imaginative leap, Rohmer emplots the ordinary space of Limehouse with an Oriental plot, the "Yellow Conspiracy" that will then emplot all of his Limehouse fiction: from his *Tales of Chinatown* (1922), in which Chinese criminals undermine the peace and safety of the metropolis; to the opium books: *The Yellow Claw*, 1915; *Dope*, 1919; *Yellow Shadows*, 1925, in which Chinese smugglers threaten the West's survival by turning thousands of Anglo-Londoners into drug-slaves; to the Fu Manchu series, in which the evil doctor and his band of Eastern assasins attempt to establish a "Yellow Empire" in the West. In every case, Limehouse is the Western headquarters of a worldwide Eastern conspiracy, a portal through which we glimpse the silent, plotting Yellow hordes. These are often represented by Limehouse's yellow fog; thus the narrator of *The Si-Fan Mysteries* says, "I had closed the window to exclude the yellow mist, but subconsciously I was aware of its encircling presence, walling me in" (2). Limehouse is furthermore a site of contagion where unwitting English people catch the "Yellow vices" of opium-smoking and lecherousness and fall prey to exotic, often erotic, forms of cruelty. An extreme example is *The Trail of Fu Manchu* (1934), where the doctor, his world-domination schemes hampered by lack of funds, uses opium and beautiful Asian women to capture and kill Englishmen, then feeds their bodies into a giant gold-making furnace—hidden, of course, beneath the ordinary-seeming squalor of Limehouse.

Rohmer's emplotment of Limehouse arose from the genuine conspiracism of a deeply-inscribed Orientalist interpretive frame. But it was also a market-savvy move in a deliberate game of self-invention. In an anecdote that may be a fiction (and all the more cunning if it is), Rohmer claimed that one evening, before he had ever heard of Mr King or imagined Fu Manchu, he asked his ouija board "How can I best make a living?" and in reply it spelled out "C-H-I-N-A-M-A-N" (quoted in Van Ash 63). A year or two later, when, searching for Mr. King, he envisioned his Limehouse-centered Yellow Conspiracy, he knew he was "on the right track": "Conditions for launching a Chinese villain on the market were ideal," he recalls; "the Boxer Rebellion had started off rumors of a Yellow Peril which had not yet died down. Recent events in Limehouse had again drawn public attention east-wards" (quoted in Van Ash 75). Villain and setting were thus chillingly calculated to suit market conditions; to further stack the deck, Rohmer then wrote a self-perpetuating role for himself within the fiction: from the start, his Limehouse stories overwhelmingly insist that, since the Orient is Here, Orientalist expertise is the West's only effective weapon in the battle against it. The Metropolitan Police fight bravely, but one or two "brilliant" and "dar-ing" Orientalists—who are always, like Rohmer himself, amateurs—save the world from destruction every time. We recognize them as Kipling's White Men (Rohmer's narrators even quote Kipling), and if the Empire needs them in the East, it needs them—and Rohmer—even more at home, where Burmese *dacoits*, Indian thugs, Chinese torturers and other "Yellow Devils" fill the secret passageways of Limehouse, of London, the heart of the Empire and of Western Civilization.

Rohmer finally did find Mr King in Limehouse, and his tale of the encounter encapsulates both the role he invented for himself and the Chinatown he invented for his readers. When he at last glimpsed the "elu-sive Oriental," it was from the mouth of a dark, foggy alley where, acting on a tip, Rohmer crouched, watching a dilapidated building across the street. Suddenly,

> The headlamps of a glossy limousine … lighted up the dark, narrow street. I ducked back into the shelter of my alley as … [a] uniformed chauffeur—some kind of Asiatic—jumped out smartly and opened the car door. … A tall, digni-fied Chinese, wearing a fur-collared overcoat and a fur cap, alighted and walked in. He was followed by an Arab girl wrapped in a grey fur cloak. I had a glimpse of her features. She was like something from an Edmund Dulac illus-tration to *The Thousand and One Nights*. The door closed. … Minutes passed and I continued standing there in the grip of such excitement as I had never felt before. For a mere instant while the light flooded out from the opened door, I had seen the face of the man in the fur cap, and in that instant my imaginary monster came to life. … I knew that I had seen Dr. Fu Manchu! His face was the living embodiment of Satan. (quoted in Van Ash 76-7)

This is the archetypal Orientalist posture of Western seer to Eastern seen, of the Intrepid Explorer infiltrating, at some personal risk, the territory of a mysterious and wholly alien Other and finding that it corresponds not only inevitably, thrillingly with what was sought—but in excess of it. That gap between the second- and first-hand experience of the Orient is an erotic one for the Orientalist, and the erotic excess is (as Roland Barthes might find) the narrative itself—not only the narrative of the event, but all the narratives to follow, for which this narrative is generative and prototypical. But Rohmer also captures and carries home from Limehouse something else besides its narrative potential, and that is the strong image he needs to actualize it. The image he takes is a face, a Chinese face flooded with light, exposed, and—and this was Rohmer's triumph—not merely exotic but *shocking*. Shocking precisely because it is surrounded by the conventional trappings of a wealthy Englishman—cap, coat, limousine, chauffeur, and beautiful woman in fur. To Rohmer it is an Eastern wolf in Western clothing, representing in condensed form Chinatown's insidious relation to London and, on a larger scale, the Orient's imperilment of the Empire, the threat of a "huge yellow claw reaching out to strangle the West" (*The Mystery of Dr Fu-Manchu*). Playing the explorer, Rohmer discovers what he needs to believe is the real Chinatown, uncloaks the "enemy within." It could have come to nothing; instead, 25 years later, Rohmer's Limehouse fiction had made him one of the most popular and highest-paid writers of his time. Pulp fiction it is, but its very success testifies to the brute strength, if not the truth, of his interpretation, to the forcefulness with which he lay imaginative claim to the terrain in question.

But though widely accepted, that claim did not go unchallenged. Although Thomas Burke never (to my knowledge) mentions his contemporary or otherwise alludes to him, his emplotment of Limehouse stands in curious counterpoint to Rohmer's. Burke's Chinatown is, like Rohmer's, wholly Other, but its otherness is its virtue, that which gives it the power to impress itself upon—and thus help write—the self. When Burke insists, through his stories, that the Orient is Here, he points at once to Limehouse and to his own heart, which is the heart of a child of the city, a heart crisscrossed by London streets and especially by Limehouse Causeway, which made the first and most important mark. In this sense, of course, Burke's invention and use of Limehouse amount to merely one more example of the West's enthnocentric pursuit of self-knowledge via a racial Other; but his engagement with place (however imaginary) and his larger purpose—to map out and give meaning to a fragmentary urban experience—condition this pursuit and the version of Limehouse that results. Though it can be maddeningly racist, this version is more often poignantly confused, as an attempt at cross-cultural communication that gets undone by the message Burke expects to receive. Believing that Limehouse holds the key to the puzzle of the self, he returns to it repeatedly, straining to grasp—and thereby perpetuating an idea of—an Orient that never has existed except in the West's (fertile) imagination.

Thomas Burke (1887-1945) was an East End orphan who grew up next door to Limehouse, in Poplar (Ferguson 41). Throughout childhood, Burke suffered the disappointments of poverty, but he found relief and refuge in the public library, where he discovered literature. He aspired to write fiction and, in his late teens, when he had become a city clerk, wrote his first short story after-hours on his office typewriter. He sent it to *T. P.'s Weekly*; the editor rejected it but encouraged him to keep writing. He struggled to do so and mostly failed—until 1915, when *Nights in Town*, a book of essays and sketches, finally established his reputation as a London travel writer, paving the way for *City of Encounters* (1932), *London in My Time* (1934), *Living in Bloomsbury* (1939), and the autobiographical *The Wind and The Rain* (1924). But it was a book of short stories, *Limehouse Nights* (1916), that made his career. By 1926, three of its stories had been adapted for Hollywood films, after which (says one critic) "arose the singing of 'Limehouse Blues' and 'Chinatown, My Chinatown,' while a good deal of chinoiserie was worked into decorations and *objects d'art*" (Ferguson 41). Despite his complaint that the book had been "tied so tightly round [his] neck that [he was] sick of ... the word Limehouse" (*City of Encounters* 66), Burke turned out *Twinkletoes, A Tale of Limehouse* (1918), *More Limehouse Nights* (1921), *A Tea-Shop in Limehouse* (1927), and *Abduction: A Story of Limehouse* (1939).

Burke's Limehouse fiction shares with his other London travel writing the narrative voice and sensibility of the lone flâneur obsessed with observing his city and its scenes, its shifting character and moods, and the spectacle of its often chaotic phenomena. To convey the unfathomable mystery and complexity of his metropolis, Burke and his narrators employ the flâneur's conventional tropes: the city is like a woman, or God, or the human heart, like a poem or a palimpsest: "London is as unknowable as a king or as the man in the bus, and the king and the man in the bus are as unknowable as the God above them." "What one knows of London," he maintains, "is what London chooses to reveal, and even that little is only revealed to those who love it. You cannot 'learn' London by study, but you can know it by love. The taxi-driver and the smart provincial 'know London,' and at the same time know nothing of it" (*City of Encounters* 15-16). Burke came to know London by ceaselessly walking its streets and by living everywhere in it. Unlike Rohmer, who, as he came up in the world, followed the predictable bourgeois trajectory from East End to West End to high-end suburbs, Burke practiced a "continual pitching and striking of camp in sharply different districts," thereby "making acquaintance with all kinds of life and all kinds of people" (*City of Encounters* 28). He had over forty different London addresses in all, each one of which, he says, disclosed a different London. Thus, whereas Rohmer draws a binary map, dividing the city irredeemably into overworld and underworld, East and West, Burke's map is decentered, multiple, and necessarily incomplete.

Like Rohmer, Burke had a defining moment of encountering the Oriental Other in Limehouse. Unlike Rohmer's, however, Burke's encounter was not a premeditated Orientalist one, the result of a deliberate quest for an Oriental Experience. Burke spent his childhood in Limehouse, wandering its streets and alleys, wondering at its shops and populace, and musing, in the unfettered way of a ten-year-old, on the meaning of what he saw. When he writes of this time as an adult, however, we hear a telling clash of terms, his memory having become a battleground where authentic event and Orientalist discourse vie for control of the representation:

> In moments of restlessness ... I would escape down the road and wander in a street of no-time and no-place; a street of spices and golden apples, where men, dark or lemon-faced, wearing the raiment of pantomime, swam through the mist or held the walls in living statuary. There lived all wonder and dismay, and the rewards that come to us in dreams. What drew me to it I do not know, but I loved to be there, to touch shoulders with its shadows, or to stand at the window of Quong Lee's [shop] filled with a Want I could not name. ... I would often go down to [the river], and stand on the wharf for an hour, staring at the water and the boats, wondering what it all meant and whether Quong Lee's shop-window would explain it. (*The Wind and The Rain* 20-1)

Chinatown as timeless and placeless, as shrouded in mist and peopled by "living statuary"—these are standard images from the Orientalist repertoire, images so omnipresent in Western culture they would have been available even to a writer like Burke who (unlike Rohmer) never made the Orient an object of deliberate study. Convenient and comfortingly familiar, these images imply for the adult writer who resorts to them exactly what they were designed to imply, and always have implied: that the Orient and Orientals are passive, unchanging and inscrutable, and that they conceal, behind silence and immobility, an essential Mystery, the Secret, the occult meaning of life. And yet we hear another voice in the passage, straining to be heard above this borrowed one: the voice of the inquisitive child, a budding flâneur, drawn not so much to an ideologically determined Orient as to difference itself.

When Burke writes of his first actual meeting with Quong Lee, the voices compete even more strenuously. One day, as the young Burke gazed into Quong's shop window, the merchant suddenly beckoned, inviting him in:

> With a sense of desperate adventure, as of cutting myself off from the friendly world, I went in. He smiled. I smiled; though not easily: I was trembling. Then he turned and ... held out to me a piece of ginger.

Again I hesitated; and in the moment of hesitating the thing happened. In that moment I knew a joy sharper than any I had known, and with it came a sense of time arrested and crystallised; a sense of eternity; a fancy that always, behind the curtain of time, this thing had been; that always Quong Lee had been sitting [there]; that for all time he had been holding out a piece of ginger and I had been standing before him, with the pins-and-needles of emotion in the back of my neck, holding out my hand to him. With it came, too, something more than joy; something that I know now was at once joy and knowledge and understanding and serenity. The Secret. I knew then all the beauty and all the evil of the heart of Asia; its cruelty, its grace and its wisdom. And I felt that whatever else might move or change, ... Quong Lee and I would not change. Always he would be sitting behind the counter of that shop, beckoning to me, and always I would be holding out my hand.

Then it was gone. ... I was back in the world of time and place; but a world with a difference. Something had happened to me ... I had achieved contact, and the [Limehouse] Causeway would forever be a part of me. I had turned my first corner. (*The Wind and The Rain* 21-3)

The language here shifts markedly from describing a genuine frozen-time moment when a child enters into subjectivity—recognizes that I am I and You are You—to rewriting that recognition as dogma, as the formula "West is West and East is East, eternally." The reasons for this shift are, I think, complex and worth considering. The young Burke probably *did* make "contact" with Quong Lee (it began a friendship that would last 12 years) and that initial experience—first of a cultural divide and then of connection across it—was no doubt formative. It was, in fact, a triple border-crossing: into subjectivity, into adulthood, and into non-Chinese identity. In memory, then, Burke's lost childhood and the Chinatown and Chinese man he knew as a child are inextricably knotted together.

And thus he falls—conveniently and unfortunately—into an Orientalist trap, which is the long-standing tropological pairing of childhood and the East (a pairing that Joyce's "Araby," for example, gently and movingly ironizes). Hence in Burke's writing, Chinatown and childhood become interchangeable objects of desire: outside of time and change, shrouded in mystery and consigned to oblivion, they are yet forever sought after, inviting recovery but irrecoverable, having divulged only once the Secret that the adult/West eternally tries but fails to grasp again.

That was the meaning of [Quong's] friendship; through him I peeped and saw and understood the beauty and sorrow of things. He opened the outer door, and for one moment he showed me the inner door and gave me its key.

But I could not turn it. And though I have tried and tried, I never have turned it. Never has the magic of the artist guided my hand to help me to show what I knew in that moment when the ginger was held out to me. (*The Wind and The Rain* 26)

Having experienced once, during that epiphanic moment in childhood, the "joy and knowledge and understanding and serenity" of the Secret, Burke longs to experience it again, to return to the mental or spiritual place where it happened. He has tried to get there through art, tried "to show what [he] knew in that moment," and this has made his art a kind of wandering, a quest characterized by the act and language of urban exploration. In Burke's restless London travel writing, Limehouse, where he "turned his first corner," is a frequent point of return. In his autobiography, too, he cycles back to it: *The Wind and The Rain* opens and closes with chapters both called "Causeway"—the first about his youthful haunting of Limehouse Causeway and his meeting with Quong Lee, the last about his return to Limehouse as a struggling twenty-three-year-old writer. And he revisits it, of course, in his Limehouse fiction itself, where his lifelong desire to reclaim the lost "Orient" of his childhood is dramatized in tales of frustrated desire between English people and Chinese.

A particularly revealing passage is the first paragraph of his first and best story in *Limehouse Nights*, entitled, unhappily, "The Chink and the Child." It is the story that D.W. Griffith adapted for his early silent film *Broken Blossoms*. Burke's story, set in Limehouse, is about a doomed romance between Lucy, a motherless English starveling of 12, and Cheng Huan, a Chinese shopkeeper who falls in love with Lucy and tries to rescue her from her abusive father. Cheng installs Lucy in an altar-like bed in his room, adorns her with Chinese clothes and trinkets, and, sublimating his sexual desire, vows to love and protect her, platonically, forever. In the end, the father beats Lucy to death for having "gone with a Chinaman"; Cheng then kills the father and himself. Burke begins the story like this:

> It is a tale of love and lovers that they tell in the low-lit Causeway that slinks from West India Dock Road to the dark waste of waters beyond. In Pennyfields, too, you may hear it; and I do not doubt that it is told in far-away Tai-Ping, in Singapore, in Tokio, in Shanghai, and those other gay-lamped haunts of wonder whither the wandering people of Limehouse go and whence they return so casually. It is a tale for tears, and should you hear it in the lilied tongue of the yellow men, it would awaken in you all your pity. In our bald speech it must, unhappily, lose its essential fragrance, that quality that will lift an affair of squalor into the loftier spheres of passion and imagination, beauty and sorrow. It will sound unconvincing a little—you know ... the kind of thing that is best forgotten. (22)

Like the waters that connect London to "darkest Africa" in Conrad's *Heart of Darkness*, a "waste of waters" here connects Limehouse to China. Water carries the "yellow men" to and fro, and the yellow men carry—not conspiracies, as in Rohmer—but stories, tales such as this one about Lucy and

Cheng Huan. As a form of cultural exchange, the tale-telling is ubiquitous, anonymous, and uncontrolled, and our narrator seems to appreciate, without fear, the latent power it represents, which is the power *of* representation, the power not of strangling yellow claws but of speaking lilied tongues. In this particular story of interracial love, child abuse, poverty, and murder, Anglo-Londoners appear brutal, bigoted, and perverse; and that *this* representation circulates—in Chinese—from Chinatown to China and back again, suggests that London's disturbing secrets do not stay locally confined, but leak out, rumored by the Other, in his own language, only to return later, "so casually," to haunt us in our own. Here, as throughout Burke's Limehouse fiction, Chinatown is the site of this daily, ungoverned exchange, the busy space of cross-cultural translation and the sometimes comic, but more often tragic, misunderstandings that attend it.

This tale itself, our narrator tells us, is both a product and instance of such (mis)translation. In the "bald speech" of English, the Anglo-Chinese romance is merely an "affair of squalor," a bit of naturalistic detail reduced from the "loftier" Chinese original, which, he implies, had the status and transformative power of poetry and myth. Just as Lucy and Cheng Huan perish in their respective border crossings, their tale loses its "essential fragrance" in crossing from Chinese to English, turns "unconvincing," loses the truth-power it once had. The differences insisted upon here—between "bald" English and "fragrant" Chinese—condense and invoke a whole series of oppositions: functional/ornamental, rational/irrational, clear/mysterious, and so on, that in Orientalist discourse, "eternally" distinguish West from East, and by activating them the narrator effectively Orientalizes the tale he is about to translate. And because the English version is not merely unconvincing but "the kind of thing that is best forgotten," its Chinese original represents for him not only the Orient but everything (such as childhood and the low-Other) that the West forsakes for the sake of its civilization and identity. In this connection, "best forgotten" sounds both prescriptive and wistful: what is forgotten and best forgotten is still desired, and hard to forget entirely. Some whiffs of it remain, to tantalize, to remind, to sadden. In these few introductory lines, then, the narrator not only encloses the tale within, and thus reproduces, the Orientalist fiction; he also effects, quite effortlessly, a complex transcoding between that fiction's "Orient" and an imagined "original" (pre-Westernized) self.

If the perceived differences between English translation and Chinese original occasion this inscription and transcoding, those processes are underwritten by the fact that the whole "translation" business is a fiction, an elaborate frame. The Lucy-Cheng Huan story is Burke's own: it did not originate among the Chinese of Limehouse and then travel to China and back again, changing hands and tongues along the way. So why this particular frame, this faked foreign intervention? We could say that being a Westerner,

Burke needs his fragrant frame as an opiate—that is, to get into the only frame of mind, an altered and illicit one, where the low-Other can be met or imagined. We could say further, as might Stallybrass and White, that this low-Other is himself, that the "Oriental" frame he erects and steps into is the carnivalesque stage that enables him to transgress the prefabricated boundaries segregating his present self from all those Other or past selves that threaten it and so are best forgotten. This stands to reason, since the story is also his "own," a version of his own "chink and child" experience—that is, his intense childhood love-affair with Limehouse and Quong Lee. Writing it as fiction, Burke recasts his childhood/Orientalized self as Lucy and his adult/Westernized self as the body of cultural forces that inevitably stalks and kills her. By providing the distance that enables intimacy, this self-othering fiction and its Orientalizing frame allow Burke to forget-remember his (illicit) Limehouse experience. However, they also entangle him further in the overcoding of that experience *as* an "Oriental" one, thereby repeating the process of designating, rejecting, and desiring the Other that was set in motion the moment he placed himself on the Western side of the "I am I, You are You" equation.

The Chinatown that Burke and Rohmer invent is, of course, phantasmal and hopelessly overdetermined, a territorialization machined by the mutually-reinforcing discourses of Orientalism and social exploration, which together ground, structure, and provide a language for both the xenophobic conspiracism that inspires Rohmer and the ethnocentric self-searching of Burke. The two discourses also authorize the process by which both men "make a career of the East" by cashing in on their Limehouse experiences—Rohmer to redeem, well, *cash* (as he admits) and an idea of England, Burke to redeem something like a unified self that preceded his fall into subjectivity.

It is tempting to think of Burke's cashing-in as more redeeming than Rohmer's since Burke's is less patently opportunistic, since his relation to Limehouse is more fraught, thoughtful, and ambiguous, and since his writing style is more nuanced and "literary." It is even more tempting when we learn that while Burke was pensively haunting the Limehouse he loved and living modestly as a publishing-house clerk, Rohmer was busy selling Fu Manchu to Hollywood and cooking up entreprenurial schemes exploiting the image of Limehouse he had made—by, for instance, inventing an "Oriental" perfume, employing a dozen Chinese men to manufacture it in Limehouse, then selling it in a department-store stall, using one of the men as a prop, complete with hammed-up "Chinaman" costume and gestures (pigtail, robe, lots of bowing).

But the very thematic, stylistic, and autobiographical elements that make Burke's writing more attractive also make it, because it is attractive, the more potent agent of the ethnocentric ideology it tenders. The codes seem more natural, are harder to crack. In its role as local Orient, a

Limehouse that (with)holds the secret of the self is more uncanny and more plausible, more "strangely familiar," than one that houses an evil Chinese doctor's corpse-fueled alchemical furnace; in its role as flâneur's signifying terrain, a Limehouse limned as one of London's many marginal centers seems more modern, and potentially more free, than one mapped according to the old, rigid, overworld/underworld hierarchy. Yet Burke's Limehouse is still a mirror for the West, an Other that exists primarily for the Western self's consumption, a means rather than an end.

Still, in the end, and unlike Rohmer's, Burke's Limehouse hints at more, trapped in self-reflection though it is. Alfred Kazin remarks (in his introduction to the 1973 reissue of *Limehouse Nights*) that although Burke "was hardly a great writer ... he had the root of real writing in him" because "he was hypnotized by his subject" (19). Kazin's choice of "hypnotized" is felicitous. Entranced, Burke believes he has received an other-worldly message from Limehouse, although "never has the magic of the artist guided his hand" to help him carry it across intact. He cannot resort to Chinese, the way that Eliot resorts to Sanskrit at the end of *The Waste Land*, since his goal is translation, a way of rendering "the Secret" into his English here-and-now. Yet while and because it fails, Burke's translation admits another reality, entirely lacking in Rohmer, which is that of a polyglot urban scene, with its innumerable dramas of immigration and assimilation and the messy, makeshift mappings that try and fail to contain them. Although London's Chinese residents remain muted in, or are muted by, his representation, the suggestion of lilied tongues at least begins to unsay Rohmer, turning readers' attention away from the fantasy of yellow claws and toward the possibility, however unrealized, of speech.

References

Barthes, Roland. *The Pleasure of the Text*. Trans. by Richard Miller. New York: Farrar, Straus, and Giroux, 1975. Originally *Le Plaisir du texte*. Paris: Éditions du Seuil, 1973.
Besant, Walter. *East London*. New York: The Century Company, 1901.
Burke, Thomas. "The Chink and the Child." *Limehouse Nights*. London: Grant Richards, 1916.
——. *The Wind and the Rain: A Book of Confessions*. New York: George H. Doran Company, 1924.
——. *City of Encounters*. Boston: Little, Brown, and Company, 1932.
Choo, Ng Kwee. *The Chinese in London*. Oxford: Oxford University Press, 1968.
Ferguson, Malcolm M. "Thomas Burke of Limehouse." *The Romanticist* 2 (1978): 41.
Kazin, Alfred. Introduction. *Limehouse Nights*. By Thomas Burke. New York: New Horizon Press, 1973.
Lucas, E.V. *A Wanderer in London*. New York: MacMillan, 1924.
May, J.P. "The Chinese in Britain, 1860-1914." *Immigrants and Minorities in British Society.* Ed. Colin Homes. London: George Allen & Unwin, 1978.

Rohmer, Sax [A.S. Ward]. *The Mystery of Dr. Fu-Manchu.* London: Methuen, 1913.
———. *The Si-Fan Mysteries.* London: Methuen, 1917.
Said, Edward. *Orientalism.* New York: Pantheon Books, 1978.
Stallybrass, Peter and Allon White. *The Politics and Poetics of Transgression.* New York: Cornell University Press, 1986.
Van Ash, Cay and Elizabeth Sax Rohmer. *Master of Villainy: A Biography of Sax Rohmer.* Bowling Green, Ohio: Bowling Green University Popular Press, 1972.
Walkowitz, Judith. *City of Dreadful Delight: Narratives of Sexual Danger in Late-Victorian London.* Chicago: University of Chicago Press, 1992.

2 *Over the Frontier* and into the Darkness with Stevie Smith: War, Gender, and Identity

Diana Austin

The twentieth century opened in Britain as it would continue to unfold, with public and private life enmeshed in the discourse of war. The Boer War (1899-1902), the product of imperialist expansion and recent gold discoveries (although waged under the banner of securing fair treatment for British citizens in what is now South Africa), produced heavy casualties, and many British families were still dealing with the resulting shockwaves of loss and suffering as 1914 and World War I approached. This war, frequently referred to at the time (with more hope than prescience) as "the war to end war," solidified the domination of the war discourse over all aspects of British private and public life in the twentieth century. As Paul Fussell persuasively argues in his cultural-literary study *The Great War and Modern Memory*, "the dynamics and iconography of the Great War have proved crucial political, rhetorical, and artistic determinants on subsequent life. At the same time the war was relying on inherited myth, it was generating new myth, and that myth is part of the fiber of our own lives" (ix). This pervasive influence of World War I on the following decades is explained by historian Eric Leed in *No Man's Land: Combat and Identity in World War I* as part of a pattern shaping the social context within which individual identity is formed: "the cessation of hostilities did not mean the end of the war experience but rather the beginning of a process in which that experience was framed, institutionalized, given ideological content" (xi).

Although Fussell and Leed focus almost entirely on men, the impact on society that they describe is of particular interest to women, because, of course, as Margaret Higonnet and others have emphasized, war is "a gendering activity ... [with] implications for women and men ... linked in symbolic as well as social and economic systems" (4). A "culturally produced activity ... rigidly defined by sex differentiation and ... committed to sexual exclusion," war is, as the organizers of a Dartmouth College Institute have pointed out, "a crucial site where meanings about gender are being produced, reproduced, and circulated back into society" (Cooke ix). Males are automatically at the center of the war discourse, because, whether soldiers or non-combatants, they have to position themselves actively in relation to what is seen by many as the quintessential test of their culture's values and of their own manhood. Women, however, are

35

automatically relegated to the margins. As the political philosopher Jean Bethke Elshtain observes, man is assigned the active role of the "Just Warrior," and, adapting a Hegelian term, woman is constructed as the passive, "Beautiful Soul ... positioned as a mourner, an occasion for war, and a keeper of the flame of nonwarlike values" (144). This role, Elshtain points out, by "[e]mbodying ethical aspirations but denying women a place in the corridors of power" (141) has the effect of "lodging women solidly in the domain of *Privatrecht*, or 'private right', a sphere that exists in tension with the *Kriegstaat*, or 'war state'" (141), always as the poor cousin.

Throughout the twentieth century, however, various British women writers have refused to accept the ways that the dominant war discourse, excluding them from decisions and actions, constructs them in the margins instead. For example, one of the earliest published voices of dissent against Britain's idealistic World War I fervor is heard in Rose Macaulay's 1916 novel *Non-Combatants and Others*; a young woman who has accepted her prescribed passivity, cocooning herself within a suffocating domestic space, suddenly joins her mother's pacifist campaign after her brother dies at the Front. The assigned safety of domestic space, this time doubly protected by class privilege, is also turned into an emotional battlefield in Rebecca West's 1918 novel, *The Return of the Soldier*, where the female narrator's observations of her amnesiac soldier-cousin lead her to a new understanding of the ways in which war is entangled with class and gender.

Moving further into the century, we see that World War II, with its routine bombing of London and other cities, extended the boundaries of the physical battlefield without altering women's exclusion from the world of power determining those boundaries. Issues produced by this paradox are central to novels about the period, like Elizabeth Bowen's 1949 *The Heat of the Day* (begun 1944) and Mary Wesley's 1984 *The Camomile Lawn*. Both novels indicate in passing that the female protagonists have been assigned useful jobs in important areas, such as intelligence-gathering, but the books also make clear that such jobs do not correlate with either political power or agreement with the war's values. Bowen and Wesley focus not on the translating and decoding done *for the war* by their female characters, but on the implied decoding *of the discourse itself* by these women who refuse to accept the constructed social script with its rigidly defined women's roles. Bowen's Stella, for instance, insists on privileging her individual "narrative of love" (94) over the master narrative of gentlemanly codes, patriotism, and treason, in which she finds herself a mere pawn. Similarly, Wesley subversively opposes the political with the personal in a dramatic image of Polly's bombed house: the only thing unharmed amidst the destruction is the canopy bed she shares with twin lovers she refuses to choose between (299). This festively decorated challenge to the rules of patriarchal order anticipates the post-war new order she establishes, a family unit within which neither she, her twin lovers, nor her children know or care about identifying paternity. In Elsh-tain's terms, both novelists are challenging *the "Kriegstaat,* or 'war state'" by subordinating its claims to those of the *"Privatrecht,* or 'private right'" (141).

More recent examples of the twentieth century's dominant war discourse are also treated as gendered sites of negotiation and resistance in British women's fiction. Doris Lessing, for instance, tackles the nuclear Cold War in her 1974 *Memoirs of a Survivor,* and in the 1991 *Gates of Ivory,* Margaret Drabble focuses on Pol Pot's murderous battle to take Cambodia "out of his-tory" (13). These novels destabilize traditional notions of war by revealing both how deeply war's violence is embedded in all aspects of social life and how war's social construction assumes our complicity if it does not encounter our questioning. Lessing's narrator, rejecting the marauding gangs and faceless bureaucrats equally responsible for turning her external world into an urban wasteland, looks inward for change. Gradually the enclosing walls of her flat are transmuted into entrance rather than barrier, a chance to start over in a new world "filled with industry, usefulness, hope" (141), cel-ebrating "variations on the human theme" (133) rather than continuing to entrench "stale social patterns" (121). Similarly, Drabble stresses the con-structedness of the war story by focusing on examples ranging from Pol Pot's vicious social engineering to the dangerous "ideological dreams" (82) of the gentle left-wing writer Stephen Cox, who also believes that humanity requires "a deep, violent, volcanic shift" to reach its "sweet natural level" (83). Like the previous writers, Drabble offers competing discourses through various female characters who either sorrowfully ask "Why must it go on for ever and ever, death and destruction, tragic empire after tragic empire?" (438), or confidently claim "'We make new history'" (78).

Whether dealing with the officially declared world wars or with the more recent bellicose situations mentioned, many British women writers insist on finding a way to participate in challenging this cultural force affecting their lives even as it excludes them; by engaging with issues other than purely military ones they demonstrate that war is more than just a temporally and spatially specific physical activity limited to males. Common strategies, as seen in the books just mentioned, include reconfiguring the physical war space by shifting the focus to the homefront from the battlefront, exposing war as constructed rather than inevitable, and raising the possibilities of a new discourse to replace that based on war, with the key to the changing of values being the dispossessed woman rather than the active warrior.

However, within this tradition of twentieth-century British women writ-ers challenging their period's privileging of far-reaching war values, the work of one writer in particular stands out. Stevie Smith, the author of two quirky novels between the world wars, *Novel on Yellow Paper* (1936) and *Over the Frontier* (1938), tackles the effects of war on society in general, and on women's identity construction in particular, with an approach that is as risky as it is unusual. She deliberately chooses to site her exploration of the issues at the source, placing her perplexed author/narrator/heroine, Pompey Casmilus, at the intersection of the political and military contexts constructing women as marginal beings. Attempting to define herself as a woman within a context that is itself defined by post-World War I masculine values, Pompey struggles for a sense of validity and purpose. Tense with desires and doubts, she negotiates within a system of gender construction which makes her private identity inseparable from the public pressures of the age; even her own "nervous irritability" at her lack of self-definition, she recognizes, demonstrates "the pulse of our time. For we have in us the pulse of history and our times have been upon the rack of war. And are, and are" (*OF* 94). In two Shandean novels that are by turns entertaining, puzzling, and disturbing, Smith ruptures the hold of the war discourse over the construction of female identity; in a daring strategy, she writes her narrator, who has refused (=failed) to secure her assigned feminine role as passive wife, into the *other* gendered position created by the binaries of war, that of active soldier.

As both Arthur Marwick (*Women at War, 1914-18*) and Gail Braybon (*Women Workers in the First World War*) have demonstrated in their studies of the labor demands on English women during World War I, the war undeniably affected women's social and economic roles. Women in the 1920s and 1930s, however, were caught between these potentially emancipating changes and the traditional pressures to see men as their only route to self-definition and a role in the world: "the unmarried girls have an idea, that if only they were married it would be all right, and the married women think, Well now I am married, so it *is* all right" (*NYP* 149). Resisting this route, Pompey makes an early, tentative effort to define herself within the public (i.e., masculine) world of action. On a German holiday in the early 1930s, roused to anger and fear by the menacing nationalism of "the Hitler campaign ... just getting on the way" (*NYP* 99), she takes a stand of public bellicosity based on her private anguish:

> it makes you feel: God send the British Admiralty and the War Office don't go shuffling on with their arms economies too long-o.... Ugh that hateful feeling I had over there, and how it was a whole race gone mad. Oh heaven help Deutschland when it kicks out the Jews. (*NYP* 103)

However, as her train leaves Germany, despite worrying "about what the Nazis might and certainly would do" to her Jewish friends (*NYP* 109), Pompey can find no role for herself as a woman in changing the public circumstances. As a result, she first bursts into tears, and then retreats into her female powerlessness: "Well, there is nothing to be done about it, about the Jews and the atavism and the decadence, no there's nothing to be done about it. So help yourself to another helping of apple sauce, Pompey, I said" (*NYP*

111). Unable to see how to define herself as a political activist, Pompey accepts her society's gendered construction of her as merely a passive object of desire, a role re-confirmed when a stranger propositions her in the midst of her dilemma.

But success in this role, too, eludes Pompey. She does attempt to construct an identity for herself along her society's approved lines of a "right-thinking girl" (*NYP* 50). Despite becoming engaged, however, she finds herself resisting the cozy domestic routines of her fiancé's family: "I am grateful to Freddy and to his mama. But I feel that I wish only to be a visitor, I cannot always be in that atmosphere, it is warm, but by and by it is too warm and too close. And if you are married it is very difficult to make it to remain always a visit" (*NYP* 234). Marriage, then, society's route to a stable identity for women, is eventually rejected by Pompey, who decides that the self-definition it offers is a form of suicide:

> Married to Freddy, in the high floating exaltation of these moments when imagination working on generosity all seemed so well between us, and all well lost for that life together, married to him in the morning, in the evening I should be dead. Dead and covered with shame and dishonour. (*NYP* 218)

Pompey is thus caught in the binary struggle that Hélène Cixous characterizes as common to women endeavoring to find a significant identity and role in a world organized on masculine principles, where "*activity*" automatically equates with "Man" and "*passivity*" with "Woman" (559-60). Unable to situate herself in this cultural script, since she has declined the allocated passive identity of wife and cannot see any route to masculine agency, Pompey feels herself disappearing into Cixous's "shadow" (565) of the powerless; to combat this she refuses to establish any fixed identity at all. Instead she opts for a fluidity that allows her to "sample" the lives of friends who are "so very different … they … cannot even safely be set down in front of each other" (*NYP* 196-7). Of course, Pompey realizes that the masculine is the normative in her society, so she recognizes that her refusal to restrict or be restricted in her relationships jeopardizes her claim to validity: "Show me a man's friends and I will show you the man. Then what sort of a *man* is Pompey whose friends are 'all of different kinds'? Is there any Pompey at all?" (*NYP* 197). In *Novel on Yellow Paper*, then, Smith allows Pompey to speculate about many aspects of society and gender, but in the end the book is dominated by a quietism created by her sense of public powerlessness and private fragmentation.

Picking up where the previous novel left off, *Over the Frontier* begins with the emotionally exhausted, jilted Pompey presented as both invalid and in-valid, living in a fog of sleeping pills provided by her doctor. Conspicuously portraying this passivity to emphasize its coming rejection, Smith immediately starts her protagonist on a journey that, as the title suggests, allows her to seek self-knowledge and agency by a new strategy in a new arena. Instead of trying to find meaning in the private female world of the heart, Pompey crosses the gendered boundaries restricting women's identity; she actively explores her sense of self in the space of public policies and action that have hitherto defined her without allowing her full participation. Because of the historical period, this means that Smith shows Pompey purposefully choosing to enter the central space of the war values defining her times, and, by extension, her. Smith's strategy recognizes that, as Carol Cohn has pointed out, even "if we are positioned *by* discourses, we can also take different positions *within* them" (230) and, by extension, *against* them, even from the inside; a military campaign is therefore a logical place for Pompey to contest the restrictive gender boundaries of her time and thus attempt the reconstruction of her private and public identity. The entire novel becomes a self-reflexive analysis of oppressive power by a narrator who simultaneously occupies the positions of victim and oppressor; Pompey's "voracious consciousness" (*OF* 43) leads her to investigate and expose the masculine world of power-hunger even as she herself participates in it.

Over the Frontier opens in an elegant art gallery, its presentation suggestive of the "towers" where women have traditionally been imprisoned by male power. As in fairytale allegories about the dangers of female sexuality, the gallery has restricted access to its "princess"—a statue of Venus—by placing her up a flight of stairs with a uniformed guard standing watch; an unauthorized, drunken "suitor" is brutally thrown down the stairs, falling into the clutches of a witch-like figure of unmanaged sexuality lurking at the bottom, a "horrible whore" (9-10). Of course, as discussed in John Berger's *Ways of Seeing*, the art displayed in galleries often continues the fairytale practice of locking women up, because society's male gaze constructs woman as a "social presence" defined by "what can and cannot be done to her" (46-7). Internalizing this gaze, women can be trapped by appearing to themselves as well as to their societies as mere objects: "One might simplify this by saying: *men act* and *women appear*. Men look at women. Women watch themselves being looked at" (Berger 47). Smith quickly establishes the significance of this dynamic for Pompey and other women by showing that art, as part of the social discourse, joins with the period's war rhetoric to make women see themselves constructed as passive other. The gallery's main exhibition is by Georg Grosz, a German whose previous portfolio, called "A Post-War Museum," had served as a moving "dark memorial" (*OF* 15) for Pompey, allowing her to share an awareness of the pain, poverty, and hopelessness inflicted upon Germany by the victors of World War I. However, since the victors prefer to deny "all of the ignobility and shameful pain of war suffering" (*OF* 15), the earlier, compassionate art has been denigrated as the flawed product of a mere "war neurotic" (*OF* 15). Grosz has, consequently, customized his artistic vision to fit demand. His current light-hearted exhibition has found favor by transferring the power motif from criticism of war cruelty to celebration of gender cruelty. Three of the paintings Pompey singles out for comment mock women: a frumpish prostitute is cheapened by the gaze of a stingy potential customer, two plump Girl Guides with exposed thighs and knickers provoke a lascivious gaze by viewers, and an "extremely ugly ... extremely amorous" (*OF* 14) old woman on a beach casting longing glances with "little eager pig eyes" (*OF* 14-15) at "a fine nordic specimen ... [of] masculine buck" (*OF* 15) is herself pinned in the ridiculing gaze of gallery spectators.

Pompey links this aura of cruelty to her own social position as a woman who has refused/"failed" to accept the scripted role of marriage to Freddy: "And coming out of this picture-gallery I must think of my own situation that is so heavy upon me" (*OF* 18). She recognizes that her private suffering is inseparable from the period's constructed public fascination with power, pain, and cruelty: "this cruelty is very much in the air right now, it is very dangerous, it is a powerful drug that deadens as it stimulates" (*OF* 58). Just as there are exploitative writers who "make a lot of money writing about pain" (*OF* 52) and readers and movie-goers drawn to works about torture and cruelty (*OF* 56), so even the ordinary person in this era is likely to be visited by "dreams that come to us in the night that are full of cruelty. And the effect of cruelty upon the imagination is fear. And the result of fear is death. There is nothing noble in this, it is something hateful and to be endured and to be resisted" (*OF* 58). Since the construction of identity in this period is inseparable from war's emphasis on power and pain, Smith shows Pompey exploring this dark region as a full, but self-analytical, participant so that she can gain a degree of agency in her own identity construction by acquiring an empowering understanding of the cultural forces affecting her whether she agrees with them or not. The strategy is risky, since both the mere "cruelty-fan" and the artist are drawn to this dark area, but while the first is enjoying the power over the victim, the second is "creating and brooding upon the darkness of pain" for a nobler purpose, choosing to tip the paintbrush "with the colours of physical agony to portray the more subtle agony of the spirit" (*OF* 62). Pompey, then, will venture over a frontier normally closed to women so that, like the artist, she can limn for herself and others the lure of darkness and dominance. The experience may enable her to strengthen resistance with the powers of recognition; the danger is that, like her society, she may succumb to the values she starts by interrogating.

Pompey begins her exploration of power and pain, suitably enough, in the stereotyped private area of romantic relationships. Like a ruthless military commander, she devises a campaign to overthrow Freddy's conquest of her heart. Forcing a reconciliation, she puts on the protective armor of a deceptively feminine "meek and docile" attitude (*OF* 34), encouraging him to take her to all the "bungaloid" (*OF* 33), suburban places she loathes:

> Well, imagine that it is a sunk submarine from which you will escape. But first
> you must stand quietly and without panic until the flood-water in the escape-
> room is covering your shoulders, is creeping up to your mouth, and only then
> when the whole of the escape-room is flooded to drowning point will you be
> able to shoot up through the escape-funnel, to shoot up for ever and away. ...
> Not until I am flooded with a dislike pointing to hatred can I escape, can I shoot
> up for ever and away. ... I must escape from him, must get completely free of
> him. (*OF* 35)

She then moves into the public realm, appropriating the qualities of the
very same British Empire that she has frequently mocked for its greedy con-
quests rationalized by elevated language ("And here for folly is the Commission from Heaven, and here for casuistry the Sole Good of the Resident
Population" [*OF* 100])—all in aid of such aims as "cheap sugar" (*OF* 98).
Going to a costume party dressed in "shorts and shirt, solar topee and sandals
and representing the bounds—limit to you—of Empire" (*OF* 71), she creates
her own mental music of imperial determination in an enormous room:

> I dance, faster and faster. ... with an intensity of concentration, an exaltation,
> an exhilaration of the spirit, and at centre a heart of darkness, of darkness and
> désespoir.
> ... And within the music there is moving now a more insistent clamour, a
> harsh grating sound, a clashing of steel on steel. It is very menacing, very mil-
> itary, this rapidly increasing metallic clamour, thrusting, driving, marching.
> (*OF* 49-50)

The increasingly martial music of this strange dance and the dark world it
represents, the same hunger for power behind both empire and war, is, like
Pompey's energetic and often criticized "pseudo-military style of riding"
(*OF* 83), a route of escape from the restrictions of her gendered identity; this
discourse of desire and action "takes a girl right out of herself" (*OF* 51).

At the urging of her doctor and friends, the invalid/in-valid Pompey
agrees to take a rest cure at a Schloss just over the border from northern Germany, and here she seeks the next stage of empowerment, a way into the
world of agency, defined in the period by masculine values. The novel begins
to embed a destabilizing double-voicing in its very structure, refusing to fix
its status as either realistic or surrealistic, enacting what it is interrogating.
Pompey dreams herself into the center of a clichéd, clandestine war scene,
as a figure so important that any slip on her part will result in both "penalty
of conscience and a general calamity" (*OF* 135). This dream, like the earlier
Empire dance, is an identity strategy marked by distinctive dress and action
appropriating masculine power: "I am in uniform. But it is a secret, this uni-

form, it must not for a moment appear that I am in uniform" (*OF* 135). Freddy as ex-fiancé appears in her dream to challenge her new role, but Pompey now controls the dynamics of their relationship:

Why Pompey, you are in uniform. No, Freddy, my sweet darling Freddy why you are raving, Uniform? Why certainly you are dotty. This is not uniform, why these for instance are my riding clothes. What are the stars on your collar? Why these are not stars, these are the pin heads of the pin that keeps my tie in place. From whom is your commission? Why I hold no commission, why surely you could not be so dippy, to think that I am sitting here under orders from an authority I do not know I do not recognize to exist? I hold no commission. (*OF* 135)

The intensity of desire in this recurring dream eventually produces its own reality: she encounters a mirror image of the scene in her everyday life, but this time featuring another Schloss guest, the dashing Major Tom Satterthwaite, in the role that Pompey is preparing to appropriate. Although Tom's precise plans for Pompey are deliberately left unclear, he seems to want to use her in behind-the-lines decoding and military strategy. Pompey, then, like Elizabeth Bowen's Stella or Mary Wesley's Polly, is recruited for a supporting role in the war effort, but she reverses expectations, allowing herself to become an "agent" so that she can gain agency. As Tom trains her, she uses him as her entry into the world of action normally denied her gender and thus is able to experience—and challenge—the war discourse from the inside. Long rides discussing political views and military strategy follow, reminding Pompey of the way such topics usually drive "a wedge between the sort of work that is man's work and the sort of work that is women's work, and all that line of reasoning that is so a part of unhappy fighting times and of cheap newspaper correspondence columns" (*OF* 149). Such gendered divisions need to disappear, she asserts, to meet the needs of modern times: "Never again in England I think shall we breed exclusively masculine and exclusively feminine types at any high level of intelligence, but always there will be much of the one in the other" (*OF* 149).

Now that she has a sense of her own agency, Pompey can begin a dramatic reconstruction of her identity. No longer needing to take refuge in the quietism of female powerlessness, she can confront the dark complexity of her own desires and attitudes, including those involving public issues like anti-Semitism. As Tom and others prompt her to parrot their authorized views, she finds her own voice and dares to articulate the despicable lure of racial hatred that they gloss over: "Do we not always hate the persecuted? Would any but they have survived their persecutions? Oh devilish hateful jibe, oh how it tugs at my assent. 'None but the Jews would have survived their persecutions.' Immense differentiation of the would and could" (*OF* 158). Exclaiming, "But I have had some very dear Jewish friends," she recognizes "the final treachery of the smug goy. Do not all our persecutions of Israel follow upon this smiling sentence?" (*OF* 158).

Pompey ignores the changeable propaganda of the war discourse and decides for herself that "friendship is a more final truth than policy or the argument of history" (*OF* 159). She admires a courteous, intelligent old man who is a Jewish business associate in the nearby university town of Ool: "by now we are great friends" (*OF* 196). Siding with the "essentially civilized, urbane and international ... cultured" (*OF* 197) group that he represents, she publicly declares her position by intervening in one of the engineered anti-Jewish demonstrations becoming more frequent in the region. When a "rather threatening" (*OF* 201) crowd of students comes to harass Aaronsen, she takes his place on the balcony, and their catcalls are silenced by surprise. Pompey tastes real power for the first time as her presence makes the anti-Semitic mob disperse, but presented simultaneously with her swelling right-eous anger against "Allemagne barbare" is her own awareness that even the most justified fury has a dangerous dark side:

> But in permitting myself to become so destroyingly furious and so intolerant, is it not to find in myself a little of this very barbarismus I so much should like to wipe out for all time from all people? No, I do not think this in me, and in those who feel as I do, is barbarismus, intolerance yes, but it is the sharp spear of defence against infamy that must bear for a sharp point the uttermost sharp point of a righteous pure intolerance. (*OF* 197)

Before she crosses the nearby frontier with Tom to join an unspecified war, Pompey takes leave of her gendered identity by crossing the boundaries of propriety at a formal Schloss social evening. In a defiant demonstration of non-conformity, she dances wildly with a female friend, ignoring Tom and outraging the other guests: "Why surely this is not at all *conforme* that Josephine and Pompey should race together through the wide long room ... a little incorrect in the thought" (*OF* 210). She responds to the angry Tom's "tiresome masculine bully-dog mania" at this apparent frivolity first with typically feminine tears and then with the laughter of power (*OF* 213-14), finally allowing him to help her prepare for the journey by acting as her valet/maid. Glimpsing herself in a darkened mirror as she leaves, Pompey realizes that she is now "in uniform" (*OF* 217), and this change of costume newly positions her within the power discourse. Another guest bids them farewell, not by giving Tom the expected chivalrous instructions to protect his weaker companion: "Take care, do not keep her too long in the saddle," but by saying instead, "'Look out she doesn't pinch your job'" (*OF* 220).

Pompey has been in conflict over the restrictions of her gendered iden-tity throughout the novel, so eager for escape that she deliberately stifles any inclination to question the nature of the operation she is joining: "I am indeed anxious not to know, in apprehension that it might prove to be something so ordinary" (*OF* 222), like the humdrum life previously trapping her: "I ... thank the God of War to be rid of the tea-cups and tattle and the boring old do-all-nothings of a finished existence" (*OF* 229). However, this transition to the world of power, with its attendant responsibilities, brings its own conflicts. Her reaction to her uniform frightens Pompey, because it forces her to confront the darkness of her own power hunger, now awakened by her participation in war:

> And wrapped in this really magnificent and close, enfolding garment, this so-military apparel, I must laugh a little about this job-pinching business, to think of all that is stirring already in my heart; that this cloak is what there is for an outward and spiritual sensation, growing growing with a strong swift growth to a full strength, that is what there is in my secret heart of pride and ambition, of tears and anger. (*OF* 220)

The uniform makes outward and visible the inward, invisible desire for power that Pompey is wrestling with, and, ironically, she retreats in fear to the very gender boundaries that have previously restricted her: "I do not like to be in uniform, to prance round and be a soldierly female, I have a sort of horror of that sort of female. ... Why must I wear this coat that is already putting such unfemale thoughts into my head?" (*OF* 227-8).

Once over the frontier, however, Pompey soon learns to savor her new position of power over troops that are "ours, to move this way and that, to command and to visit with rewards and penalties" (*OF* 234). She excels in her new role as military commander, and soon surpasses Tom: "I have succeeded where he has failed, and the messages that come through to us are for me and not for him" (*OF* 245). Despite her ambition and success, though, Pompey remains aware of the problematic nature of the change within herself, asking, "what am I now, and set to what?" She recognizes that participating in war is changing her identity, creating "an absolute darkness of ferocity about and within me"(*OF* 245). When the devastated region's unhappy citizens fling dirty looks and stones at her instead of Tom, thus paying tribute to her dominant status as commander, she responds with arrogant laughter, but is aware nonetheless that "it is not a very friendly laugh, and there is still something in me to be appalled at its hateful undertone" (*OF* 246).

The turning point in Pompey's analysis of both her new identity and its validating context comes when, on an ambitious solo mission, she is caught by a sentry. Confronted with the difference between ordering murder from a distance as a military commander and committing murder herself, she has to rationalize her action in the time-honored way, by diminishing her opponent with an objectifying gaze, seeing him as "rat-like, so wizened, so remote from all accepted standards of a dignified old age" (*OF* 248). Quieting her "liberalistic world-conscience, that is still persisting in Opposition" (*OF* 250), she draws her revolver, although with a self-mocking awkwardness, but she has no voice, either her own or one appropriated from war rhetoric, for the moment of killing; the text falls silent. Beginning to speak of the deed in retrospect almost immediately, however, she reveals her horror at what she has done, the novel once again demonstrating both Pompey's continuous murmuring resistance to her new identity as warrior and her open questioning of the war discourse itself. She cannot forget

> something so fleeting-familiar ... something that did not at all belong to the essence of the heart of Rat-face, that was flashed upon his eyes by a thought, it must have been my own, from some far place of a dark memory, to rise up with an impertinent incongruity, an altogether out-of-character impertinence; to rise up, to question, to question my commission, with a surge-back to a voice that never spoke, but in a dream of weakness: *From whom do you hold your commission?* (*OF* 252)

Lying at night with the ill Tom, Pompey tries to revel in her strength and her successes, but always with an undercurrent of self-challenge. She reassures herself that all the bloodshed is necessary to wash away "the dotty idealismus" of the enemy, that is "a deceit of the black devil, that will have us all to destroy us." On the other hand, she recognizes the arrogance of such a claim to power: "But is not the devil also in the hands of the destroyer, that shoots and slays, to destroy, to make an end, that can make no end, that only God can make?" (*OF* 253). Pompey is caught in the war discourse, trying to act simultaneously its conflicting but co-dependent gendered identities, Elshtain's "Just Warriors and Beautiful Souls" (4). Although as a Beautiful Soul she has to deplore the killing, as a Just Warrior she has to rationalize the slaughter. After all, the "dotty idealismus" of Nazi Germany marches with the enemy on this side of the frontier, making Pompey feel justified in crying, "Death to the dotty idealismus, death to all ideologies," and yet her language reveals uncertainty. Although she reassures herself that "we are right, we are right," she immediately undercuts this confidence with a recognition that exposes the flimsiness of the Just Warrior construct, "however riff-raff our armies, however base our honey-voiced Headquarters." To buttress her shaky loyalty, Pompey falls back on the traditional demonizing of the enemy as the hated and feared Other: "I grind my teeth to think of Germany and her infection of arrogance and weakness and cruelty that has spread to our own particular enemy, has set on foot this abominable war, has brought us all this to pass" (*OF* 255-6).

Pompey's search for identity in a society dominated by war values has led her to seek self-validation in the acceptance of the rhetoric traditionally used to validate war, but she questions this even as she tries to employ it; she is aware that her authorized "hatred ... is not without guilt, is not, is not a pure flame of altruism; ah, hatred is never this, is always rather to make use of this grand altruistic feeling, to bring to a head in ourselves all that there is in us of a hatred and fury upon a less convenient truth" (*OF* 256). Given war's binary divisions and their associations with her society's gendered activity/passivity models, she has gone after the sense of agency provided by power. However, her self-reflexive participation in the very system that she has viewed as oppressive allows her to come to a recognition not only of her own collusion but also of the system's reliance on such either-or choices. Even before her successes win her the right finally to meet her military masters at Headquarters, she has realized that re-positioning herself within her society's hierarchy does not change its ability to define her, but merely makes her complicit in that definition: "How apt I was for this deceit, how splendid a material, that recognizing the deceit must take commission under it, forever following darkness" (*OF* 256). The cruel and self-centered Archbishop and Generalissimo, whose midnight summons reveals to Pompey that the war is being waged merely for their own "advantage ... to a hateful end" (*OF* 263), confirms her awareness that, despite the lure of dominance for the marginalized, choosing to become "'one of us,'" as the Generalissimo calls her (*OF* 267), merely perpetuates inequities. Although she has previously "despised utterly and avoided the mentality that clings to privilege," she has let herself "be for a moment attracted, conceited to have the cloak of *their* privilege, for *their* purpose, thrown about my shoulders"; since "all holders of privilege" are "ruthless and cruel in their tenure" and will hold "at any cost whatever of pain and suffering to other people, the power of their privilege" (*OF* 271), she has thus allowed herself once again, this time knowingly, to be constructed by the war discourse.

The novel seems to have come full circle as it closes, since instead of various women locked in an objectifying gaze on an art gallery wall, it shows one woman locked in a room at military Headquarters, where Pompey's masters no longer entirely trust her. The crucial difference, however, is that the power-hunger at the center of both imprisoning forces has been exposed and its hold disrupted by Pompey's continuous interrogation of the very process in which she has been participating:

> Is then power and the lust for power the very stuff of our existence ...? And if we cannot achieve in our individualities this power are we any less guilty if we pursue it, or again, abandoning the sweet chase, identify ourselves with a national ethos, take pride in our country, in our country's plundering, or, if the mood takes us, in our country's victories upon other fields less barren, in science, art, jurisprudence, philosophy? (*OF* 271-2)

Having traveled in the novel from the shame of "Pompey very very bad soldier" (*OF* 137) in a world where even injections in a doctor's office were judged by masculine norms, to a world where her success as a military commander gave her the power of life and death over multitudes, Pompey has concluded that the cost of this route to identity is unacceptable, the result *more* shameful: "is there not this very frightfulness of an unsatisfied personal lust for power, identifying itself with a national arrogance, my country's successful delinquency? How base, despicable, how unutterably base" (*OF* 272).

Thus a novel that begins as one individual's search for agency becomes a commentary on the binary pressures within the period's pervasive war discourse shaping identity, private and public, individual and societal, particularly in the gendered scripting inseparable at the time from issues of power. In some ways, then, Smith takes the assertions of Fussell and Leed about war's influence even further, revealing that the habit of bellicosity is, as described by Lynne Hanley, "a structure of consciousness ... a mental habit of creating arbitrary categories that are presumed to be mutually exclusive and hostile (self/other, masculine/feminine, white/black, us/them), and of then insisting on the supremacy of one category over the other" (7). Frustratingly, as Hanley says, this model of bellicosity has sometimes seemed almost self-perpetuating because "For the most part Fussell's premise that war literature is by and about men at the front remains the operative premise .... And since soldiers write our story of war, theirs is the perspective that prevails" (6). *Over the Frontier*, however, changes the gaze *from/of* and the narration *by* war, stripping away the protective rhetoric.

As the participants in the Dartmouth College Institute on Gender and War suggest, one strategy for disrupting war's cultural dominance is to "expose the historical constructedness of the war story that must eliminate the feminine to survive" (Cooke ix), and *Over the Frontier* accomplishes this in a variety of ways. For instance, by the unusual strategy of taking her female protagonist into the combat zone as active participant, Smith challenges the basis of what Daphne Spain calls "'Gendered spaces.'" Spain, a scholar whose work connects the areas of architecture, sociology, and gender, links social institutions and their spatial corollaries with gender segregation and status, arguing that such spaces "separate women from knowledge used by men to produce and reproduce power and privilege" (3). War is, in effect, one of these social institutions, with the combat zone inextricably linked to the political zone that declares war in the first place, and women's exclusion from the Front has seemed to justify excluding them at home as well. Pompey's transformation from broken-hearted invalid to ruthlessly successful soldier in a non-existent war that nonetheless has all the recognizable markers of the period's military and political tensions disorients any conditioned response to war, whether within the narrative or in actual historical assessment; the simultaneous participation in and analysis of war further denies the reader the stability of custom. In addition, by placing her protagonist in the forbidden zone, Smith raises the thorny issue of female collaboration in the ideology of war, an awkward subject that critics like Claire Tylee (211) and Sharon Ouditt (3) have also broached in comments on Vera Brittain's well-known World War I work *Testament of Youth*, which they argue actually reproduces the very ideologies of class, gender, and military romanticization that Brittain viewed herself as exposing.

By having Pompey consciously choose the lure of power behind the gendered war discourse, Smith succeeds in challenging simplistic divisions scripting women as "the custodians of life" and men as "destroying machines" (Macaulay 268). Despite its different emphasis from Elshtain's "Just Warriors and Beautiful Souls" (Elshtain 4), Macaulay's rhetoric similarly perpetuates the gendered stereotyping by which society symbolically manages war—even when protesting against it. Pompey accepts full responsibility for her choices:

> But you see it is my fault I am in this galère, I have brought myself to this absurd pass. I may say I was shanghaied into this adventure, forced into a uniform I intuitively hated. But if there had been nothing in me of it, nothing to be called awake by this wretched event, should I not now be playing, in perhaps some boredom, but safely and sanely enough, with those who seem to me now beyond the frontier of a separate life? (*OF* 267)

Although her relationship with Tom has mirrored war's systemically divisive values, with Pompey first the neophyte under his tutelage and then in the reverse position of power ("as I grow stronger Tom grows weaker" [*OF* 246]), she has by the end of the novel tried to dismantle the binary structure in this private sphere, as she has by analyzing the public sphere of war itself. Dropping her competitive secretiveness, she tells Tom of her summons to Headquarters for a promotion, and he in turn, while uneasy, wishes her luck: "watch your step. I don't say, Stay with me. If I did I was raving" (*OF* 268). Locked in a tower at the end by her unscrupulous military masters, she calmly begins to plot her escape, including planning how to succeed without endangering Tom by returning to him. Refusing to assume blame for her recent actions, she also refuses dependency.

Over the Frontier is, as I have shown, a thought-provoking exploration of war and gender, yet its critical reception has been disappointing both in scope and quality. The last few decades have seen a steady, if modest, flow of commentary on Smith's work, but the focus is usually on her poetry; when the novels are examined, *Novel on Yellow Paper* and *The Holiday* dominate the discussion. It is as if the blurring of boundaries in *Over the Frontier* discourages commentary by offering no secure place to comment from: should the style be judged by the standards of realism or surrealism? How is one meant to react to the implausible metamorphosis of the nervous young woman into the ruthlessly successful military commander? Most of its contemporary reviewers, sympathetic but prepared by *Novel on Yellow Paper* to be amused, were instead bewildered. As *The Times Literary Supplement* reviewer said perplexedly, "The design is not that of a novel.... But it is not easy to describe what it is all about" ("The New Novels" 43); the *London Mercury* reviewer similarly tried to puzzle through the "fantastic symbolism" in the last third of the novel, before giving up with a despairing "We do not know" (Scott-James 456). Victoria Glendinning, a discerning recent reviewer, finds the book's wide-ranging military fantasy disconcerting, since Pompey is obviously exploring only "the wilderness of her own *animus*" (54). Recognizing that "[f]rontiers are inconclusive and uncomfortable places," however, Glendinning falls back on her general admiration for Smith and praises the novel despite the faults that stem from its being "an inconclusive and uncomfortable book."

These tentative, if well-disposed, reactions are at least understandable, unlike the determination of a number of modern commentators to read the book as just one more example of the romance plot. Sanford Sternlicht says coyly that

> Although Stevie does not explicitly relate their sexual acts, Pompey and Tom are energetic, often tender, sometimes angry lovers. ... Pompey sometimes is wearing the uniform that converts her into someone hard, fierce, and aggressive; but sometimes she wears a feminine nightgown. (22)

Catherine A. Civello, on the contrary, focuses on the *lack* of sex in *Over the Frontier*, arguing that Pompey is a case of arrested psycho-sexual development, with "no taste for sex" (111). Read (and misread) as a romance plot in both cases, the novel produces the standard reinscribing of male activity and female passivity: "In the end Tom belittles and leaves Pompey" (Sternlicht 23); "Tom abandons her when she becomes successful" (Civello 118). (In fact, he doesn't, as I have indicated above.) In contrast, Laura Severin, one of the more perceptive recent critics of Smith, asserts that *Over the Frontier* should not be read through the romance plot, but in the twentieth-century tradition of fictions of female development examined by such writers as Rachel Blau duPlessis and Elizabeth Abel. Severin's astute reading of the novel, however, does not push far enough; she is still reading within the binary constraints of the romance plot by seeing the novel only as an unsuccessful rejection of that convention: "Smith does not succeed in presenting a new set of choices in *Over the Frontier*, but we do see her using the traditional quest form to avoid ending her novel in marriage or death, both of which threaten her heroine Pompey throughout the novel" (475).

Stevie Smith's exploration of twentieth-century gendered identity construction goes beyond the simple conventions of either the romance or the quest plot; it tries to break away from binary distinctions by refusing to situate itself in a single recognizable space, realistically, stylistically, or morally. Pompey's self-reflexive participation in war's sanctioned violence gives the novel simultaneous multiple voicing; the rallying cry of the power/war discourse, "Have you no pride, no ambition?" is made to contain within it another set of values: "And are there no tears?" (*OF* 272). This is why the novel's closing words are so disturbingly enigmatic: "Power and cruelty are the strength of our life, and in its weakness only is there the sweetness of love" (*OF* 272). Binary rhetoric is employed, but a single clear meaning is refused.

The novel began as an attempt by Pompey to go from the margins to the center of society in a search for self-hood, a process which, as Helena Rubenstein points out, always involves negotiating the physical and social boundaries constructed on the basis of gender (4-6), but the emphasis is on "process"; this is not a simple matter of choosing between opposites as words like "margin," "center," or "frontier" might seem to imply, with a safe distinction between "here" and "there." The roots of the "liminal rites" (14) which Eric Leed, following Arnold van Gennep's model, has identified as marking the soldier's transition from civilian to military life, are exposed in *Over the Frontier* by its insistence on liminal writing: Pompey, yearning "for a change to be inside-of, instead of perpetually and draughtily outside-of" (*OF* 247) does not end up moving *herself* from margins to center but instead, through her experience, moves the war discourse *itself* into interrogating liminal space. The result is that the novel offers a unique perspective on gender and war, speaking from neither center nor margin in opposition, but from Teresa de Lauretis's "'elsewhere' ... the elsewhere of discourse here and now, the blind spots, or the space-off, of its representations. ... it is there that the terms of a different construction of gender can be posed—terms that do have effect and take hold at the level of subjectivity and self-representation" (25). Smith's novel employs binary rhetoric with stereotypical positions, showing Pompey apparently crossing the frontier between them, but this movement is not "between" so much as it is "within." As de Lauretis says of the "movement back and forth across the boundaries of sexual difference," this is not "a movement from one space to another beyond it, or outside" (25) but "a movement from the space represented by/in a representation, by/in a discourse, by/in a sex-gender system, to the space not represented yet implied (unseen) in them" (26). By refusing to occupy a single site, *Over the Frontier*, with ambiguity and self-interrogation, tries to re-configure the gendered spaces affecting identity within the twentieth-century war discourse, raising what Dale Spender calls "possibilities for alternative ways of making sense of the world" (3).

References

Abel, Elizabeth, Marianne Hirsch, and Elizabeth Langland, eds. *The Voyage In: Fictions of Female Development*. Hanover, New Hampshire: University Press of New England, 1983.

Berger, John. *Ways of Seeing*. London: British Broadcasting Corporation and Penguin, 1972.

Blau duPlessis, Rachel. *Writing Beyond the Ending: Narrative Strategies Of Twentieth Century Women Writers*. Bloomington, Indiana: Indiana University Press, 1985.

Bowen, Elizabeth. *The Heat of the Day*. London: Cape, 1949.

Brittain, Vera. *Testament of Youth*. London: Gollancz, 1933.

Civello, Catherine A. "Stevie Smith's *Ecriture Feminine*: Pre-Oedipal Desires and Wartime Realities." *Mosaic* 28.2 (June 1995): 109-22.

Cixous, Hélène. "Sorties: Out and Out: Attacks/Ways Out/Forays." *Contemporary Critical Theory*. Ed. Dan Latimer. New York: Harcourt Brace Jovanovich, 1989.

Cohn, Carol. "Wars, Wimps, and Women: Talking Gender and Thinking War." *Gendering War Talk*. Ed. Miriam Cooke and Angela Woollacott, eds. Princeton: Princeton University Press, 1993. 227-46.

Cooke, Miriam and Angela Woollacott, eds. "Introduction." *Gendering War Talk*. ix-xii.

De Lauretis, Teresa. "The Technology of Gender." *Technologies of Gender: Essays on Theory, Film, and Fiction*. Bloomington, Indiana: Indiana University Press, 1987.

Drabble, Margaret. *The Gates of Ivory*. London: Penguin, 1991.

Elshtain, Jean Bethke. *Women and War*. Brighton, England: Harvester, 1987.

Fussell, Paul. *The Great War and Modern Memory*. Oxford: Oxford University Press, 1975.

Glendinning, Victoria. "Sturm in a Teacup." Review of *Over the Frontier*, by Stevie Smith. *Times Literary Supplement* 18 January 1980: 54.

Hanley, Lynne. *Writing War: Fiction, Gender, Memory*. Amherst, Massachusetts: University of Massachusetts Press, 1991.

Higgonet, Margaret, *et al.*, eds. *Behind the Lines: Gender and the Two World Wars*. New Haven: Yale University Press, 1987.

Leed, Eric. *No Man's Land: Combat and Identity in World War I*. Cambridge: Cambridge University Press, 1979.

Lessing, Doris. *Memoirs of a Survivor*. 1974. Toronto: Bantam, 1981.

Macaulay, Rose. *Non-Combatants and Others*. London: Hodder & Stoughton, 1916.

Marwick, Arthur. *Women at War, 1914-18*. London: Fontana, 1977.

"The New Novels: Miss Pompey Casmilus." Rev. of *Over the Frontier*, by Stevie Smith. *Times Literary Supplement* 15 January 1938: 43.

Ouditt, Sharon. *Fighting Forces, Writing Women: Identity and Ideology in the First World War*. London: Routledge, 1994.

Rubenstein, Roberta. *Boundaries of the Self: Gender, Culture, Fiction*. Chicago: University of Illinois Press, 1987.

Scott-James, Marie. "News from Nowhere." Review of *Over the Frontier*, by Stevie Smith. *London Mercury*. 37 (February 1938): 456.

Severin, Laura. "Recovering the Serious Antics of Stevie Smith's Novels." *Twentieth Century Literature* 40.4 (Winter 1994): 461-76.

Smith, Stevie. *Novel on Yellow Paper*. 1936. London: Virago, 1980.

——. *The Holiday*. 1949. New York: Pinnacle, 1982.

——. *Over the Frontier*. 1938. London: Virago, 1980.

Spain, Daphne. *Gendered Spaces*. Chapel Hill, North Carolina: North Carolina University Press, 1992.

Spender, Dale. *Man Made Language*. London: Routledge and Kegan Paul, 1980.

Sternlicht, Sanford. *Stevie Smith*. Boston: Twayne, 1990.

Tylee, Claire M. *The Great War and Women's Consciousness*. Iowa City: University of Iowa Press, 1990.
Van Gennep, Arnold. *Rites of Passage*. 1908. Translated by Monika B. Vizedom and Gabrielle L. Caffee. Chicago: University of Chicago Press, 1960.
Wesley, Mary. *The Camomile Lawn*. 1984. London: Black Swan, 1989.
West, Rebecca. *The Return of the Soldier*. 1918. London: Virago, 1982.

Further Reading

Barbera, Jack and William McBrien. *Stevie: A Biography of Stevie Smith*. London: Heinemann, 1985.
Barton, E.M. *Eve in Khaki: The Story of the Women's Army at Home and Abroad*. London: Nelson, 1918.
Berkin, Carol R., and Clara M. Lovett. *Women, War, and Revolution*. New York: Holmes and Meier, 1980.
Brittain, Vera. *Chronicle of Youth: the War Diary 1913-17*. Ed. Alan Bishop. London: Gollancz, 1981.
Cadogan, Mary, and Patricia Craig. *Women and Children First: The Fiction of Two World Wars*. London: Gollancz, 1978.
Carr, K. *Women Who Dared: Heroines of the Great War*. London: Partridge, 1920.
Di Stefano, Christine. *Configurations of Masculinity: A Feminist Perspective on Modern Political Thought*. Ithaca, New York: Cornell University Press, 1991.
Dick, Kay. *Ivy and Stevie*. London: Allison and Busby, 1993.
Gelhorn, Martha. *The Face of War*. London: Virago, 1986.
Graddol, David and Joan Swann. *Gendered Voices*. Oxford: Blackwell, 1989.
Haste, Cate. *Keep the Home Fires Burning: Propaganda in the First World War*. London: Lane, 1977.
Hynes, Samuel. *A War Imagined*. New York: Atheneum, 1991.
Jesse, F.T. *The Sword of Deborah: First-Hand Impressions of the British Women's Army in France*. London: Heinemann, 1919.
Kenyon, Olga. *Women Novelists Today*. Brighton, England: Harvester, 1988.
Khan, Nosheen. *Women's Poetry of the First World War*. Hemel Hempstead, England: Harvester-Wheatsheaf, 1988.
Macdonald, Lyn. *The Roses of No Man's Land*. London: Joseph, 1980.
Mitchell, David. *Women on the Warpath: The Story of the Women of the First World War*. London: Cape, 1966.
Poynton, Cate. *Language and Gender: Making the Difference*. Oxford: Oxford University Press, 1989.
Reilly, Catherine, ed. *Scars Upon My Heart: Women's Poetry and Verse of the First World War*. London: Virago, 1981.
Spalding, Frances. *Stevie Smith: A Biography*. New York: Norton, 1989.
Waugh, Patricia. *Feminine Fictions: Revisiting the Postmodern*. London: Routledge, 1988.
Wiltsher, Anne. *Most Dangerous Women: Feminist Peace Campaigners of the Great War*. London: Pandora, 1985.
Yaeger, Patricia. *Honey-Mad Women*. New York: Columbia University Press, 1988.

3 Citizenship in the Salon: The Public Private War of Violet Hunt

Debra Rae Cohen

To discuss Violet Hunt as a writer of Great War literature seems at first glance almost perverse. As Douglas Goldring points out, she was unremittingly self-absorbed, unable to let even the war distract her from the "circumference of her own griefs" (118); according to her biographer, Barbara Belford, for Hunt the war was a "personal inconvenience" (221). When her lover Ford Madox Ford enlisted, Hunt burst out bitterly in the middle of a theatre review, condemning the "eas[y]" heroics available to the artist in time of war: "The author has only to throw down his pen, shoulder a rifle, and putting himself into the hands of his colonel instead of his publisher, address himself to the Front" ("Half" 332).

Hunt was undoubtedly obsessed with the ongoing drama of her relationship with Ford (then still Ford Madox Hueffer[1]), the man to whom she may or may not have been married—at least, the man whose name she felt morally entitled to use. But the very ferocity of her concentration prompted her, even as the war served as the catalyst and mechanism of their severance, to recast that war for her own purposes, appropriating the languages of patriotism and citizenship for use in her own "propaganda" campaign. In *Zeppelin Nights: A London Entertainment*, the book she published with Ford in November of 1915, she relocates these discourses within a narrative "salon space," blurring the boundaries of public and private discourse in order to legitimize herself in both spheres. Like many of the female novelists writing on the British home front during the war, she uses this narrative safe haven as a testing-ground for models of female citizenship—not, however, in order to critique them, but to marshall them in the service of her own posterity. Although such power proves to be merely transitory—vanishing outside the "salon"—within this novelistic space she turns to her advantage the very propaganda discourses that are too often thought of as simply constructing from above women's wartime identities. Hunt's rhetorical strategies point up not only the period's charged and complex relationships between gender and nation, public and private, but also the vexed and contested nature of wartime self-fashioning.

While Trudi Tate has convincingly traced the influence of wartime propaganda practices on Ford's 1924-28 *Parade's End*, pointing to an economy of gossip as one of the novel's "organising principles" (42), in fact the mobilization of public opinion had always been crucial both to the uneasy legitimacy of the Ford-Hunt menage and to its precarious balance of power. Throughout their affair—especially after Ford's wife Elsie, enraged and humiliated by his conduct, made it clear she would not give him a divorce[2]— the two released disinformation to the media, learnedly rewrote history, claimed legitimacy based on secret and privileged information, issued confusing and contradictory statements designed to mislead the "enemy," circulated "atrocity" stories, and courted the intervention of influential neutrals. In short, they had long since faced the question that Tate asks rhetorically about *Parade's End*: "How do people imagine themselves as subjects, or indeed as citizens, in a culture which is mobilised around rumors, lies and official secrecy?" (43). For Ford and Hunt the answer was, you collaborate.

Just as the Great War brought about not the invention of propaganda, but the development of a "rationalized, professionalized, modernized" propaganda (Haste 2), so too, then, did it serve as a crucible to heighten and refine the discourse of Ford's and Hunt's private propaganda battles.[3] In their relationship the power politics of authorship, nationality, and gender had always overlapped in uniquely complex ways. Ford tried to get around Elsie's refusal of divorce, for example, with a peculiar strategy of exile, in which by regaining the German citizenship his father had relinquished, he could somehow "legally" marry Hunt; after several months spent trying to establish himself with the German authorities, he announced their marriage to a reporter—in order to promote their new books.[4] Later, the identification of Hunt as "now Mrs. Ford Madox Hueffer" in a *Throne* review of *The Governess* (1912)—a book to which Ford had lent his imprimatur by writing a preface—led to a lawsuit that publicly destroyed the "trumped-up story" (Belford 197) of their German marriage, and thus Hunt's respectability. But by then Hunt had already written *The Desirable Alien* (1913)—a travel book that extolled the joys of Germanness, published, with Ford's authorizing assistance, to legitimize their joint position—both national and domestic. Within Ford's and Hunt's orbit, in other words, nationalism was articulated through gender, gender through authorship, authorship through nationality— and vice versa. The often-overlooked truth that discourses rarely operate singularly was here inescapable.

As war neared, then, the discourses of power surrounding the relationship became ever more charged, the relationship itself ever more strained. Ford blamed Hunt for the German citizenship debacle, and the resulting suspicion in which he was widely held (this despite his own continued reluctance even in August 1914 to fall into line with pro-war sentiments[5]). For her part, although the reassurances Ford received from C.F.G. Masterman that he was "a British subject in good standing" (Mizener 250) could also be read as an official disavowal of their marriage, Hunt clung to her spurious German name as a symbol of English bourgeois legitimacy. Each, meanwhile, used his or her considerable literary authority to buttress personal claims, even as they continued to "collaborate."

Ford's and Hunt's 1915 *Zeppelin Nights*—their last literary collaboration, assembled in the midst of national and personal crisis—is a densely palimpsestic document in which all the mingled, mangled discourses that characterized their relationship are superimposed under the guise of "A London Entertainment." Prepared and published in the months between Ford's enlistment and his departure for the front, the book repackaged a series of historical vignettes previously written by Ford for the *Daily News* and the weekly magazine *Outlook* (Harvey 50, 161, 171). Its linking narrative—written by Hunt[6] as Ford slogged around training camp with subalterns half his age—depicts an intellectual crowd that gathers under the threat of German air attack at the home of the "young widow" (9) Candour Viola to listen to the stories recounted by her lover, the writer Serapion Hunter. In crafting the "packaging" of Ford's tales, wielding control for the first time over his fictions, his rewritings of history, Hunt is able to harness the discourses of nationalism, gender and authorship for her own purposes. The interior space of the novel—a controlled and tamed version of her own literary salon—becomes a "small world [she can] shape her own way" (Blair 216), within which she can restage her own public private history in order to reclaim a private public status.

Hunt's manner of recasting Ford's discourse in her memoirs offers a clue to her methodology in *Zeppelin Nights*. On the first page of *I Have This to Say* Hunt renders a conversation she had with Ford during the Great War:

> Not, said a soldier to me, walking along the pier at Redcar in the days of the bitterness of the war—when words flowed from the mouths of deeply tried men, ebullitions of a deep and desperate cynicism that seemed to sour the sunlight—not, said he, till a person comes to lie on his deathbed and is faced with that five minutes' unrolling of the Book of Judgement—that feverish access of memory, including full clarity of vision, of which all who have been brought back from the gates of death have spoken and written—does a person know which is *the* affair of all. (3)

In this paragraph Hunt performs in miniature the rhetorical appropriations that characterize *Zeppelin Nights*: she brackets the war and its broader significance, subserviating it to personal drama; she serves as arbiter and impresario of Ford's discourse; manipulating Ford's argument, she uses his words to emphasize the lasting connection between them—thus "naming" herself, implicitly, as Ford's "real" wife in the eyes of posterity even as she, paradoxically, renders him anonymous.

The linking narrative of *Zeppelin Nights* mobilizes the war itself to enable these appropriations. Written with Hunt's characteristic "brilliant, untidy cleverness" ("New Novels"), the opening pages evoke the anxious oppression of a hag-ridden, darkened London under the threat of Zeppelin attack, "profoundly wretched and uneasy, filled with a restlessness that was worse than pain" (2).[7] Though Hunt's narrative roots itself in contemporaneity by its reference to wartime lighting regulations and air raid precautions ("the baths kept full, the respirators, the pails full of sand upon the landings" [7]), its real concern is with what Caroline Playne calls "the instability of the war mind" (102) as a narrative impetus for the formation of a new defensive space. Hunt floridly summons up the tensions of the artistic temperament under assault, "a sense of unbearable things taking place at a great distance, punctuated by sudden and hideous pains of realisation" (7). The atmosphere is claustrophobic, with England itself "a beleaguered city, walled in with a wall of blue water beyond which strong men made sorties and did not always come back" (2). For such fears, "cellars [are] no refuge; no cellar can hide you from the thought of millions of men in danger of death or of civilisations crumbling like the inner craters of volcanoes in eruption" (7). Rather (as in so many home front novels written by women during the war) conventional, claustrophobic enclosures are replaced by an idealized, phantasmic one—here the "carefully regulated" (Relyea 125) yet porous space of the salon. Here intellectual discussion can flourish unfettered[8] and yet serve as a verbal edifice to exclude "all the hateful thoughts that make life unbearable" (6).

In its reference to narrative as "anodyne," to tales told against the fall of night, *Zeppelin Nights* self-consciously invokes Boccaccio's *Decameron*—and indeed, most reviewers of the novel seized on the comparison, temptingly offered up in the opening pages. But the reference is a red herring; *Zeppelin Nights* is more than simply a distracting "Entertainment." The comparison serves to establish the world-weary pretension and resultant unreliability of the unnamed "joint" narrators (138), who refer to *The Decameron* as that "dreary institution" (7); but it serves as well to disguise the nature of Hunt's own project. *The Decameron*, after all, really does offer an anodyne; after a "brief exordium of woe" (I: 4), the backdrop of plague and civic disorder falls away almost completely, banished by tales of romance and cuckoldry told by virtually indistinguishable youths and maidens. Certainly the frame narrative rarely reshapes the narratives it contains; in fact, the plague is only invoked—and that only once—to justify the falling-away of customary restraints on narrative.[9] In *Zeppelin Nights*, by contrast, the conversation of a coterie of recognizable intellectuals (modeled on Ford and Hunt's South Lodge circle) serves as commentary on historical vignettes ostensibly "composed" as commentary on the war itself. The model here is not Boccaccio, but E.T.A. Hoffmann; the name Serapion Hunter is a clear allusion to his collection *The Serapion Brethren*, in which a group of aesthetes hone their artistic theories through the telling of tales. Like that work, *Zeppelin Nights* is a testing ground for ideologies; like Hoffmann's band of aesthetes, striving to counter prevailing "Philistinism" (9) with a commitment to fully conceived artistic expression, the Serapion of *Zeppelin Nights* attempts to use impressionistic storytelling to give a truer picture of the war.

The name Serapion, then, as an emblem of aesthetic brotherhood, seems only fitting for Ford, whose early qualms about the war had centered around its possible debilitation of the arts ("For goodness sake, buy a book a week, and economise in socks," he urged in his *Outlook* column [quoted in Tomlinson and Green 140]); the name stands as an implicit test of Ford's own commitment to art. But the model from whom Hoffmann's group derives its "Serapiontic" principle is actually a deluded young nobleman who believes he is the historical martyr Serapion,[10] having survived and transcended his own martyrdom; thus he embodies the "Fixed Idea" (16) as the source of true poetic inspiration. As such the name is also appropriate to Ford, but with a nasty edge: what better emblem for a man who clung always to the notion of aesthetic martyrdom, and whose impostures were lived with the verve of true belief?

By affixing this name to the storyteller hero of *Zeppelin Nights*, then, Hunt seems to be giving Ford his due as champion of the artist, all the while positioning herself to undermine his preeminence; as a spokesman for the artist, Serapion, like his namesake, will finally prove impassioned but deluded. The name also adds to the instability of the storyteller's (and Ford's) position as any sort of spokesman for the nation: Hoffmann, after all, was a Prussian functionary (McGlathery 1-20), a representative of the very culture Ford had recently excoriated in the propaganda books he wrote for C.F.G. Masterman.[11]

Given the anti-German hysteria of the early war years[12] (and in particular at the time *Zeppelin Nights* was assembled, the months following the sinking of the *Lusitania*), it's not surprising that the use of Hoffmann as model is elided and disguised; the narrators' opening pages feature then-standard nationalistic denunciations of German *Kultur*, the "gruesome melodrama" and "coarse touch of … crude, undisciplined fancy" (2).[13] Yet these are the narrators' words, not Hunt's; *she* allows the model to be clearly glimpsed through her use of the name Serapion. A great deal hangs on a name here, but names, for both Ford and Hunt, were always significant: by 1915 both had been pilloried in court over the use of the name "Mrs. Hueffer." As Hunt once wrote to H.G. Wells, "one's name seems to matter so much when one has to fight for it and been ruined for it" (quoted in Belford 246). By imposing the name Serapion on the "Ford" character Hunt reinforces the Germanness already implicit in the name "Hueffer," leaving the door open to uncertainty about Ford's ethnicity, and thus his citizenship—the very uncertainty Ford already blamed on her desire for marriage, had tried to dispel with his two propaganda books, and hoped to have put to rest for good with his enlistment (Farrar 146; Saunders I: 479).

Hunt dubs her own *Zeppelin Nights* alter ego "Candour"—a significant move for one of this pair of accomplished fabulists—presenting herself as self-evidently the better citizen. Her relationship with Ford, too, is legitimated by making Serapion's last name a version of Hunt's own; within the frame text this move is recapitulated when the narrators refer to the couple: "the Violas, or the Hunters, as we called them" (8). Not only does Candour share Serapion's name within the text, but she does so symmetrically, thus bettering Hunt's own dependence on Ford for respectability.

The self-referentiality of *Zeppelin Nights*'s structure allows Hunt leeway to reenact her life with Ford—with a difference. By 1915 the war had exacerbated the financial, personal, and sexual tensions in their relationship to the point that some of Ford's biographers claim that he enlisted only to escape her;[14] but within the fictional space of the Violas, or Hunters, all is serene. A "relatively pleasant, rather extravagantly embowered dwelling" (8) in the vaguely disparaging opinion of the narrators, Candour's house is a version of South Lodge, Hunt's family home where Ford had been a "paying guest" since 1910 under the uncertain chaperonage of Hunt's senile mother. In recreating the menage, Hunt manages to stress its respectability[15] as well as Ford's financial dependence (then steadily worsening as the war cut down on his Herculean productivity). Hunt allows the narrators to comment suggestively about her alter ego, though; in what reads irresistibly as a *double entendre*, they note that Candour grants her favor to Serapion by "according his manuscripts the hospitality of her bureau" (9). Paradoxically, such rhetoric empowers Hunt: it establishes her as the undeserving victim of public calumny; it, again, reveals the lack of sensitivity (relative to her) of even the intellectual élite; and it recreates her as an equal partner in Ford's—or Serapion's—literary career.

This literary authority is enacted most clearly in Candour's position as *salonnière*, hostess to the gatherings of artistic sensibilities. In real life Hunt and Ford were both known for being almost voraciously social—"You *are* Society," Henry James wrote to Violet in 1907 (quoted in Secor 8)—with what Douglas Goldring refers to as "a complex about celebrities" (33). Even before she and Ford met, Hunt's "conversational brilliance—and the sharpness of her tongue—were legendary: she was credited, by those who did not know her, with being the centre of a dazzling metropolitan circle, which combined 'smartness,' in the social sense, with intellectual distinction" (42).[16] At South Lodge she and Ford had maintained, even in the face of scandal, a hectic schedule of entertainments for "a new generation of artists and writers" including Ezra Pound, Wyndham Lewis, D.H. Lawrence and Rebecca West, as well as "fashionable people who liked a dash of ink with their tea or to pick a bright brain for dinner" (Belford 166; Patmore 51).

Ford himself enjoyed presiding over these gatherings, a "flabby lemon and pink giant" (in Wyndham Lewis's terms) "happiest when his rooms are jammed with people (for preference of note)" (quoted in Mizener 228). Around Ford, says Goldring, every goose became a swan, and "one was tempted to think that almost anybody who turned up at his receptions, whether invited or not, became a 'celebrity' merely by being present" (33). But within the fictionalized literary salon of *Zeppelin Nights*, it is Hunt, not Ford, who serves as the artistic enabler, as impresario, she who promotes his career: "Nothing, in the ordinary course of events," say the narrators, "would have persuaded us or our friends to listen to Mr. Hunter," a man with "literary ambitions." Yet the salon assembles because "so many cultured people knew Candour and liked her" (9, 11). The group conceives the gatherings as a way to face down imaginative demons, as a kind of counter-*Kultur*, but that artistic culture is embodied not in Serapion, but in Candour.

Concatenating the South Lodge social circle with the historical tradition of the literary salon (and legitimizing that merger by re-privatizing it within her own narrative space) Hunt avails herself of a model that emphasizes both meritocracy and female-centeredness. The salon of the *ancien régime*, some historians have argued, accorded women an unprecedented public role legitimized by its location within the private realm.[17] Paradoxically, then, reinventing the salon might make it possible to use the private sphere to change the public balance of power; indeed, Hunt, a vocal and intermittently active supporter of the Women's Social and Political Union, had offered as entertainment in her real-life "salon" speeches by Mrs Pankhurst (Saunders I: 382, 586n). Now, in wartime, with such issues rendered even more fraught by the uneasy alliance between militarism and feminism, Hunt—herself excluded from most available models of female citizenship by age or temperament—invoked the template of the salon to destabilize resurgent distinctions between male and female spheres, recapturing an art-centered (and notably anti-maternalist) version of female power, and creating a safe space for her own self-definition as citizen, *salonnière*, spouse.[18]

According to Landes, *salonnières* functioned as power brokers, facilitating the "integration of new individuals into the elite" (24). In invoking this model, then, Hunt not only awards to herself Ford's power to make swans from geese, but also implicitly robs the judgmental bourgeoisie of its power to denounce her: *salonnières*, as Hunt well knew,[19] "were largely unconcerned with the bourgeois norms of domestic propriety" (Landes 2).

The paradox here—that Hunt uses an idealized aristocratic model partly to secure herself bourgeois legitimacy—is telling. The "salon space" Hunt creates in *Zeppelin Nights* undermines the doctrine of separate spheres by remaining simultaneously public and private, thus allowing Hunt to replay public events on (as it were) her home court. But in its precarious balance between the domestic and the historical, in its modernist reinvention of the feminine literary power of the *ancien régime*, the salon also figures Hunt's own precarious position between worlds. What Robert and Marie Secor have seen as Hunt's "conflicting impulses" towards bohemian adventurousness and middle-class respectability (8) can be traced to her situation as a transitional figure, late-Victorian in upbringing, pre-Raphaelite in sympathies, and modernist mostly by association; as she admitted a bit ruefully in her autobiography, having been the "New Woman" of the nineties made her far from being "the Newest Woman of all" (*I Have This* 73).[20]

Thus the "South Lodge" Hunt recreates in *Zeppelin Nights* is simultaneously an idealized élite gathering-place and a more conventionally bourgeois home than the original. Significantly, the house is denuded of its modernist appurtenances—the crimson mural by Wyndham Lewis in Ford's study, Hunt's own Vorticist-inspired garb, the Gaudier-Brzeska bust of Ezra Pound that loomed, like a huge penis, on the lawn (Mizener 247-8; Belford 211-13); "the Violas" instead go in for mirrored sconces and Chippendale (46-7). Friends who had fallen by the wayside during Ford's and Hunt's legal troubles are here restored to their hearth: Henry James, who had squeamishly withdrawn his friendship when the word "divorce" was first bruited, is here unmistakably rendered (Belford 162-5); Violet's sister Silvia, who had banned her daughter from South Lodge, and in real life conducted most of her correspondence with Violet through lawyers, is also present (largely so she can be derided as uncomprehending). The house and its visitors are tamed, domesticated—both smartened up and dumbed down—in the service of Hunt's self-legitimization.

Hunt's salon space (constituted, in the Foucauldian sense, by the scandal it excludes) works as a more complex version of the sort of "prefatorial politics" (Kineke 298) at which Ford and Hunt had always been so adroit. By 1915, Ford already had a reputation (gained as editor of the *English Review*) as a discoverer and encourager of literary talent; Sheila Kineke has written provocatively of his later sponsorship of Jean Rhys, showing how such modernist mentoring often bore overtones of a kind of gendered imperialism. Hunt, however, less vulnerable than Rhys (in a professional sense, at least) and an accomplished novelist long before her affair with Ford, understood as well as he the thrust and parry of literary reputation; each had mastered the use of introductions, footnotes, even dedications, as propaganda tools, mechanisms of containment and control, and each had mustered them characteristically in their ongoing "collaboration."

Ford's additions to Hunt's work are often blatantly patronizing, offering or deliberately withholding approval—his footnotes to *The Desirable Alien*, for example, often snidely rebuke Violet for her observations (one begins, "This, of course, is nonsense" [42]). His introduction to the same work notes that "if I had not very much admired the kindly, careless, inaccurate, and brilliantly precise mind of the author, I presume the book never would have been written" (x)—simultaneously disparaging Violet's efforts and annexing them by reading her literary life as *merely* a function of their personal situation. Hunt is often slyer in her marshalling of this literary apparatus; dedications, for example, often function as a sort of implied chaperonage, so that her invoking "Mrs. Oswald Crawfurd, who led me into Germany" to begin *The Desirable Alien* confers an aura of retrospective respectability to the tale of her travels with Ford (even as it testifies that her reputation survived her earlier affair with Mrs Crawfurd's then-future husband). *Zeppelin Nights* itself is dedicated to "Mrs. Francis Hueffer"—clearly yoking Ford and Hunt together by invoking his mother in a way that implies her sanction of their union.

Hunt secures her artistic preeminence within the book by establishing Candour as the best "reader" of Serapion's tales. The vignettes themselves, ranging chronologically from the Battle of Marathon to the coronation of King George, are presented as Serapion's impressionistic diagnosis of "how it comes that we are here and that Civilisation is what it is" (48)—a tracing of what Robert Green has characterized as Ford's devolutionary view of history. Ford's own imaginative identification with the landed classes, says Green, led him to see history as a "decline from distant glory" (40), from a time when "order and ritual were central" (41).[21] In the vignettes, individuals burn brightly for a moment before being doused by history's ironic tide; heroes go unrecognized; small victories are won. Ford's approach is sidelong, miniaturist: Henry VIII's rebellion against the Church is presaged, in the eyes of a dogmatic housewife, by the importation of "infidel foods"; a lord's house is protected from the anti-Catholic riots of 1780 by an Italian harpsichordist; the death of Nelson is witnessed by an uncomprehending bullfinch.

These vignettes bring the past into focus in brief moments of illumination—like the searchlights that sweep the sky, looking for Zeppelins, in the opening pages, "long arms of light" that find their corollary in the "white streamers" of page proof from which Serapion reads (15-16). Serapion defends Ford's own theory that history is best seen through "minute contacts with immense happenings" (quoted in Saunders I: 70); "We [are] all of us too given to running to textbooks," he says, and thus our minds are "tinny and thin" (45).

Using the narrators as cat's-paw, Hunt is able to portray Ford's "slightly conceited and magisterial air" (169), his "rather intolerable egotism" (200), while distancing herself from that portrayal; it's clear from their defensive irony, after all, that the narrators don't really get the point. Indeed, most of Serapion's intellectual audience seems to miss the "general sense of things" (45) that he is trying to convey; they seize on specific details, fly off on literary tangents, or critique the vignettes as insufficiently "radian[t]" (86). "Serapion, old chap," says one listener (modeled on Ezra Pound), "you shouldn't have brought all that stuff in about naturalisation and aliens; it's too topical; too dragged in to suit the evening papers of June, 1915. It's not up to your usual poetical standard" (31). In other words, *The Serapion Brethren* sets a standard for an artistic "union" that Serapion and his listeners in *Zeppelin Nights* signally fail to match.[22]

As Serapion's reputation grows, the evenings become a kind of intellectual war-work, raising money for "destitute Belgians" or "stricken Montenegro" (198);[23] the crowd of listeners is swelled by non-intellectuals who test Serapion's stories against various forms of political rhetoric, and find them wanting. "It isn't you know to glorify ourselves that we are here tonight," he finds it necessary to remind them (72). He is rebuked for failing to include in a vignette on Joan of Arc the words "Votes for Women"; "I don't see how any old anachronism can matter," exclaims his critic (83-4). To an Irish lady novelist, Serapion's values are "all wrong.... I simply don't believe that flirtations will be a bit less delicious if the policeman on the corner is German instead of English" (242). And Candour's sister sweeps out of one reading exclaiming that it is not the sort of thing "one ought to be asked to bring one's children to hear" (83). Others attempt to decode his "historic parallelisms" to yield "occult" messages, "omens of return or of happy deaths at least" (200).

By contrast, Candour's simple comments both aesthetically and philosophically legitimate Serapion's enterprise. Although she is apt to simply characterize the tales as "very beautiful" and defer to Serapion's artistic genius (44), to watch him "from her seat below among the audience, like a mother proud of a clever child" (240), she also intuitively recognizes the applicability of his stories, and is drawn particularly to a tale of the English Civil War for its evocation of the way in which "great wars" sweep through the lives of "simple people" (158). A "candid" (71) and feminine creature, Candour is Violet without the claws, a Violet unbesmirched by scandal, untinged by what D.H. Lawrence called Hunt's "devilish" cleverness (Nehls 412), and thus, potentially, a sympathetic victim, a martyr to Serapion's enlistment as Violet felt she was to Ford's.

Nowhere is this aura of martyrdom made more apparent than in the way the frame narrative recasts one particular vignette, the story of Madame de Combray, relic of the French nobility, whose devotion to the remnants of the royalist cause brought her to the pillory in 1809. Serapion introduces this tale as one he was prompted to write by Candour (the only time she's acknowledged as any kind of collaborator), but one that interests him only minimally; "he seemed," say the narrators, "rather in a hurry to get done with it" (248). The vignette presents the image of the elderly woman, one of a handful of "moles undermining the subsoil" (250), as Serapion puts it, of Bonapartist rule, who had maintained hiding places, plotted and schemed, harbored deserters—all in the service of a possible glorious restoration. Tricked into betraying the conspiracy, she is brought to the humiliation of the public pillory, where she is silently honored by a host of "such women of the ancient nobility as remained alive in 1809" (249), all wearing black in tribute. Returning to prison, she remarks with aristocratic reserve, "My reception ... has been very well attended" (254). Serapion gently ironizes Madame de Combray's devotion to her royalist dream as "romance; for what after all is romance but the imbecile upholding of lost causes, the ignorant setting out upon impossible adventures?" (252).

Framed as this story is, it's impossible not to read it as Violet's image of herself, pilloried for her devotion to romance, a martyr to her faith in Ford, tricked into self-betrayal because, as Serapion says, "she was a noble and high soul, and such characters are usually at the mercy of the clever tricks of ... clever knaves" (253). The vindication of Madame de Combray, too, becomes Violet's vindication; within this fictional space she is able to triumph over "social opprobrium" (Secor 8) as she could do only wishfully in real life—as in her pitiful boast to posterity in her journal during the height of the *Throne* scandal, "Home, and my yearly garden-party never so well attended" (*I Have This* 241), which Madame de Combray's reference to her "reception" seems to echo.

In conflating herself with Madame de Combray, Hunt achieves the vindication that part of her still craves through imaginative merger with the aristocracy; those who are as "noble" as she respect her and do her honor. Before the war, both Ford and Hunt had used the image of foreign aristocracy to renegotiate their symbolic position with respect to bourgeois Edwardian England[24] (and as discussed earlier, Hunt's use of the salon is itself a gesture to an aristocratic continental tradition); part of their bohemian proto-Modernism involved a stance simultaneously élitist and internationalist.[25] The days when Ford ran the *English Review* were those in which he boasted most flamboyantly of his (fictitious) claims to a German barony (Goldring 37-8). In a sense, Ford pursued his nostalgic dream of a place among the Tory aristocracy by way of these foreign connections.

Although it was quite common among prewar intellectuals to define one's Englishness with respect to Frenchness or Germanness, by weighing the claims of those cultures in defining "national" traits and qualities,[26] few went as far in their cosmopolitanism as Ford; "if anyone in pre-war England could have been regarded as pro-German," says Samuel Hynes, "it was Hueffer" (*A War* 72). It was Hunt, not Ford, who wrote the effusions in praise of Germany—warblings about Heine and forests and cleanliness and strudel—that fill the pages of the unpropitiously-timed *The Desirable Alien* (1913 was hardly the moment for a book subtitled "At Home in Germany"). But the book's opening page makes it clear why Ford, rather than Hunt (even after his very public reversals in his propaganda books), retained a whiff of pro-German taint: she has become German, she says, "with no reluctance, but through no fault of my own" (1).[27]

In prewar England, national identity for a woman, as Jane Mackay and Pat Thane remind us, was relational rather than inherent (191-2);[28] for Hunt to call herself German was the same as asserting her married status—another way of "naming" herself Mrs Hueffer. The more German she becomes, the more "married" she is: "I had said to Joseph Leopold that I could never feel truly German until I had ... lived in a house taken in our own name" (17). Similarly, she refers throughout the book to Ford's mother as "Mutterchen," since to render the relationship German is to render it true.

Now, during wartime, Hunt reconfigures herself as Madame de Combray—who also derives her national identity from her lord—becoming imaginatively French, and thus, in relation to the discourse of the war, authentically patriotic. Being willing, like Madame de Combray, to sacrifice herself in the service of a forlorn hope also makes her, paradoxically, more *English*—aligning herself with the rhetoric of Christian sacrifice that underlay much of the propaganda of the early war years. If such rhetoric, merging Biblical iconography and Victorian pseudo-medievalism, identified soldiers with holy crusaders, their deaths with the sacrifice of Christ,[29] it also, as Claire Tylee points out, confirmed that "women's lot [was] one of passive suffering" (73): the "knightly ideal leaves women on the sidelines[,] and the mythology of the Crucifixion represents woman as *mater dolorosa* or weeping daughter of Jerusalem—in other words, as ancillary mourner" (Montefiore 56). In this discourse the nurturant mother becomes transfigured by the "sacrifice" of her menfolk—giving life "in a double sense," as the famous 1916 letter from "A Little Mother" exulted (quoted in Tylee 70).

Such sacrifice, as Jean Bethke Elshtain explains, is mobilized by the durable historic representation of women as "Beautiful Souls"—"essentially caring, concerned, nonviolent beings who can, however, be mobilized as wartime civic cheerleaders and home-front helpmeets" (140) as epitomized in the famous recruitment poster "Women of Britain Say—GO!" Her sacrifice actually constitutes the woman as citizen:

> To the extent that she has become a civic person, to the extent that the other imperatives ... that make her who she is can be at least temporarily jettisoned, overridden, or themselves mobilized for combat, she is available as a civic republican mother whose call is not to arms but to dis-arm, to break the protective enfolding of her children, to cherish "public freedom" above "private devotion." (93)

Within the space of *Zeppelin Nights*, Hunt bolsters her claim to Beautiful Soul-dom not only by portraying herself as Serapion's potential chief mourner, but by creating for herself a fictional brother[30] so that he can be suitably sacrificed, his company "wiped out. ... Not a man left alive" (97). Candour receives the phone call telling her of her brother's death during one of Serapion's readings, and it serves as the spur for her own artistic flight—imagining a heaven for all the dead "boys," a place "somewhere like Rumpelmayer's. ... With the tea, and the little cakes ... and the nice young girls, and the little orchestra playing. ... Can't it be done for them, don't you think?" Here, too, she proves herself more sensitive than the narrators, who observe, "It was a little harrowing and a little unlike Candour to harrow us" (168).

But in imagining a heaven, Hunt is also once more upstaging Ford, offering an answer to his 1913 poem "On Heaven." Violet had asked him to write her "a plain, workaday heaven that I can go to some day and enjoy it when I'm there" (*I Have This* 218); he responded with a modernist idyll set in a Provençal paradise, complete with the Virgin Mary, who says to the woman, "It is sad that you have no child" (III 134).[31] In altruistically imagining a "workaday heaven" for doomed youth, Hunt earns the status of mourner, of *mater dolorosa*, by simultaneously awarding herself the "child" Ford's poem assumes she feels she lacks and killing him into art.

In clearly envisioning the suitable heaven for the lost boys, however, Hunt also claims recognition as the better artist, giving herself the role of the God of Ford's poem, who "knows well what each man has in his heart" (III 185). Moreover, her selfconsciously middlebrow vision (winsomely presented as simple and unpretentious) punctures the grandiosity of Ford's, which delivers a catalogue of possible heavens with the assurance that "God is a very clever mechanician" (III 175)—a locution Hunt mocks through the narrators, who assure Candour that "God is a pretty rich man. ... He can afford to run several tea-shops, all white, with the little orchestra playing Hitchy Coo" (168).

Added to Candour's status as artistic impresario and best "reader" throughout the book, this underscoring of her artistic preeminence goes far to establish her/Hunt as another aspect of the paradigm of the Beautiful Soul—the "keeper of the flame" of artistic values during wartime. The Beautiful Soul, says Elshtain, is "custodian and conserver of elemental chords of memory whose echoes are foreordained to be drowned out by the guns of war" (141). This second model of citizenship (conflating, like the salon, elitism and female-centeredness) is one, I suspect, that comes closer to Violet's own real views; certainly it echoes the position she takes on the matter in *The Desirable Alien*.

At the end of that book's first chapter, having traveled down the Rhine, Hunt says that she is now no longer a British subject because she has "tasted of these grapes, drunk of this wine, and heard the flow of this ... river" (16). Citizenship, she implies, is largely a matter of aesthetic appreciation; one *loses* one's specific national identity when one's aesthetic sense is broadened. It may be as a woman—or rather, "through no fault of [her] own," as a "wife"—that Hunt is now become "German," but it is not as a woman (with apologies to Virginia Woolf), but as an artist, that she has no country, or all countries.

By this transnational definition of citizenship, Serapion's decision to enlist—a decision Candour has anticipated and that she protests because "art alone is too valuable" (306)—is at least a mistake, if not a betrayal. The text, as it must, given both the demands of wartime publication and Hunt's desire to trump Ford as both artist and citizen, overtly supports Serapion's enlistment; two entire pages are given over to his self-justification, phrased, in Ford's own language, as what he owes for enjoying the "privileges" of "the ruling classes of this country" (306).[32]

But it is Candour who has the last word, rebuking the sneering habitués of the salon, who assume that Serapion has taken some cushy War Office assignment. Tellingly, she reveals that Serapion has been able to enlist because he has lied about his age—and then she exits the room, crying. This last act ensures that her martyrdom (Violet's martyrdom) constitutes the reader's final impression of the book. Candour, in this last exchange, embodies both models of citizenship offered by the text: by enacting the ideal of self-sacrificing English womanhood, she proves herself worthy of inclusion in Serapion's heroic vignettes—one more brave soul bucking the devolutionary tide; by preserving the space of culture that Serapion "deserts," she proves herself the artistic "citizen" beyond shallow nationalism. While Serapion perverts his artistry into patriotic lies about his age—thus configuring his enlistment as just another act of propaganda—Candour will tend the flame of art. As the best and most supportive reader, she remains custodian of Serapion's manuscripts, legitimized both as impresario and as "wife."

As when she wore Ford's tin helmet to an air raid party, tied under her chin with a pink bow (Saunders II: 41; Belford 240), Hunt in *Zeppelin Nights* symbolically declares herself a citizen with both feminine and artistic sensibilities—at the same time tying up both the war and Ford himself into a neat domestic package. Within the temporary "salon space" of the novel, she secures his love, the narrators' admiration, the reader's pity. Yet even within the book, these aims are often contradictory, the definitions of citizenship at uneasy odds, working not in harness, but in a "collaboration" much like Ford's and Hunt's own. In a wartime propaganda economy, when Ford's *The Good Soldier* could be attacked for its title's "profanation" of the military, or dismissed as "of some value to the specialist in pathology," the overdetermined, conflicted text of *Zeppelin Nights* was unlikely to be understood;[33] reviewers tended to dismiss the book as "turgid" or overly "highbrow" ("Fiction," "Novel Notes"). One controversial critique seized upon the book as an excuse to disparage Ford's patriotism, condemning him for cowardice and being un-English by quoting words that Hunt had actually written—thus, like many later critics, occluding her participation (Prothero, "Mr. Hueffer" 293; Foster 38).

Certainly Hunt's propaganda proved ineffective with Ford himself. As the war dragged on, it provided a mechanism for him to withdraw ever further from her, presenting this as in some senses a patriotic act: in 1917 he told her he was no longer "the sort of animal who makes love to women. ...I have one passion now, the Army & that England should win" (Secor 52). Later, he justified himself to Masterman by invoking the "Scaremonger" incident, stating that since Violet had stayed friendly with people "whose chief claim to patriotic activities ... had been the denouncing of myself as a German agent," he "saw no other way open than to retire from the scene" (quoted in Mizener 278).

This strategic withdrawal, with its "patriotic" overtones, set the pattern for Ford's and Hunt's post-war propaganda efforts, in which each, in effect, painted the other as Prussian—Hunt by stressing his brutal treatment of her in her memoirs, Ford with his scathing portrait of her as Sylvia Tietjens, whose insidious use of personal propaganda undermines her husband's military service. Indeed, in the preface he wrote from "somewhere in Belgium" for Hunt's 1916 novel *Their Lives* he claims that her characters—overtly based on Hunt's own family—*are* Prussians, "without remorse or pity. ...that horrible family of this author's recording explains to me why to-day, millions of us ... are enduring torture it is not fit human beings should endure" (3-4).

Merging "prefatorial politics" and patriotic self-justification, Ford withheld his name from the preface to *Their Lives*, denying Violet a last "collaboration." He signed it instead, with "bitter, ironic anonymity" (Saunders II: 19) "Miles Ignotus"— "Unknown Soldier." When, after the war, he moved in with Stella Bowen, he changed his name to Ford Madox Ford, thus both expunging his German ties and rendering moot any claim of Violet's to the name "Mrs Hueffer."[34] "So," she lamented when she heard of his renaming, "I am not now even the wife of his pen!" (quoted in Belford 246).

Janet Lyon's recent work on the twentieth-century salon has suggested that the transitory social power of women within the salon serves largely to bring into relief the degree to which they are disempowered outside its space. So it was to prove with Hunt, whose control over her private circumstances and public image in *Zeppelin Nights* was rapidly overwhelmed outside its pages. Within the space of the novel Hunt had exploited the rhetorics of wartime to win herself the last word, but it was Ford who had the last laugh. The image of Candour crying was to prove prophetic; Hunt, frozen into a posture of abandonment, maintained it for the rest of her life.

Notes

1. Ford Hermann Hueffer, later Joseph Leopold Ford Madox Hueffer, changed his name officially to Ford Madox Ford on June 4, 1919. Although I refer to him throughout this essay as Ford, as the name most familiar to readers, it is essential to remember that the name in dispute throughout this period, the name Violet Hunt claimed as her own and the name under which Ford fought for England, was his original name, Hueffer (anglicized by his father from the German Hüffer).

2. Ford's hopes that Elsie would agree to a divorce—a course her Catholic family opposed—were dashed when she caught Ford and Hunt at Charing Cross station, returning from a 1909 trip to France. According to Hunt's memoirs—in which, characteristically playing to posterity, she protests that the trip was "chaperoned to the nines"—Ford "delivered me into [my maid's] hands saying simply 'It's all up, old girl! You will see. There'll be no divorce'" (*I Have This* 84-5). See also Mizener 194-5; Belford 160.

3. I here nod to—rather than endorse—James Longenbach's argument in "Men and Women of 1914." Heavily influenced by Sandra Gilbert's depiction of the modernist sex wars, Longenbach sees the war as a gendering experience that, for Ford, "made the already complicated issue of sexual difference intractable" (112). Although he points out how, in Ford's and Hunt's wartime rhetoric, "each war nurtured the others" (111), he does not mention *Zeppelin Nights*. Like Gilbert, he oversimplifies these issues, failing to acknowledge the way in which for Ford and Hunt national identification, gender questions, and literary authority are *always* inextricably intertwined.

4. The article appeared in the *Daily Mirror* 22 October 1911. What actually happened between Ford and Hunt—whether any marriage ceremony actually took place—has never been determined, and the issue is a controversial one. Ford's biographers generally maintain that it was a fiction in which Violet knowingly colluded ("they had committed themselves to the bluff that Violet was Mrs. Hueffer," says Mizener [219]; concludes Goldring, "Violet agreed to it with her eyes open" [97]). Hunt's biographers are more likely to endorse her claim that she went through some sort of ceremony. Robert and Marie Secor claim that "Violet was even more of a victim than has been recognized" (19); Hardwick calls her "naive and guilty of wishful thinking in believing that her marriage had any standing in law" (105). Belford reserves her scorn for Ford, whose indiscreetness with the *Daily Mail* reporter in an "atmosphere of male clubbiness, bragging and pontificating ... destroyed forever Violet's dream of respectability" (182).

   Ford never went back on his story that a ceremony took place, although most of Violet's versions of the incident have them marrying in France, not in Germany, as the initial newspaper article had it; but he certainly undermined any claim Violet had to *legal* possession of his "abandoned patronymic" (quoted in Mizener 337) by stating in 1927 that "I never became a German citizen for legal or illegal reasons or for any reason. ... I always was and shall always be a British subject" (quoted in Mizener 211). Hunt herself says in her memoirs that "I have been rudely taught since that it was not so—that I never did become a legal wife." Hinting at secrets which "to explain is death," she implies that whatever proofs she did have are now "at the bottom of the well at Selsey" (*I Have This* v-vi).

5. See Hardwick 130. Nora Tomlinson and Robert Green's "Ford's Wartime Journalism" offers a fascinating overview of the evolution of Ford's political rhetoric as expressed in his weekly articles in *Outlook* (the series began in September 1913 and ended with his enlistment in August 1915). Ford, who had told C.F.G. Masterman as late as August 3, 1914 "The German troops will never cross the German frontier. ... Never. ... Never. ... Never" (quoted in Buitenhuis 43), was publicly "distressed by the prospect of war, feeling that 'whichever side wins in the end—my own heart is certain to be mangled in either case'" (Tomlinson and Green 139). Despite his unpopular anti-jingoism early in the war—expressed in an August 1914 *Outlook* piece as a call to acknowledge the "gallant enemy"—he was, says Mizener, "nonetheless astonished that anyone should question his loyalty to England" (250).

   The situation was exacerbated by "The Scaremonger," a story Ford published in November 1914 that satirized invasion fears through an obvious portrait of Edward Heron Allen, Hunt's neighbor at her summer home at Selsey, Sussex. Possibly at Allen's instigation, Ford was officially asked to leave the area—an order quickly canceled by his influential friend (and Selsey neighbor) C.F.G. Masterman, but which continued to rankle, especially since Violet remained friendly with Allen (Saunders I: 473-4, Mizener 250-1).

6. Although reviewers often misattributed parts of *Zeppelin Nights* (see especially Prothero, "Mr. Hueffer's"), Ford's bibliographer, David Harvey, and his major biographers agree on the division of labor as I have given it.

7. The first Zeppelin attacks over England occurred in December 1914; London was first hit in May 1915. Early press reports tended to downplay the dangers—in March the "Science Jottings" column of the *Illustrated London News* concluded that "the monster airship is a bogey calculated to frighten rather than to hurt" (344)—and to stress the "effrontery" ("The Zeppelin Raid") of the attacks rather than the damage they caused. See Sillers 107-10 for some examples of editorial cartoons mocking the Zeppelin threat. In May 1915 G.K. Chesterton wrote scornfully of the "blundering Zeppelin" and the "indiscriminate bomb":

    > When the Superman drops about a hundred bombs and kills but one woman in Southend (which is not exactly the brightest jewel in the British crown), we mourn for the woman but we laugh at the hundred bombs. We laugh because they are funny.... The present enemy wants to make our flesh creep even more than to make our blood flow ... [but] the flesh of Englishmen is not a creeping thing. (653)

    It was Chesterton's future sister-in-law (writing in his brother Cecil's paper, the *New Witness*) who later attacked *Zeppelin Nights* for demonstrating just such un-English fleshcreeping.

    The official Home Office statements after later attacks on London reinforced this theme of British phlegm:

    > As for the moral effect, for which presumably the enemy is seeking, that was all to his disadvantage.... The population of London, though hundreds of thousands heard the sound of the bursting bombs and the guns, remained cool and free from panic. There were, if possible, even less signs of excitement than on previous occasions. (quoted in "Cowardly" 517)

    Michael MacDonagh describes the promotion of "Moony Nights" for Zeppelin-free entertainment (143). See also Peel 138-6; Haste 96-7; Marwick 136-7; Wilson 156-7.

8. Joan Landes stresses that the salon of the *ancien régime* "offered one way around the problem of censorship, by holding public discussion in private" (57); Hunt's modernist restaging of the salon appeals to this tradition, offering the illusion of an intellectually free discussion as a means of configuring her as the truest citizen. See note 19 below for Hunt's own fascination with eighteenth-century France.

9. "I wot that the times are such that, so only men and women have a care to do nought that is unseemly, 'tis allowable to them to discourse of what they please. For in sooth, so out of joint are the times that the judges have deserted the judgement-seat, the laws are silent, and ample license to preserve his life as best he may is accorded to all. Wherefore, if you are somewhat less strict of speech than is your wont, not that aught unseemly in act may follow, but that you may afford solace to yourselves and others, I see not how you can be open to reasonable censure on the part of any" (II: 90-1).

    The notable parallel here to Hunt's true enterprise is not the use of narrative to bring "solace," but the restoration of respectability through the staging of fictions.

10. The name Serapion carries resonances from the "several celebrated holy men of that name" (Hoffmann I: 14), one of whom, Serapion the Martyr, was a well-known opponent of Manicheanism before being driven into the desert. One can easily read echoes of this history in Ford's career—the anti-dualism in his initial opposition to vilifying the Germans; the forced exile of both his expulsion from Selsey (see note 5 above) and his time served abroad trying to win German citizenship; the martyrdom in the eyes of public opinion. But these resonances are undercut and ironized by Hunt's use of the *Serapion Brethren* model; as will be clear later, *she* is the true martyr in this text.

11.   In August 1914 Masterman, a Liberal minister, became head of the War Propaganda Bureau, which was initially run out of his office at Wellington House; many of his early efforts involved the participation of noted literary figures. (See Buitenhuis, especially Chapter 4, and Sanders and Taylor 39-43, 107-12.) Ford's books for Masterman, *When Blood Is Their Argument* and *Between St. Dennis and St. George* (both written in the period from September 1914 through July 1915) concentrate on painting the Prussian state—as distinct from South Germany—as a "blind, gross and imbecile machine," and Prussian education as ultimately destructive of culture: "The province of Prussian education has been to teach the Germans that the ideal man is a millionaire like a pig living in a vast and gilded hotel" (*When Blood* 9, *St. Dennis* 192). With these books he both improved his financial position and shored up his standing as a patriot; Farrar also points out that he scored points against critics of his work by linking them with "the baleful influences of Prussia on British intellectual life" (147; Buitenhuis 44).

12.   Haste gives some excellent examples of extreme rhetoric after the *Lusitania* sinking: on May 15, 1915 the demagogue Horatio Bottomley called for "a vendetta—a vendetta against every German in Britain—whether 'naturalised' or not. ... You cannot naturalise an unnatural abortion, a hellish freak. But you *can* exterminate him" (126). And the 16 May 1915 *Weekly Dispatch* declared:

> We are so sick of the Germans, of their treachery, their sneaking, their spying, their lying, their brutality, their arrogance, their loutish conceit, their cold blooded dastardly cruelty, their murderous bitter hatred, that we never want to see or hear a German again, nor to touch anything made by Germans. To every decent Briton, a German is an unclean dangerous and bloody monster. Such is the fact. And the people are right to demand that every Hun should be put behind wires or bars ... [.] It is not only that the Germans are enemies and spies. We loathe them. We feel they pollute our air. We see blood on their hands ...[.] We demand that the wretched creatures be removed. The thought that there are 20,000 of them walking in our streets was enough to make all London sick. (108)

See also Peel 34-8; Marwick 131; Wilson 160-1 on the *Lusitania* riots. On contemporary "spy mania" see Posonby 152-3; MacDonagh 32-5; Peel 39-43.

13.   Hynes has the best description of the "Culture Wars," (*A War Imagined* 67-78); he points out that Modernism itself was regarded as German, and that therefore 'it was right and patriotic that English critics should declare war on Modernism wherever it could be detected' (58)—yet another reason why Ford needed to affirm his patriotism.

14.   See for example Saunders I: 481; Longenbach 110. Mizener says that *Violet* believed Ford's decision was "motivated by his desire to escape from her" (280)—which for present purposes is much the same thing.

15.   Serapion, for example is referred to as Candour's mother's "prospective son-in-law" (30).

16.   Hunt retained this reputation even after the split with Ford; in 1928 A. St. John Adcock wrote gushingly that "you may frequently meet her ... at literary dinners and social gatherings, or at more fashionable salons where men and women distinguished or becoming distinguished in art or letters are wont to congregate and rub shoulders with persons of importance in the business and political worlds" (126). But South Lodge's era as a literary salon ended when Ford went to war.

17.   See for example Goodman 18. Joan Landes has argued that the bourgeois public sphere was largely constructed "in deliberate opposition to ... a more woman-friendly salon culture" in which "women out of place" were seen as having excessive cultural power, including a "willful and unnatural control over language" (Fraser 59; Landes 30). While Landes's argument has been widely criticized, largely on methodological grounds, even her detractors tend to agree with her conclusion that "women were excluded from the

public sphere that developed out of the French Revolution" (Goodman 15). Janet Lyon's recent work suggests that twentieth-century versions of the salon continued to serve as a nexus of anxieties about female power, situating themselves in a critical relationship to modernity by putting pressure on the failed practices of equality outside their female-run spaces. For characterizations of the salon through history see Tinker.

18. The WSPU, in particular, quickly subsumed its prewar militancy into the war effort, with Mrs Pankhurst announcing "Our country's war is our war" (quoted in Elshtain 112). The massive WSPU-organized march "demanding" access to a public-sphere war-work role (and including women whom, according to the *Illustrated London News*, "nothing but a clear conviction and a strong sense of duty would draw from their quiet homes into the glare of publicity") was actually encouraged, if not instigated, by Lloyd George ("Women's" 109; Pugh 9).

The increasingly publicized role of mother-citizen, in particular, was one Hunt could not hope to play in real life (although, as I discuss below, she secures herself a version of this mourner's role in *Zeppelin Nights* with a fictional brother-sacrifice). For the fullest treatment of this subject see Grayzel; also Mackay and Thane 218-19, Ouditt, and Tylee (especially Chapter 2). Kent (Chapter 1) argues that the war restored the centrality of motherhood for both pro-war and anti-war feminists; see also Elshtain 140-9 for pro- and anti-war mobilizations of the image of the "Beautiful Soul." See Landes 26-38 for the way *salonnières* were configured as anti-family.

19. Goldring, who was one of Hunt's executors, describes her library as dominated by books on "the history of the French Revolution, folklore, feminism, archaeology, and the bypaths of sexual psychology" as well as French erotica and "French and English classical literature" (201).

20. Goldring says of Violet's memoirs that their most "valuable quality" is the way they attest to the lasting power of Victorian conventions—a power, he says "from whose grip neither of the principal protagonists ever wholly freed themselves" (76-7). Still, Violet was never *merely* a late-Victorian; as David Garnett says, she had "something of the Elizabethan pirate in her" (183) that pushed her to defy convention, in opposition to her very real desire for respectability. It is important to remember in this connection that Ford, so identified with the advent of Modernism, was born in 1873, a generation earlier than the many writers he helped to "discover"; Violet was eleven years his senior.

21. Ford's politics are difficult to codify, largely because his rhetoric was so sweeping and so seemingly contradictory; in *The Spirit of the People*, for example, he alludes to "the true Toryism which is Socialism" (291). Saunders sees Ford's distaste with "the levelling tendency of the unpleasant times we live in" not as an "anachronistic form of fantasy feudalism"—which is how he characterizes Mizener's views—but as a contempt for liberal capitalism and the Liberal party (quoted in Saunders I: 215; I: 467).

22. This may help explain why the "South Lodge" of *Zeppelin Nights* has been shorn of its Modernist trappings; their presence might convey a sense of shared artistic ideals which would undercut Violet's presentation of "Candour's" preeminence.

23. Carolyn Playne observes that "For a time, 'Belgians' were the excuse for such social functions as might still be held. There were bazaars to get money for Belgians, parties and concerts to amuse them" (131). Such recontextualizing thus acts as a legitimization—but also a fundamental misreading—of Serapion's enterprise.

24. It is sometimes difficult to see this as other than an intellectual's version of Edwardian "class insecurity"; see Waites 47-54. Certainly Ford's description of the coronation of George V (the last vignette in *Zeppelin Nights* [285-303]) dwells fawningly on the panoply of aristocratic personages as much as it celebrates ritual.

25. See Hynes, *The Edwardian Turn of Mind* (307-45) for an indication of how Edwardian modernism defined itself against late-Victorian artistic isolationism.

26. This sort of "typological negotiation" (Peppis 390) had always been central to Ford's vision of Englishness: in the 1906 *The Spirit of the People*, for instance, he claims that England can best all other nations because of the elements of those other cultures that have been absorbed into its own (279). And in his introduction to Hunt's *The Desirable Alien* he writes that the book shows that "there is no such thing as Germany as distinct from England" (xi). For Ford, argues Paul Peppis, such negotiations were self-serving; by fashioning the persona of a "cosmopolitan imperialist" (380) who advocated a non-racialized British supremacy, he implicitly legitimized his own "mongrel" heritage.

27. Hunt's memoirs, published in 1926, backpedal substantially on her prewar enthusiasm for Germany by stressing that her 1913 journey to Germany with Ford (after *The Desirable Alien* had been published) pointed up the changes that had already occurred there; naturally, she has hindsight to inform her here, and posterity in view. But Ford was already distancing himself from *The Desirable Alien* when it came out (as he was distancing himself from Violet); oddly, he devoted one of his *Outlook* columns to an extremely mixed review of the book that emphasized the "comparatively valueless" nature of Violet's social observations—without mentioning his own participation in the book ("Literary" 498).

28. Similarly, Raphael Samuel states that "Nationality, like class, is doubly mediated for women" (xiv). As Jean Pickering and Suzanne Kehde put it, "Nationalism is the field over which gender differences are played out, making possible what otherwise seems an irrational if common disposition of putative gender differences: women are determined by biology, men by their free wills" (6). Such assumptions were hotly contested during the war, but, as Susan Pedersen argues, largely reaffirmed by the system of soldiers' allowances that figured women's relationship to the state as mediated by her relationship to her husband.

29. Paul Fussell first and most influentially delineated the way that the literary culture of the war was shaped by the image of the Crucifixion (see especially Chapter 4); as Tylee has clearly argued (6-8), Fussell leaves women out of his analysis altogether.

30. Many novels written by women during the war contain the image of the brother-sacrifice—possibly because many of the authors were not old enough to have sons of military age. But as Angela Woollacott points out, middle-class brothers often "mediated the outside world for their sisters" and thus served as their surrogates; the death in wartime of a brother "became not just a personal loss, but a loss of their own person" (137, 136). Ironically, Hunt employs this trope—one might even say cynically—to legitimize and empower herself by establishing her sacrificial bona fides.

31. Hunt blasted the poem in her memoirs as "Not the fabled love that moves mountains, faces the seven deaths of boredom, but the mild, watery variety that, rather than attempt to move the thwarting mass of opposition, sits down in front of it and repeats the great word Agony three times, taking up all one line!" (*I Have This* 220). Saunders (I: 397) suggests that much of Violet's disappointment with the poem may have come from the recognition that its heroine, "very tall and quaint / And golden, like a *quattrocento* saint" (I: 5-6), is less like her than like Brigit Patmore, with whom Ford was currently and temporarily enamoured.

32. Saunders claims that Ford must have been "at least collaborating" on this concluding section of the frame narrative, since it "seems to capture his voice" so well (I: 485); Buitenhuis seems to agree, calling the book "a public airing of the couple's long quarrel over Hueffer joining the army" (117). But Ford had been recycling the same arguments since his enlistment; indeed, virtually the same phrases appear in an August 1915 letter to his mother that Saunders quotes only a few pages earlier (479). Given Ford's penchant for grandstanding and for self-plagiarism, it's probable that Violet had heard his explanations often enough to achieve a high level of ventriloquism.

33. Quoted in Prothero, "Reply" 416; Review of *The Good Soldier* 117. I am reminded in this connection of the difficulty with which neighbors "decoded" the Gaudier-Brzeska bust in the garden of South Lodge in relation to the war, unable to decide if it would attract German bombs or ward them off.
34. According to Saunders, the name change was crucial to Ford's self-reinvention after his wartime experiences: "Postulating the death of Ford Madox Hueffer was a necessary stage in the rebirth of Ford Madox Ford" (II: 26). Just as crucial to this reinvention was the symbolic break with Hunt.

References

Adcock, A. St. John. "Violet Hunt." *The Glory That Was Grub Street*. New York: Frederick A. Stokes, 1928. 125-34.

Belford, Barbara. *Violet*. New York: Simon & Schuster, 1990.

Blair, Juliet. "Private Parts in Public Places: The Case of Actresses." *Women and Space: Ground Rules and Social Maps*. Ed. Shirley Ardener. Cross-Cultural Perspectives on Women 5. Rev. edn. Oxford & Providence: Berg, 1993.

Boccaccio, Giovanni. *The Decameron*. Translated by J.M. Rigg. Everyman's Library 845. 2 vols London: J.M. Dent, 1930.

Buitenhuis, Peter. *The Great War of Words: Literature as Propaganda 1914-18 and After*. 1987. London: Batsford, 1989.

Chesterton, G.K. "Our Notebook." *Illustrated London News* 22 May 1915: 653.

"The Cowardly Zeppelin Raid of Oct. 13." *Illustrated London News* 23 October 1915: 516-7.

Elshtain, Jean Bethke. *Women and War*. 1987. Rev. edn. Chicago: University of Chicago Press, 1995.

Farrar, L.L., Jr. "The Artist as Propagandist." *The Presence of Ford Madox Ford*. Ed. Sondra J. Strang. Philadelphia: University of Pennsylvania Press, 1981.

"Fiction." Review of *Zeppelin Nights*, by Ford Madox Hueffer and Violet Hunt. *Times Literary Supplement* 25 November 1915: 430.

Foster, Richard. "[Forward to Stories from *Zeppelin Nights*]." *Critical Essays on Ford Madox Ford*. Ed. Richard A. Cassell. Boston: G.K. Hall, 1987. 37-8.

Fraser, Nancy. "Rethinking the Public Sphere: A Contribution to the Critique of Actually Existing Democracy." *Social Text* 25/26 (1990): 56-80.

Fussell, Paul. *The Great War and Modern Memory*. London: Oxford University Press, 1975.

Garnett, David. *The Golden Echo*. New York: Harcourt, 1954.

Goldring, Douglas. *South Lodge: Reminiscences of Violet Hunt, Ford Madox Ford, and the English Review Circle*. London: Constable, 1943.

Goodman, Dena. "Public Sphere and Private Life: Toward a Synthesis of Current Historiographical Approaches to the Old Regime." *History and Theory* 31.1 (1992): 1-20.

Review of *The Good Soldier*, by Ford Madox Hueffer. *The Bookman* July 1915: 117.

Grayzel, Susan R. *Women's Identities at War: Gender, Motherhood and Politics in Britain and France During the First World War*. Chapel Hill: University of North Carolina Press, 1999.

Green, Robert. *Ford Madox Ford: Prose and Politics*. Cambridge: Cambridge University Press, 1981.

Hardwick, Joan. *An Immodest Violet: The Life of Violet Hunt*. London: Andre Deutsch, 1990.

Harvey, David Dow. *Ford Madox Ford, 1873-1939: A Bibliography of Works and Criticism*. Princeton: Princeton University Press, 1962.

Haste, Cate. *Keep the Home Fires Burning: Propaganda in the First World War*. London: Allen Lane, 1977.

Hoffmann, E.T.A. *The Serapion Brethren*. 2 vols Translated by Alexander Ewing. London: G. Bell, 1886-92.

Hueffer, Ford Madox. *Between St. Dennis and St. George: A Sketch of Three Civilisations*. London: Hodder and Stoughton, 1915.

———. "Literary Portraits—V.: Miss Violet Hunt and 'The Desirable Alien.'" *Outlook* 11 October 1913: 497-8.

———. "On Heaven." *Poetry* 4.3 (1914): 75-94.

———. *The Spirit of the People*. 1906. *England and the English: An Interpretation*. New York: McClure, 1907.

———. *When Blood is Their Argument*. London: Hodder and Stoughton, 1915.

Hueffer, Ford Madox and Violet Hunt. *Zeppelin Nights: A London Entertainment*. London: John Lane, 1916.

Hunt, Violet. *The Desirable Alien*. With Preface and Two Additional Chapters by Ford Madox Ford. London: Chatto and Windus, 1913.

———. *I Have This to Say: The Story of My Flurried Years*. New York: Boni and Liveright, 1926.

———. "Not Even Half a Hero." *Outlook* 11 September 1915: 332.

———. *Their Lives*. New York: Brentano's, 1916.

Hynes, Samuel. *A War Imagined: The First World War and English Culture*. 1990. New York: Collier, 1992.

———. *The Edwardian Turn of Mind*. Princeton: Princeton University Press, 1968.

Kent, Susan Kingsley. *Making Peace: The Reconstruction of Gender in Interwar Britain*. Princeton: Princeton University Press, 1993.

Kineke, Sheila. "'Like a Hook Fits an Eye': Jean Rhys, Ford Madox Ford, and the Imperial Operations of Modernist Mentoring." *Tulsa Studies in Women's Literature* 16.2 (Fall 1997) 281-301.

Landes, Joan B. *Women and the Public Sphere in the Age of the French Revolution*. Ithaca: Cornell University Press, 1988.

Longenbach, James. "The Men and Women of 1914." *Arms and the Woman: War, Gender and Literary Representation*. Ed. Helen M. Cooper, Adrienne Auslander Munich, and Susan Merrill Squier. Chapel Hill: University of North Carolina Press, 1989. 97-123.

Lyon, Janet. "Better Homes and Moderns: Salons and Modernity." Modernist Studies Association Inaugural Conference. Penn State University, 8 October 1999.

MacDonagh, Michael. *In London During the Great War*. London: Eyre and Spottiswoode, 1935.

Mackay, Jane and Pat Thane. "The Englishwoman." *Englishness: Politics and Culture 1880-1920*. Ed. Robert Colls and Philip Dodd. London: Croon Helm, 1987.

Marwick, Arthur. *The Deluge: British Society and the First World War*. 1965. New York and London: Norton, 1970.

McGlathery, James M. *E.T.A. Hoffman*. New York: Twayne, 1992.

Mizener, Arthur. *The Saddest Story: A Biography of Ford Madox Ford*. 1971. New York: Carroll & Graf, 1985.

Montefiore, Janet. "'Shining Pins and Wailing Shells': Women Poets and the Great War." *Women and World War 1: The Written Response*. Ed. Dorothy Goldman. Houndsmills: Macmillan, 1993. 51-72.

Nehls, Edward, ed. *D.H. Lawrence: A Composite Biography*. Vol 2. Madison: University of Wisconsin Press, 1958.

"New Novels." Review of *The House of Many Mirrors*, by Violet Hunt. *Times Literary Supplement* 10 June 1915: 197.

"Novel Notes." Review of *Zeppelin Nights*, by Ford Madox Hueffer and Violet Hunt. *The Bookman* January 1916: 136.

Ouditt, Sharon. *Fighting Forces, Writing Women: Identity and Ideology in the First World War*. New York: Routledge, 1994.

Patmore, Brigit. *My Friends When Young*. London: Heinemann, 1968.

Pedersen, Susan. "Gender, Welfare, and Citizenship in Britain during the Great War." *American Historical Review* 95 (1990): 983-1006.

Peel, C.S. *How We Lived Then 1914-1918: A Sketch of Social and Domestic Life in England During the War*. London: John Lane, 1929.

Peppis, Paul. "Thinking Race in the *Avant Guerre*: Typological Negotiations in Ford and Stein." *Yale Journal of Criticism* 10.2 (1997): 371-95.

Pickering, Jean and Suzanne Kehde. Introduction. *Narratives of Nostalgia, Gender, and Nationalism*. Ed. Pickering and Kehde. New York: New York University Press, 1997. 1-8.

Playne, Caroline E. *Society at War 1914-1916*. Boston and New York: Houghton Mifflin, 1931.

Posonby, Arthur. *Falsehood in War-Time*. London: Allen & Unwin, 1928.

Prothero, J.K. [Ada Elizabeth Jones]. "Mr. Hueffer and his Cellar *Garnis*." Review of *Zeppelin Nights*, by Ford Madox Hueffer and Violet Hunt. *New Witness* 6 January 1916: 293.

——. Reply to letter of E.S.P. Haynes. *New Witness* 3 February 1916: 416.

Pugh, Martin. *Women and the Women's Movement in Britain 1914-1959*. Houndsmills: Macmillan, 1992.

Relyea, Suzanne. "Aggression, Enclosure and the Caress: L'Honnete homme chez ses amies." *Actes de New Orleans*. Ed. Francis L. Lawrence. Paris: Papers on French 17th Century Literature, 1982. 125-52.

Samuel, Raphael. Preface. *Patriotism: The Making and Unmaking of British National Identity*. Ed. Samuel. Vol 1. London: Routledge, 1989. x-xvii.

Sanders, Michael L. and Philip M. Taylor. *British Propaganda During the First World War, 1914-18*. London: Macmillan, 1982.

Saunders, Max. *Ford Madox Ford: A Dual Life*. 2 vols. New York: Oxford University Press, 1996.

"Science Jottings." *Illustrated London News* 13 March 1915: 344.

Secor, Robert and Marie Secor. *The Return of the Good Good Soldier: Ford Madox Ford and Violet Hunt's 1917 Diary*. Victoria: English Literary Studies, University of Victoria, 1983.

Sillers, Stuart. *Art and Survival in First World War Britain*. New York: St. Martin's, 1987.

Tate, Trudi. *Modernism, History and the First World War*. Manchester and New York: Manchester University Press, 1998.

Tinker, Chauncey Brewster. *The Salon and English Letters*. New York: Macmillan, 1915.

Tomlinson, Nora and Robert Green. "Ford's Wartime Journalism." *Agenda* 27.4-28.1 (1989-1990): 139-47.

Tylee, Claire M. *The Great War and Women's Consciousness: Images of Militarism and Womanhood in Women's Writings, 1914-64*. Iowa City: University of Iowa Press, 1990.

Waites, Bernard. *A Class Society at War*. Leamington Spa, United Kingdom: Berg, 1987.

Wilson, Trevor. *The Myriad Faces of War: Britain and the Great War, 1914-1918*. 1986. Cambridge: Polity, 1988.

"The Women's Right-to-Serve Demonstration: A Great Procession." *Illustrated London News* 24 July 1915: 109.

Woollacott, Angela. "Sisters and Brothers in Arms: Family, Class, and Gendering in World War I Britain." *Gendering War Talk*. Ed. Miriam Cooke and Angela Woollacott. Princeton: Princeton University Press, 1993. 128-47.

"The Zeppelin Raid of May 10: Damage at Southend and Leigh." *Illustrated London News* 15 May 1915: 615.

Part II—There *IS* a Story There: Literary Forms of Protest

4   A Feminine Conspiracy: Contraception, the New Woman, and Empire in Rosamond Lehmann's *The Weather in the Streets*

Andrea Lewis

In 1935, Neville Chamberlain, then Chancellor of the Exchequer, commented on Britain's declining birth rate:

> I must say that I look upon the continued diminution of the birth-rate in this country with considerable apprehension ... the time may not be far distant ... when ... the countries of the British Empire will be crying out for more citizens of the right breed, and when we in this country shall not be able to supply the demand. (Branson 165)

In a novel of the same period—*The Weather in the* Streets by Rosamond Lehmann—Olivia Curtis reflects, in very different terms, on her impending abortion:

> Enter into the feminine conspiracy, be received with tact, sympathy, pills and hot water bottles, we're all in the same boat, all unfortunate women caught out after a little indiscretion. (260)

Britain's declining birth rate in the late nineteenth and early twentieth centuries is by now a well-documented fact. Ethnographers and social historians point to a good deal of empirical evidence—including the mass deaths of World War I, the entry of an increasing number of women into the workforce, and the rise of contraception—to explain the phenomenon. In the political imagination of the time, however, the way in which the issue gained significance tells a somewhat different narrative. In Chamberlain's mind, for example, the declining birth rate is tied up with global power, national identity, eugenics, and the commodification of people. In Lehmann's, the issue raises questions of female transgression, abortion, the disenfranchisement of women, and social class.

The extent to which national calls for an increase in population clashed with various social practices that resisted that call reveals the population issue in Britain during the inter-war years as a vexed one. Placed side by side, the political and social spheres raise questions about the relationship between state power and female sexuality. The two quotations above—one from a male politician, and one from a female novelist—suggest that the call to increase population as it was framed by the male, official sphere was not always consistent with what many women were experiencing in their lives. While the state was encouraging women to bear children, many women had reason to see childbearing as something to be avoided. During the inter-war years, abortion became increasingly publicized, discussed and attacked as a means of avoiding childbearing. And while abortion gained currency in social and political rhetoric, fiction of the time was slow to address it in any sustained way. Rosamond Lehmann's *The Weather in the Streets* is one of the few contemporary novels to address abortion. And it does so provocatively by exploring the specific ways in which abortion intersects with class structures of the period. For it is the middle-class Olivia Curtis's constant concern with discretion that propels her counter-reproductive, counter-national, and illegal act of abortion. Lehmann's novel thus raises compelling questions not only about the dynamic interplay of female sexuality and national ideologies of reproduction, but also about the extent to which class structures imposed on those dynamics.

The Weather in the Streets was published in 1936—the year following Chamberlain's observation. It was the fourth of Lehmann's seven novels. Four of her novels—*Dusty Answer, A Note in Music, Invitation to the Waltz,* and *The Weather in the Streets*—were written during the interwar years. In 1953, she wrote *The Echoing Grove* and in 1976, she wrote her last novel, *The Sea-Grape Tree.* Lehmann also completed a collection of short stories, *The Gypsy's Baby,* in 1946, and her memoir, *The Swan in the Evening,* in 1967. Broadly speaking, one might say that all of Lehmann's work treats the romance plot in unconventional ways. These explorations lead, in one sense or another, to a statement of disillusionment, primarily on the part of women, characteristic of the personal and political wasteland that was perceived to comprise so much of early twentieth-century existence. Lehmann's novels address lesbianism, failed marriages, abortion, alcoholism, madness, and death. None plays out a conventional marriage plot. It is this pervasively ironic nature of her fiction that makes the critique of social and political structures so powerful.

Yet during her career, Lehmann never won the respect accorded even to less-read writers of the modernist period such as Dorothy Richardson and May Sinclair. Indeed, in her own life, she existed on the periphery of the Bloomsbury group. That her writing incorporates no innovative narrative technique undoubtedly contributed to her relative lack of success during a literary era privileging radical artistry. Such a modest approach in most of Lehmann's work places her amidst that group of novelists whose work is situated part way between the bourgeois realism of the nineteenth century and the radical avant-garde of writers such as Joyce and Woolf. Lehmann's early work, particularly, does not exhibit the bold narrative fragmentation and authorial absence of better-known modernist literature. Moreover, because her narrative technique does not harbor a hypersensitivity to the novel as a work of art, it remains somewhat realist in its renditions of life. Yet it is important to note that Lehmann worked in the realist tradition because it served her purposes: she wanted to show social and class conflict more than she wanted to explore the inner workings of individual consciousness, and she used a narrative mode that enabled her to make an ironic commentary on an iniquitous world.

To be sure, Lehmann does not entirely disregard modernist literary techniques. She is experimental in her use of narrative perspective, to name just one technique. Shifting between first, third, and sometimes second, person point of view, she explores the nature of subjectivity and questions the meaning of individual identity. In *The Weather in the Streets*, for example, the shifting perspective is a function of a given level and nature of the protagonist's emotional and psychological anxiety. At the moment in the novel when Olivia is most anxious, deciding what to do about her pregnancy, we see such narrative shifts in Lehmann's prose:

> She remembered Kate unfamiliar and touching in a grey maternity frock with white ruffles. Such dignities will not be for me. To be rid, to be rid, to be rid of this ... To be not sick ... I should be hanging on doors, lifting wardrobes and pianos, trying to fall downstairs, doing everything I can ... Instead, day after day, inert, she rested, strolled, sank down in chairs, crawled to the bathroom, fell into bed again: protecting herself against her own designs against nature, lowering herself unresistingly to a vegetable standard: A maggotty spoiling vegetable ... I don't weep, I don't fret. I regulate my life. I hope only as a marrow might hope for sun and rain: a dull tenacious clinging. (293)

Today, Lehmann is not mentioned in otherwise inclusive anthologies, such as *The Norton Anthology of Women Writers* and *The Gender of Modernism*, and barely noted in Mary Loeffelholz's *Experimental Lives*. Several critics, however, have built convincing cases for Lehmann's literary merit. Among them, James Gindin, in a 1974 article in *Contemporary Literature*, attempts to understand critical neglect of Lehmann and argues that her fiction contains a "density of experience" (201) comparable to other major works written by her contemporaries. Valentine Cunningham, in *British Writers of the Thirties*, declares Lehmann the "most important fiction-writing sister" of her time after Virginia Woolf, "inexplicably ignored in all standard accounts of '30s writing" (26). And Sydney Janet Kaplan's *Feminine Consciousness in the Modern British Novel* devotes a chapter to Lehmann who is placed alongside Woolf, Richardson, Sinclair, and Lessing. Judy Simons's

1992 *Rosamond Lehmann* is the only recent book-length study to celebrate Lehmann's literary contribution to the period. Simons approaches Lehmann's oeuvre through a blend of psychological and social perspectives:

> The contradictions and confusions that confront the protagonists of Rosamond Lehmann's fiction reflect, however, not only the vicissitudes of her personal fortunes but also the political and social upheaval of the times in which she lived ... Lehmann's sensitivity to her times and her acute political awareness are fused with her insight into the personal lives of women caught up in the processes of history, and one of her major achievements as a novelist is the way in which she explores the response of individuals to the cultural shift of the age. (2)

In extending Simons's idea of Lehmann's women as "caught up in the processes of history," I would like to suggest—as the two opening quotations of this paper do—that Lehmann's novels reveal more than just the fall-out from World War I and a changing Edwardian society. Lehmann's novels also address the conjunction of political issues—larger imperial goals and national identity—and contemporary attitudes and behavior regarding female sexuality. Particularly, I suggest that the contradictory ways in which female sexuality was constructed by competing ideologies—of imperialism and nationalism, on the one hand, and of class, on the other—during the inter-war years is made evident in her novel, *The Weather in the Streets*. Because the novel raises questions of reproduction, contraception, and abortion in association with class structure in a way that runs contrary to the imperative to breed British citizens, Lehmann's novel reveals the extent to which women faced a double-bind regarding reproduction.

The Weather in the Streets traces this double-bind through its sympathetic treatment of its protagonist, Olivia. On the one hand, the novel is subversive to the extent that it challenges official male discourse advocating reproduction. Olivia rebels against middle-class values by rejecting marriage and children because she wants to guard her independence. Even when Olivia does identify with middle-class values—in her overriding preoccupation with discretion—she chooses to have an illegal abortion, an act in defiance of official discourses on reproduction at the time. On the other hand, however, by showing that middle-class status is also an ideal that Olivia fears will be compromised by her potential associations with lower-class indiscretion, the novel simultaneously reinforces discriminating distinctions within the class structure. Because ideologies of personal respectability and class weigh in more heavily than do ideologies of reproduction, the novel ironically affirms the class structure upon which reproductive ideologies depended. Thus the novel comes full circle by shifting between the indictment of and complicity with hegemonic social and political modes of thinking. *The Weather in the Streets* thus occupies a double space with regard to women and reproduction in British society at the time: it suggests that for middle-class women of the thirties, both convention and transgression could exist side by side, making it likely that women would realize only partial success in changing their positions within the system.

The Weather in the Streets returns us to Olivia Curtis—the protagonist of Lehmann's earlier novel, *Invitation to the Waltz*—after her separation from her husband, Ivor. *Invitation to the Waltz* takes as its focus the day of Olivia's seventeenth birthday. The Curtises are a middle-class family who live in the picturesque village of Little Compton. About half the novel takes place in the Curtis's house, where Olivia is surrounded by adults to whom she can barely relate. Her Uncle Oswald, her father, and her mother all bore the polite Olivia with their tiresome concerns. The second half of the novel moves, with Olivia and her sister Katie, to the coming-out ball of Marigold Spencer, daughter of the neighboring aristocratic Lady and Sir John Spencer. Here, the frenzy of Marigold's artistic and youthful friends contrasts with the earlier dullness of Olivia's home life. The two settings in *Invitation to the Waltz*— Olivia's parents' home and Marigold's ball—function to suggest Olivia's growing sense of marginalization in the society in which she lives; she finds herself on the periphery of both the stuffy adult world of her parents' gener- ation and the fast-changing world of her peers. Olivia is left, in this novel, alienated from both options of female sexuality available to her—the dowdy tradition of her mother and the defiant social behavior of the New Woman. Too youthful to be disillusioned, Olivia nevertheless is aware of her own dis- placement in a changing world. The novel ends with this displacement unre- solved—it offers no alternative choice for its protagonist but to exist in a suspended state.

At the opening of *The Weather in the Streets*, ten years after the end of *Invitation to the Waltz*, Olivia is living with her cousin, Etty, in a small Lon- don apartment. Both Etty—the cheerful flapper who appeared in *Invitation to the Waltz*—and Olivia embody the New Woman and changing gender roles—they smoke, drink, live independently, and work to earn their livings; Olivia has attended Cambridge's women's college. Olivia embodies the enhanced freedoms available to women—she is able to separate from her husband with relatively little scandal, she is able to work for her money, and she is able to go out at night and travel alone. But this has come at a price. Olivia has vowed to be financially independent, which means a "poorer" existence for her. The apartment she shares with Etty is rather shabby. The somewhat bohemian lifestyle of the two women and their friends seems far removed from the comfort of their parents' homes. Thus while both Etty and Olivia come from middle-class backgrounds, this is overshadowed in the novel by the material realities of their current lifestyle. Olivia worries about earning enough money to keep herself, cannot afford to replace worn clothes, and sacrifices dinner to spend the money on a film instead.

Near the opening of the novel, Olivia's ailing father forces her to return to Little Compton for a few weeks. On the train journey there, she meets Rollo Spencer—brother of Marigold Spencer and son of Lady and Sir John Spencer of *Invitation to the Waltz*—who is also returning home for a family visit. Although alone on the train, Rollo is now married to the beautiful and frail Nicola, only ever alluded to in *The Weather in the Streets*. The novel takes as its focus Olivia's affair with Rollo Spencer, a series of illicit meetings kept hidden from friends and family. The novel ends with Nicola pregnant, a pregnancy that is carried to term. When Olivia too becomes pregnant, however, she has an abortion. Her own and Nicola's respective pregnancies lead Olivia to break off the affair with Rollo. After Olivia announces her decision to break off the relationship, Rollo is hurt in a car accident. In the final scene in the novel, Olivia goes to visit Rollo, who is recovering from the accident; the scene is ambiguous as to whether the affair will continue or not.

As in *Invitation to the Waltz*, Olivia in this novel encounters the ambiguities inherent in the cultural changes of her time, ambiguities heightened in the novel by her sister Kate's, Nicola's, and her own respective pregnancies. *Invitation to the Waltz* opens with, and maintains, a focus on the breeding function of the family where the purpose of Little Compton itself is characterized by Lehmann as "primarily designed to shelter the old age and accommodate the numerous offspring of Mr James Curtis" (7). We are told, further, of the Curtis's house: "Here grows a curious plant with strong roots knotted all together: an unique specimen. In brief, a family lives here" (9). But while in *Invitation to the Waltz*, the role of women in this institution is strangely absent yet central to it, *The Weather in the Streets* provides a decisively more overt and radical critique on the place of women in the reproduction of the British family. It does so, on one level, by its confrontation with the issue of abortion—a socially subversive and legally criminal act at the time—which offers a critique of official national, imperial, and class-related discourses on reproduction by allowing women a more defiant position in relation to the nation state.

During the interwar years, the ideology of reproduction and the practices of counter-reproduction showed just how much ambiguity surrounded women's sexuality. With the declining birth rate and with Britain's imperial power beginning to wane, a certain anxiety over national identity characterized much of the nation: Britain needed people to replenish its population at home after the devastation of war, and abroad, in its colonies. In effect, British nationals, especially women, were called to serve their country by reproducing. Thus, imperial discourse came to define female sexuality largely in terms of the motherhood that was so integral to the ideology of population, and in turn so central to Britain's racial and national longevity. Women's task was, in effect, a nation-building and a civilizing one that was to take place via reproduction on both domestic and political fronts.

Such reproductive urgency, however, clashed with the simultaneous rise in awareness and use of contraception and abortion, and a high maternal mortality rate. In the late nineteenth and early twentieth centuries, Britain saw an increased demand for contraception which, though not illegal, remained largely unavailable to the majority of people. The presence of a number of birth control advocates—Stella Browne and Dora Russell, among others, along with a number of private organizations like the Malthusian League—managed to raise awareness of contraception, mostly, but not exclusively, because of increasing maternal mortality. Although contraception was available in the private sector, activists wanted the government to make it readily available. Forms of birth control had been in use for decades, but the British government refused to permit any access to contraception through its public health system until 1930 when the Minister of Health finally permitted existing maternity and child welfare clinics to give contraceptive advice to women in cases where pregnancy endangered the health of a woman (Lewis 34). Even though the service was not widely publicized, it was an important step in the campaign for contraception because it marked the official recognition of the importance of women's reproductive health on a state level. Arguments against contraception persisted, however. Conservatives were worried that liberalizing access to contraception would result in greater sexual immorality. But many opposed contraception as essentially unpatriotic because it curtailed the population which Britain needed desperately to increase in the face of its declining birth rate. It was not until 1949 that birth control became fully sanctioned by the Royal Commission on Population and thus freely available to the public (Lewis 44).

Some birth control advocates succeeded in turning to their advantage the argument that birth control was unpatriotic; they did this by blending specific demographic facts and class-based fears about the declining birth rate with current theories of eugenics, which gained immense support during the 1930s. Class ideologies became embedded in different theories about contraception. Before the Great War, the decline in birth rate had been greater in the middle and upper classes than in the working classes. This was generally thought to result from the use of birth control. During the interwar years, this gap narrowed slightly. But the fact that it was the lower classes who were having most of the children was exploited by birth control advocates of the time. Advocates raised concern over the supposed quality of society, arguing for the burden that an exploding working class would place on the rest of society. Such arguments won over even conservatives who had been reluctant to embrace contraception in the past because of concern about sexual "immorality." Thus contraception was able to win favor in the face of the call to reproduce because it played on class-related fears in the political imagination to which eugenics posed an equally imaginary solution.

Eugenics found further support by weaving together medical and scientific knowledge with patriotism. Marie Stopes, a doctor of science by training, was probably the most influential advocate of "family planning" in the 1920s and 1930s because she succeeded in popularizing this stance. She wrote numerous books promoting women's sexuality and birth control, including *Married Love, Radiant Motherhood*, and *Contraception*, and she founded the conservative Society for Constructive Birth Control and Racial Progress (Weeks 187). Her overt argument that contraception might be used to limit individual suffering put a slightly more human face on Chamberlain's notion that only "citizens of the right breed" should reproduce. But like other eugenicists, she essentially promoted contraception not as a means of reducing the population but as a means of controlling the quality of population. Stopes contends in *Contraception* that by using birth control "unsatisfactory offspring can be avoided in the cheapest and most wholesome way" (12). This supposed positive spin on contraception was effective in gaining significant support for the birth control movement (Lewis 38).

Eugenicists' arguments were informed primarily by a class-based vision of the English nation in which contraception would curb working-class reproduction. But it is important to note that the eugenics movement flourished at a time when European imperialism promoted the assumption that the white race was the superior race. Indeed, many prominent thinkers of the time—Havelock Ellis, for one—categorized race hierarchically so as to define the Caucasian race as superior. It is then not difficult to imagine eugenics as a contributing factor to the rise of fascism in Europe in the 1930s and the breeding of an Aryan nation. What becomes evident for female identity is that despite the pervasive pro-mothering national ideology in Britain, the eugenics movement promoted only certain definitions of acceptable motherhood, motherhood that had the respectability of particular class and racial identities. So the patriotic call to reproduce under any circumstances became transformed into a patriotism that called for "responsible" reproduction.

The discriminating distinctions within this social structure were reinforced by its association with different types of contraception, most notably abortion. Even though contraception was gaining favor, and became fairly widely used in the 1930s, abortion remained a prevalent means of restricting family size. It had been illegal (although a 1929 law excepted cases where a mother's life was in danger [Weeks 195]). Yet even as a criminal act, abortion occurred extensively, increasing especially in the 1920s (Brookes 56) and raising further concern about maternal mortality. The inaccessibility of birth control forced many women to find alternative methods of controlling their fertility, one of which was abortion. Abortion had mostly lower-class associations; Stopes, in *Contraception*, writes that "Methods of abortion are most frequently used by poor and ignorant women who are denied the necessary contraceptive knowledge" (59). Yet evidence suggests the widespread use of abortion by women other than working-class women. Barbara Brookes notes that while "working-class women used abortion as an accepted method of fertility control" (97), "women of all classes resorted to self-induced abortion" (110). And Patricia Knight observes that "though there was probably a good deal of discreet middle-class abortion indicated by the extensive sale of more expensive abortion remedies, contemporaries persisted in seeing abortion as a working-class phenomenon" (58). The link between abortion and the lower classes, then, was more a function of the political imagination than a real demographic fact.

So, class- and race-specific images of motherhood and the British population, as well as certain modes of contraception and their relation to class, colored the political imagination of the inter-war years and made their way into some literature. Lehmann's *The Weather in the Streets* takes up issues of conflicting models of motherhood and reproduction and addresses the abortion issue in the context of class. Rollo's wife, Nicola, and Olivia's sister, Kate, are—according to official definitions—perfect models of motherhood: they are appropriately married and consequently have access to money that brings with it no need to work and an entourage of servants to care for their children. They have the respectability of the middle class and the Caucasian race as do the children they bear. Lehmann says of Kate, "as the wife of a young doctor. ... as the mother of four fine healthy children, she has established herself beyond question in all eyes" (61). Lehmann builds on this affirmation in a scene one evening, while Olivia and Kate are both visiting their parents' home. As Kate and her mother sit in armchairs knitting at the fireside, Olivia is sprawled, smoking, on the rug in front of the fire. The images of mothers and daughters function here as a powerful site of reproductive responsibility reinforced by the series of family portraits in the Curtis's drawing room:

> Kate had taken on and elaborated the theme unfolded in her own infancy by Mrs. Curtis. The little tables either side of the fireplace were choked now with photographs of the grandchildren at all stages: straight-fringed, neat-featured, hygienic-looking. A number of the more rococo pre-war likenesses of Mrs. Curtis' own young—plumes, curls, ribbons, frothing frills—had been put away to make room for them. (65)

The changes in generation are glued together by the continuous replacement and sequencing of children while the images of those children bear class and racial characteristics that allow them to be "citizens of the right breed": their "straight" hair, their "neat" features, and their "hygienic" looks. Such breeding, clearly the domain of women, allows Mrs Curtis and now Kate to engage in the nation building required of them to serve national goals. In this same scene, Olivia is set apart:

Olivia smoked, looked at *The Illustrated London News.* Over her head the two pairs of hands resumed their busy conspiracy, the two voices droned peacefully on ... The children, the servants, the children, Rob, Dad, James, the children. (65)

Kate has the approval necessary to become privy to the tradition of family—so much so that she and her mother have entered into a type of "conspiracy" together. The family, here, is a closed system, and Olivia's behavior—intellectual rather than domestic, rebellious rather than conformist—positions her on the periphery of the domestic space that is filled with children, husbands, and middle-class domestic details. Lehmann's slightly deprecating tone in these passages and her description of middle-class domesticity as functional routine with little social or intellectual excitement to offer suggests her endorsement of Olivia's position as outsider to a fertile but vacuous tradition.

In several other scenes in *The Weather in the Streets* where Olivia and Kate visit their parents' home in Little Compton, Kate and her children are placed more directly alongside Olivia, with the effect of showing Olivia's increasing alienation from middle-class convention. This juxtaposition becomes more poignant towards the end of the novel when Olivia is taking medication obtained from the chemist in her first attempt to induce an abortion. The two sisters' conversations and playfulness with Kate's children are punctuated by Olivia's frequent disappearing to take her next dose of pills. This distinction is furthered by the contrasting ways in which the two sisters see one another at this time. Kate sees Olivia as "hollow-cheeked, inert ... ghastly colour, greyish beneath the make-up ... thinner than ever" (265). Just a few pages later, Olivia sees Kate with "pink, soft, firmly-modelled lips ... the clear-water eyes looking up, abstracted, the wavy hair swept backwards, the long supple body that had borne four ... Beautiful still" (279). Images of beauty, here, are tied to images of motherhood and reproduction such that Kate is represented as physically fitter and more suitable for the reproduction of the Curtis family than is Olivia. The eventual pregnancy of Rollo's wife, Nicola, at which the family heaves a collective sigh of relief, allows the Spencer family, too, to fulfill its reproductive mission. It also persuades Olivia that it is time to break off her relationship with Rollo because the expectation of the baby solidifies her position as an outsider to the Spencer family. And so the novel raises questions of the fate of women who fall beyond the ideal definition of motherhood. Such questions are brought to the fore by Olivia's pregnancy and her abortion. Olivia's decision not to carry her own pregnancy to term is the ultimate counter-reproductive act that places her in stark opposition to Kate and Nicola, and the convention that the Curtis and Spencer families symbolize.

For most of the New Women in Lehmann's novel, pregnancy is a bleak and disturbing notion. By refusing pregnancy and motherhood, many women in the novel occupy a position outside of the traditional family structure. For all women at the time, abortion was a means of controlling fertility, but especially when women were officially "citizens of the right breed," their decision not to have babies can be interpreted as a means by which they defied the state's call to reproduce and turned abortion into a transgressive, politicized act. Olivia's close friend, Anna, says she would "drown herself rather than face" (294) motherhood. And Olivia's discussion one evening with her cousin Etty about the possibility of an abortion reveals the extent of a kind of underground subculture of young, unmarried, pregnant women, seeking ways to terminate their pregnancies illegally. For Etty herself, unknown to Olivia, has had an abortion, as have several of their middle-class friends. And Etty and her friends seem fully aware that their actions are transgressive. Etty rather craftily characterizes this search to terminate unwanted pregnancies by women as "the feminine conspiracy" (258). Clearly, in the context of *The Weather in the Streets*, the conspiracy appears to be against the forces compelling women to reproduce, and against legal and social institutions that punished certain women for their sexuality by forcing them underground. Given that these institutions and ideologies are aligned with national and imperial goals concerning reproduction, one could read the New Woman as conspiring, ultimately, against the imperial nation. The crisis of the declining birth rate, then—and Chamberlain's "considerable apprehension" about the loss of national and global power, to which ends population was so essential—becomes, to some extent, a function of the New Woman's disruptive sexuality and refusal to reproduce. Lehmann clearly endorses these disruptive women whom she sees as victims of their own "female humanity" (258), and Olivia elevates her cousin to divine status—calling her "Savior Etty" (261)—when she names an abortion doctor to whom Olivia can go.

The Weather in the Streets also uses middle-class abortion as a transgression of class structure and class-related fears about population quality. Certainly, for the individual woman, abortion was a means of controlling one's financial well-being. The parliamentary Birkett Committee set up in the 1930s to look into the issue of abortion found that economic factors were one of the leading reasons for abortion (Brookes, 111-12). In *The Weather in the Streets,* Olivia, who supports herself financially, would struggle if she had to raise a baby alone. This provides one incentive for Olivia's abortion. Thus codified class distinctions become blurred by the middle-class women's abortion, typically thought of at the time as a working-class women's method of contraception. And in some ways, economic realities bound together the seemingly disparate experiences of women. Etty, Olivia and their other middle-class friends draw attention to the widespread use of abortion by women outside the working-class, especially in—and perhaps because of—the notable absence of other methods of birth control in the novel. Neither Olivia nor her friends ever discuss using contraception to prevent pregnancy; they only discuss it to terminate pregnancy. The novel thus recasts abortion as very much a middle-class women's means of contraception, suggesting a sympathy with the plight of working-class women and breaking down the discriminating class lines that existed in the political consciousness of the time.

However, this rather bold transgression offered by *The Weather in the Streets* is simultaneously undermined by other configurations of class that reinforce class distinctions. Lehmann shows class identity to be more deep seated than gender identity as the novel explores Olivia's struggle to maintain a deeper difference in consciousness between herself, as a middle-class woman, and the lower classes. We see this awareness and revulsion against her shifting class position when Olivia is pondering what to do about her newly-discovered pregnancy. She realizes that being single and pregnant has significant implications for her class status, and goes through the following process of thinking about her situation: "You're not a servant girl, bound to produce illegitimately, apply for a paternity order, carry a lifelong stigma ... You can scrape up the money and go scot-free" (260). Again later, when Lady Spencer—who unexpectedly visits Olivia to ask her to terminate her affair with Rollo—asks whether she's "in any trouble" (307)—"in trouble" being the well-known euphemism for pregnancy—Olivia responds: "Do you mean—like kitchen maids?" (307). Both of Olivia's reactions to her pregnancy as an unmarried woman align her own illegitimate reproduction with the working classes, clearly an unacceptable mode of mothering in the mind of the middle-class Olivia. Olivia's hurry to dissociate herself from the servant classes suggests that her own slippage between class categories is threatening to her middle-class consciousness. Money—the resource of middle-class women—is the means of avoiding a threatening scandal and regaining respectability.

The abortion doctor, to whom Olivia finally turns after the pills from the chemist fail to work, aids in the restoring of that respectability, just as he is concerned with his own. A well-known "public benefactor" with a respectable practice, he saves "erring women from ruin" (258) as a side-line. The abortionist is, perhaps, also privy to the feminine conspiracy and as such is also in defiance of the national call to reproduce. But his interest in restoring ruined reputations suggests that he is particularly interested in the public embarrassment that pregnancy might bring to middle- or upper-class women. This becomes compounded by his reputation for offering safe abortive procedures and by the powerful secrecy that surrounds what he does. Certainly his services would not be affordable to many working-class women who might have to resort to less expensive, and more dangerous, means of abortion. And indeed Olivia is hard-pressed to come up with the money to pay for it, having to sell items of jewelry given to her by Rollo in order to foot the bill. The abortionist, then, is reinforcing a discriminatory class structure by concealing the fact that abortion is a method of contraception used by middle-class women for the purposes of maintaining the respectability associated with the middle and upper classes, and thus reinforcing abortion's visibility as a lower-class phenomenon. He is also aiding in eugenicists' goals of breeding a certain type of population by shaping acceptable types of motherhood that depended on class identity.

Class, in *The Weather in the Streets*, a consciousness of one's place that is deeper than one's immediate material status, is reinforced by Olivia's horror that her affair will jeopardize her respectability and associate her with the working-class woman's pregnancy and abortion. Class norms inform much of Olivia's affair with Rollo. At one point, Olivia reflects:

> I didn't want even the shadow of a situation the world recognises and tolerates as long as it's *sub rosa*, decent, discreet, that means a word in the ear, a wink, an eye at a keyhole ... My idea being we were too fine for the world, our love should have no dealings whatsoever with its coarseness ... (177)

Although Olivia deplores the middle-class hypocrisy that would ensure the discretion of her affair with Rollo, her fear of personal embarrassment, brought about by a deep psychological identification with class, is in fact a powerful catalyst driving her to override official calls to motherhood. Her abortion itself, while aligning Olivia in her own mind with the working classes, is also an attempt to maintain respectability and middle-class identity. Ultimately, the strong class identity prompting Olivia to conceal her abortion is a means by which the respectability of the nation and its citizenry are maintained despite her challenge to that respectability by her sexually emancipated lifestyle.

Certainly, the significant role played by abortion in *The Weather in the Streets* sets this novel apart from others of the same period. The taboo subject is confronted by Lehmann and explored in more economic, psychological, and social depth than in other literature of the period which, at best, only ever alludes to the issue. In particular, the extent to which the novel places abortion in the realm of the middle class makes this novel an exceptional contribution in a time when abortion was represented in most social and political rhetoric as a working-class phenomenon. Few critics of Lehmann's novel have explored, even briefly, the vulnerability and abuse of women's bodies in the context of abortion. Simons, for example, notes the "bitter irony" (78) in the novel as the romance plot is undermined by Olivia's termination of her pregnancy, which he reads as a function of social structures that have no acceptable place for unwed mothers. Yet Lehmann's recognition of the connection between abortion practices and highly specific national and class-based ideologies warrants more detailed scrutiny than most critics have allowed.

If reproduction—and especially reproduction for the middle-class woman—was an essential element in being a loyal female British citizen during the inter-war years, then *The Weather in the Streets* must be read as a transgressive text. *The Weather in the Streets* offers a powerful critique of this loyalty by focusing on a protagonist who does not and cannot nurture her race; she, in fact, discards all duty by having an abortion. In so far as motherhood was connected with producing offspring needed to replenish the population at home and to occupy colonial territory abroad, Olivia is subversive of national and imperial goals. Lehmann's sympathetic treatment of such subversiveness endorses Olivia's thinking and behavior as necessary to guard her independence. Certainly, much of the novel is narrated through Olivia's point of view, which allows the reader to be sympathetic to the anguish that she experiences in loving Rollo while not being able to bear his child as an unmarried woman. Lehmann also represents middle-class motherhood as a banal experience, completely unappealing to the intelligent and independent Olivia. The decision to have an abortion seems transgressive but is nevertheless supported by Lehmann and becomes a radical statement about women's power to re-negotiate, even undermine, hegemonic gender and class structures buttressed by eugenicist and nationalist discourses.

But while the New Woman defies the injunction that middle-class women marry and reproduce, Lehmann ultimately uses abortion to define, not undermine, class differences. Olivia's desire to maintain respectability in *The Weather in the Streets* proves stronger than her responsiveness to the call to reproduce, and indeed motivates her decision to have an abortion. While on one level Olivia is disinherited by her social milieu, and accepts that up to a point, on another she fights to maintain that place by avoiding any dire loss of respectability. Her class status is what is at stake, and she succeeds in maintaining it in the end. In a typical Lehmanesque closure that skirts convention while simultaneously allowing it, Olivia is taken under the wing of her friend Anna who, also unmarried and childless, offers her a home and an annual allowance at the close of the novel. Anna inherits her friend Simon's country cottage, and an allowance of four hundred pounds a year, half of which she shares with Olivia. Thus inheritance and class structures remain firmly in place, perpetuated here within the boundaries of the middle class, although outside of a traditional, closed family structure. This, too, Lehmann seems to endorse as she allows her protagonist to partake in the benefits of inherited wealth associated with Anna and Simon, two celebrated characters throughout the novel. The novel is able to claim a space for women apart from the marital and reproductive imperatives of the time, replacing heterosexual marriage with female friendship.

Much of the official discourse of the day on Britain's population problem during the interwar years is questioned, even indicted, by Lehmann because it miscasts the class- and gender-related realities of women's lives.

The narrow definition of acceptable motherhood promoted by eugenicists and supported by a rigid class structure is, according to Lehmann, hostile to many women who sought other ways to live their lives. Lehmann's fiction is important because it offers a competing discourse to the official rhetoric on reproduction, and itself enters into the feminine conspiracy against such rhetoric. While its transgression is mostly daring, it is also somewhat limited. Just as middle-class female sexuality is caught between the freedoms of the New Woman and the protocols of good citizenry, so Lehmann's novel, like its protagonist, is both daring in its bid to transgress, while at the same time unable to do so completely in its return to class-based convention at the close of the novel. Indeed, it is this very ambivalent and multi-layered experience that makes up Olivia's journey in *The Weather in the Streets*, suggesting the host of complexities and ambiguities surrounding the sexuality of the middle-class New Woman in Britain during the inter-war years, and contributing to the novel's texture and richness.

References

Brookes, Barbara. *Abortion in England 1900-1939*. Kent: Croom Helm, 1988.

Branson, Noreen and Margot Heinemann. *Britain in the Nineteen Thirties*. New York: Praeger, 1971.

Cunningham, Valentine. *British Writers of the Thirties*. Oxford: Oxford University Press, 1988.

Davin, Anna. "Imperialism and Motherhood." *History Workshop: A Journal of Socialist Historians* 5 (1978): 9-65.

Ellis, Havelock. *The Psychology of Sex*. New York: Random House, 1937-42.

Gilbert, Sandra and Susan Gubar, eds. *The Norton Anthology of Women Writers*. New York: W.W. Norton, 1985.

Gindin, James. "Rosamond Lehmann: A Revaluation." *Contemporary Literature* 15.2 (1974): 203-11.

Kaplan, Sydney Janet. *Feminine Consciousness in the Modern British Novel*. Urbana: University of Illinois Press, 1975.

Knight, Patricia. "Women and Abortion in Victorian and Edwardian England." *History Workshop: A Journal of Socialist Historians* 4 (1977): 57-68.

Lehmann, Rosamond. *A Note in Music*. New York: H. Holt and Company, 1930.

——. *Dusty Answer*. Ed. Jonathon Coe. 1927. London: Flamingo, 1996.

——. *Invitation to a Waltz*. New York: Harcourt, Brace, and World, 1932.

——. *The Ballad and the Source*. New York: Reynal and Hitchcock, 1945.

——. *The Echoing Grove*. New York: Harcourt, Brace, and World, 1953.

——. *The Gypsy's Baby*. London: Collins, 1946.

——. *The Sea-Grape Tree*. London: Collins, 1976.

——. *The Swan in the Evening*. London: Collins, 1967.

——. *The Weather in the Streets*. New York: The Literary Guild, 1936.

Lewis, Jane. "The Ideology and Politics of Birth Control in Inter-War England." *Women's Studies International Quarterly* 2 (1979): 33-48.

Loeffelholz, Mary. *Experimental Lives: Women and Literature, 1900-1945*. New York: Twayne, 1992.

Scott, Bonnie Kime, ed. *The Gender of Modernism: A Critical Anthology*. Bloomington: Indiana University Press, 1990.

Simons, Judy. *Rosamond Lehmann*. New York: St. Martin's, 1992.

Stopes, Marie Carmichael. *Contraception: Its Theory, History and Practice, A Manual for the Medical and Legal Professions*. London: Putnam, 1932.

——. *Married Love*. 1918. London: Putnam, 1940.

——. *Radiant Motherhood: A Book for Those Who are Creating the Future*. London: Putnam, 1920.

Weeks, Jeffrey. *Sex, Politics, and Society: The Regulation of Sexuality Since 1800*. Second edn. London and New York: Longman, 1981.

5 "There is No Ordinary Life": Privacy and Domesticity in E.H. Young's *Celia* and Elizabeth Bowen's *The Death of the Heart*

Stella Deen

Our dominant model of Thirties' writers is still that of male poets too young to have fought in the first world war but deeply influenced by it, a group of writers committed to making literature respond to urgent domestic and international crises such as mass unemployment and the war in Spain. One problem with this model, as critics such as Janet Montefiore, Jane Dowson, and Maroula Joannou have pointed out, is that it defines the Thirties in a way that marginalizes or leaves out altogether women writers.[1] The assumption that only one genre and one mood—the poetry of crisis—adequately captures the complexity and changes of a decade also dismisses texts perceived as inward-looking either in the "solipsism" of late modernism or in their treatment of a "regressive" or merely "feminine" sensibility.[2] The critical designation of the "woman's novel" has brought to our attention works written by and for women—impressive in number and quality—that have been bypassed by mainstream critical attention.[3] Yet the focus on women's distinctive experiences in this scholarship has undoubtedly contributed to the perception that the "woman's novel" does not or cannot address issues of national or international significance. These valuable treatments of women's writing, then, may, paradoxically, compound the effect produced by women writers' omission from so many accounts of literature of the Thirties.

The notion that Oxford educated, Red intellectuals best represent the decade also obscures the extent to which Britain between the wars was engaged in celebrating what it meant to be English in inward-looking and home-centered terms. "I shall never be one of those grand cosmopolitan authors. ... Not until I am safely back in England do I ever feel that the world is quite sane" (416), declared J.B. Priestley in his 1934 *English Journey*. This sentiment was echoed by the conservative political policies of Neville Chamberlain, who described Czechoslavakia as "a faraway country of which we know little" (quoted in Samuel xxii). "Splendid isolation"[4] was Britain's undeclared policy between the wars. Corresponding to an inward-looking political policy was a stress on new, anti-martial English virtues: simplicity, tolerance, loyalty, pride, and an indispensable, saving sense of humor. A nation of home-lovers replaced the notion of an imperial conqueror, and the typical Englishman was, arguably, a woman.

97

The interwar period thus saw a flourishing culture of domesticity, variously expressed in a terrific expansion of home ownership;[5] in the popular image of the Little Englander; in an annual "Ideal Home Exhibition" sponsored by The *Daily Mail*;[6] and in what Cynthia White has called a "sustained effort" (101) in women's magazines to curb restlessness and to popularize the career of wife and mother. Some magazines elevated housekeeping to the status of a demanding profession; others projected a cozy and sentimental image of home life (100). These magazines also recognized and responded to a variety of stresses during the Thirties—economic stagnation, declining fertility, and marital failure—by "showing women how to make themselves more physically attractive, their homes more comfortable, and their families more content. They encouraged women to look no further" (111).

While classic literary histories of the period emphasize the political engagement of a few Thirties' writers, two recent accounts of women's novels between the wars, Alison Light's *Forever England* and Nicola Beauman's *A Very Great Profession*, have begun to shed light on this culture of privacy. Both studies suggest a more complex relationship between women and domesticity than is implied by the picture emerging from women's magazines. Beauman, for example, emphasizes women's rather grudging accommodation of convention: in the novels she examines, protagonists face up to, but devalue "domestic trivia" (98); or they are encouraged to view their households "with a wry if daring detachment" (113). While for Beauman domestic life signifies material matters separate from life's real centers of interest, for Light it is the frame for finer feeling (142); domesticity in the woman's novel between the wars becomes the source of private and expressive consciousness (127).

In this essay I would like to add to and complicate the work of Beauman and Light through a study of Elizabeth Bowen's *The Death of the Heart* (1938) and E.H. Young's 1937 novel *Celia*.[7] E.H. Young was an accomplished and reasonably successful novelist, publishing eleven novels, several short stories and two children's books between 1910 and 1947. Her "modern, [witty] classics,"—fictions of female development and explorations of troubled marriages—are among those reprinted in the Virago series. Pairing an obscure writer with one of established reputation, I intend to foreground textual features that might not be noticed or noteworthy if we work within the parameters of received categories such as "political writing" and "domestic fiction";[8] in turn, these newly emerging features enable us to challenge the assumption that such categories adequately illuminate the literature and culture of the period.

Both *Celia* and *The Death of the Heart* center on family life and use such recognizable Thirties' attitudes as disillusion and the disparaging of sentiment[9] to situate private life within a meaningful contemporary context. In both novels, domestic space, furniture, and the ordinary interactions of family life are the expression of and training ground for public virtues and vices. As I will show, both novels use the private sphere to represent public, national trends. In so doing, both novelists weigh in on a question that pre-occupied commentators on national English life in the Thirties: how to con-ceptualize the changing relation between private and public realms, whose separation was so thoroughly theorized in the nineteenth century. By writ-ing novels centered on human relations within the domestic sphere, Bowen and Young were not continuing to write in an outmoded literary form but were engaged in a vital contemporary dialogue about English life and cul-ture between the wars.

In contrast to political and cultural celebrations of English privacy and insularity, both novelists are deeply skeptical about the benefits of privacy and reluctant to approve it unequivocally. Elizabeth Bowen's skepticism has been well-documented. Phyllis Lassner has described Bowen's use of domes-tic space in *The Death of the Heart* to show how "domestic arrangements of power" (105) betray both women and men seeking to create their own iden-tities. Hermione Lee and John Coates have analyzed the domestic events in *The Death of the Heart* as expressions of middle-class unease. Less discussed has been the degree to which "domestic" novelists like Young and Bowen, writing about England in the late 1930s, were participating in a national debate about the relation between private life and wider currents in politics and culture. As I will argue, both novelists credit private life with the power to represent—especially by making concrete—social, economic and politi-cal dimensions of national life. For Young, floundering marriages best rep-resent private life, and the psychological lexicon of private relations provides an anatomy of English political fear and inertia. For Bowen, more optimisti-cally, an essential civilization is learned and maintained in the furniture and domestic spaces of private homes; this civilization offers a reassuring coun-terweight to contemporary habits of private life, especially the refusal of both the past and the present.

In contrast to plentiful discussion of Bowen's attitudes toward privacy and the middle-classes, E.H. Young's participation in the Thirties' debate about domesticity and privacy has scarcely been documented.[10] In *Celia*, a novel of family life focusing on the troubled marriages of four couples at midlife, Young adopts and extends contemporary meanings of privacy by focusing on private fantasy worlds. These private spaces in the mind, Young insists, are merely the logical extension of the link we make naturally between self and house. Young's representation reveals her concern that these private spaces in the mind might function as safe havens from the demands of intimacy and as breeding grounds for egotism, possessiveness and self-deception. Having established Young's ironic analysis of privacy, I will dis-cuss the ways in which both Young and Bowen give private experiences public meaning: in *Celia*, by articulating the national climate of disillusion and instability in which they arise; and in *The Death of the Heart*, through a series of allegorical figures making the private only the most visible manifestation of the public.

Young's preoccupation with the cluster of attitudes that comprise the word "privacy" can be superficially gauged by a glance at the multiple forms it takes in *Celia*. Privacy is the ability to lock one's door against criticism from outside the family (82); it includes the tacit agreement between husband and wife to put the best face on their relationship when consulting with outsiders. Celia's family and friends frequently violate Celia's own standards of discretion by involving her in their marital affairs. Privacy is thus often linked to notions of decorum. Both Celia and her daughter, for example, are horrified when Celia's mother-in-law is seen eating gingerbread outdoors, out of a paper bag. Transgressing the unwritten law that meals are to be taken within the private space of the home, Mrs Marston betrays her place lower down on the social ladder. Thus the concept of privacy in the interwar years became a way to mark gradations within an expanding and diverse middle-class. Finally, and importantly, privacy entails the regions of the mind—memory and desire especially—which Celia understands could never bear the scrutiny of another person. Drawing on these private spaces in the *mind*, Young suggests, one might replicate *within* the family the demarcations by which a *private house* maintained its identity and status with respect to others.

In *Celia* Young drew repeatedly on the time-honored literary tradition of metonymic relationship between self and house:[11] Celia's sister, demonstrating a gift for the creation of serene spaces, betrays a depth that her speech belies; Celia's niece keeps her dollhouse under lock and key; and Celia herself displays on her desk a clipping of an elegant Georgian house where "personal perfection" might be obtained. In the absence of frank communication, such correspondences enable characters to read one another. Nowhere is this metonymic link more revealing than in Celia's attitude toward her husband.

The personal and political dislocations of the first world war led Celia Fellows to marry Gerald Marston some twenty years before the action of the novel takes place. But during the war she fell in love with Richard Milligan, the brother of a friend, and although she remained sexually faithful to Gerald, she has for twenty years cultivated a private world of romantic memory that separates her from Gerald. Celia's physical distaste for Gerald, who designs "hideous little villas" (19), is frequently expressed in the claustrophobic terms that simultaneously convey her discomfort in their crowded little flat: "In the narrow passage his bulk oppressed her" (99). Nevertheless, Celia claims that "the mind need not be bounded by walls" (17) and that her exercise of physical restraint in her relationship with Richard has provided "a scaffolding on which memory could build wonders" (217). Continuing her contrast between crass material lodgings and airy mental ones, Celia describes her home as an atmosphere in which she houses dreams (344); and her narrow life as a "little enclosure for her thoughts, [and] ... memories" (373). It is tempting to see the novel championing a rather unambitious feminism between the wars, acknowledging that women continued to be homebound but claiming their creation of pleasurable spaces of memory and desire. But *Celia* does not finally celebrate women's ability to surmount material obstacles, and in fact it gradually exposes the link between Celia's private mental world and self-deception, snobbery, and egotism. Especially through her often unwilling involvement in the marital problems of her siblings, Celia gradually confronts and acknowledges the quality and function of her private world.

It would be a mistake to understand this cluster of house images as no more than a colorful device by which Celia betrays her attitude toward Gerald and rationalizes her fantasy. If the metaphor of the house repeatedly describes the private fantasy world in Celia's mind, the tenor and vehicle mutually inform one another. The "house" says something about the domestic woman's conception of her own mind; but the fantasy world in the mind also comments on the solipsistic potential of privacy practices more generally.

At the end of the novel, Celia admits that she has made her narrow life narrower than it need have been (373), that "she had lived chiefly in the passive mood ... and the past tense, in a past episode so tenuous that it had taken all her time to preserve its being" (384). She realizes that her faithfulness to the beautiful romance of twenty years earlier, shored up each year during Richard's visit to his sister, has corresponded to no parallel nourishment of romantic ideals on Richard's part. In contrast to magazines' evocation of the rewards of private life—warmth, security, and quiet coziness—*Celia* suggests that the private world which is never checked by public life may be no other than delusion. As Celia herself remarks in a wise moment of recognition, "It was extraordinary how self-satisfaction flourished on self-deception" (243). Only the continual invasions of the little flat and of her private fantasy by family members bearing problems enable Celia to observe, judge, disapprove, condemn—and at last recognize herself in, these others.

But perhaps even more important than the preservation of a romantic ideal in understanding Celia's "little enclosure" for her thoughts are several less visible, more psychologically useful motives: Celia wishes to maintain barriers between herself and her husband, so that "the meretricious mediocrity" (395) of his architectural work might condone her mental unfaithfulness to him and at the same time might justify the "snobbishness from which she had believed she was free," but which, she discovers "had always subtly tinged her view of Gerald" (400). Searching still deeper into the "dark twisting passages" of her motives, Celia finds egotism, the expectation that Gerald serve as "a mirror which simply gave back an enchanting picture of herself" (190) and its alter-ego: insecurity. The romantic episode of twenty years earlier can be safely locked away in the mind without suffering any erosion (280), while the husband who gives evidence, as the novel progresses, that he will not function as that mirror gives her "a strange sense of insecurity" (293).

If the speeches of politicians and the columns of women's magazines celebrated a home-centered English culture, E.H. Young's *Celia* carries out the logical consequences of this turn inward. Egotism and snobbery could all be given umbrage by the domestic privacy in which women were encouraged to realize themselves. Suggesting her difference from the Victorians, for whom the home needed to be defended against a soiled public arena, Young implicitly argues that the crucial border in not between private and public space, but between self and other. "The need for kindness and the giving of it were not necessarily involved in passionate love," notes Celia. "There was just as likely to be a sort of cruelty, an antagonism set up by the determination of each lover to preserve an identity in danger" (373). Privacy in *Celia* comes to mean not the collective life of the family in the well-maintained home, but the individual's defensive retreat from intimacy.

Freud had supplied Young's generation with new insights into the nature and complexity of the self, but it was up to novelists to devise a language for the individual's strategies of retreat, concealment and defense. As we have seen, *Celia* implies—like the women's magazines of the day—that the home and its furnishings could constitute an acceptable forum for self-expression. But in *Celia* this semiotic system is turned on its head to imply that gothic conventions provide the most appropriate psychological language of the self. The deepest recesses of the mind might not be visible until the closely associated domestic space becomes suddenly unfamiliar and even phantasmagoric. In each of the four marriages portrayed, some exile from the home is necessary to absorb the implications of the marital crisis and to bring about the change in self-knowledge that it demands. This exile is an especially fitting exercise in perspective for John Fellows, who has inherited the family drapery business and the family house, and who tends to include both wife and children in the customary glance encompassing his possessions. In the first moments of disagreement with his wife, Julia, John experiences a "queer feeling, quite new to him, of unfamiliarity in his own home and isolation in it" (262). Yet John's initial discomfort leads only to the ironic reconfirmation of his possessions. Releasing himself from the house where he suddenly feels himself an intruder, John ventures only as far as the garden, where a screen of trees enhances the privacy of his domain so that "he need see nothing which did not belong to him" (270). His ego bolstered, John re-enters the house, only to overhear his wife's words of "treachery" and again to be driven out by the instinct "to leave the place where he had been injured" (272). Only when he ventures beyond the pale of the family enclave can he begin to see his wife apart from his habitual and possessive conception of her.

Young's satiric allusion to gothic conventions to portray exile from habitual perception and the attendant horror of self-recognition suggests her deep reservations about marriage, domesticity and privacy in 1937—all of which might shelter, instead of English tolerance or marital harmony, an inflated sense of ownership.

The Death of the Heart reveals the extent to which Elizabeth Bowen shared Young's skepticism about the unqualified benefits of domestic privacy so celebrated in Thirties' expressions of national culture.[12] The symptoms of this privacy are largely registered through Portia's perceptions, sometimes supplemented by narrative comment. Living temporarily in her brother's Windsor Terrace, the orphaned Portia Quayne eventually understands that it is "all mirrors and polish"; there is "no point where feeling could thicken" (42). Away from Windsor Terrace, Portia in her new surroundings gains fresh perspective on it: "[t]hey had sat round a painted, not a burning, fire, at which you tried in vain to warm your hands" (149). The Windsor Terrace rooms do not foster intimacy but are set for "strangers' intimacy" or "exhausted solitary retreat" (42), adds the narrator. Husband and wife are not united in the home but are isolated in spaces of refuge—Thomas Quayne retreating to his study on his return from business and Anna using the room-to-room telephone to greet him.

Countering the magazines' confident images of busy, successful and fulfilled wives and mothers, *Celia* and *The Death of the Heart* portray homes harmfully severed from a wider life: in *Celia*, through private fantasy, and in *The Death of the Heart*, through the cultivation of a morbid, defensive privacy: "Each person at Windsor Terrace lived impaled upon a private obsession" (171).

I would like now to consider the degree to which "domestic" novelists like Young and Bowen, writing about England in the late 1930s, were participating in a national debate about the relation between private life and political apathy. Feminist intellectuals and novelists such as Rebecca West, Winifred Holtby, and Vera Brittain all drew attention to the ways in which a contemporary ideology engineered to keep women contented in the home might jeopardize women's action as informed citizens during the European rise of fascism. In her prologue to *Black Lamb and Grey Falcon*, West interweaves her own life with an account of Balkan history, undoing her readers' assumptions that such a violent history can have little to do with the private life of a middle-class Englishwoman. Her determination not to succumb to what she calls "female idiocy" provides a partial rationale for the structure of the prologue: "Idiocy is the female defect: intent on their private lives, women follow their fate through a darkness deep as that cast by malformed cells in the brain" (3). Winifred Holtby worried that women in Germany would be lured by Hitler's proclamations of their invaluable services as wives and homemakers: "Throughout history, whenever society has tried to curtail the opportunities, interests, and powers of women, it has done so in the sacred names of marriage and maternity" (343). Holtby furthermore warns her British readers that "it is not irrelevant to compare" British fascist Sir Oswald Mosley's recent prescriptions for women "with what Herr Hitler has performed" (342). And Vera Brittain argued that British housewives were too wrapped up in their homes and families to notice what was going on in neighboring European countries: "In peace-time [women's] greatest intellectual handicap, as a group, lies in the mass of narrowly pre-occupied housewives who remain completely unmoved by the threat of catastrophe from various parts of the world" (59).

The comments of these feminists indicate one front on which interwar writers attacked the notion of an impassable border between private and public experience. That most people felt that boundary to be permeable I don't think needs to be argued: Virginia Woolf's contention in *Three Guineas* that the worm of fascism was uncoiling in the patriarchally governed private home is only the most famous example. But just how to reconceptualize the relation between private and public was a matter of considerable debate. The briefest and most random sample of Thirties' novels shows something of the range of attitudes and questions on this issue. In Richard Aldington's *The Colonel's Daughter* (1931), the home—and the protagonist's inability to free herself from it—are direct products of parental policy, which in turn Aldington traces to an exploitative economic system. Woolf's *Between the Acts* begins with a less polemical, but decidedly jolting picture of outside events intruding on the private realm when a newspaper account of the "real"—a soldier's rape of a young girl—disturbs Isa's private dream life (20). Inverting these two models, the popular *Mrs. Miniver*, first serialized in *The Times* in the late 1930s, conceived the home as the source of virtues and values that could reshape public life. Above all, domesticity provides Mrs. Miniver with the human scale necessary to apprehend events and phenomena that are not proper to the home. This is the lesson gleaned from her glimpse of the early morning sky through her chintz-curtained window: "Eternity framed in domesticity.... One had to frame it in something, to see it at all" (48).

The Death of the Heart and *Celia* are among the most interesting novels to conceptualize the relation of public and private: those that suggest parallel public and private chronicles. In these novels, the history of a family recapitulates the history of a nation, something like "ontogeny recapitulates phylogeny." How did Elizabeth Bowen, in *The Death of the Heart*, and E.H. Young, in *Celia*, imagine this recapitulation?

Both *Celia* and *The Death of the Heart* draw parallels between the national disillusion following World War I and disillusion within the private sphere, especially in marriage. Both furthermore adopt a historical model of cause and effect to describe behavior within the private home across a "historical" period of no fewer than three generations. The operation of public history is thus implied by events in the private home.

If the subject of *The Death of the Heart* is the collision of innocence and experience, we can observe that it features two forms of innocence acting on experience in parallel and overlapping ways: within the private sphere, Portia searches for "normal, cheerful family life" (15); while in the social and economic realms, Major Brutt yearns both for employment and for a place within postwar middle-class social life, pressing Thomas Quayne for an explanation of its hidden mainspring when he asks what "all you people get together about" (94). Both appeals set in motion the self-examination of the parties to experience. In making the dynamic of human relations within the family run parallel to relations in the social and economic spheres, Bowen suggests that private and public are not discrete enclaves interacting as subject and object, but function on a continuum. The private sphere synedochically represents the public.

Celia also uses the private sphere to imply public, national trends; here the two realms are reciprocally intertwined. For the onset of World War I, twenty years before the action of the novel, coincided with Celia's coming of age; and the international cataclysm gradually reveals itself as the source of dysfunctional emotions at the root of Celia's troubled marriage. In turn, these emotions, tallying in many ways with the troubles in three other marriages of the same generation, delineate a national culture of inertia and "unadventurous respectability" that supports English political insularity in the late Thirties.

Elizabeth Bowen's essays and reviews of the 1930s and 1940s indicate the degree to which the changing relation of private and public realms preoccupied her. In "Why Do I Write?" (1948), for example, the writer is besieged by a curious public gnawing at the edges of individual privacy, and must struggle against her mental image of "that closing-in circle of thousands of avid glittering eyes" (222). And in her reviews of others' work, Bowen is clearly thinking about how writers and artists can portray the rapprochement of "outer and inner," designations she uses in her review of *Between the Acts*.[13] This reconciliation of public and private is particularly at issue in "Open to the Public," a review of Harold Nicholson's memoirs. Here Bowen pays keen attention to what she considers a "new form" (143) in which public past and personal past—"history and feeling"—are made to interact (141). "The project is interesting," notes Bowen as she considers what it will mean to combine one's own past with the "public past": "He is to write a book that shall be at once informative and a work of art. He must suffuse the book in personal colour, and at the same time keep facts clear of distorting memory" (141).

Bowen uses the private-public continuum in *The Death of the Heart* to examine what happens when a nation—or a dominant class—repudiates its past. The novel envisions two sectors of the middle-class cut off from the past, discarding sentiment, obsessed with standards of behavior, and measuring themselves with the yardstick of a consumer age. The narrator makes an argument for *feeling* as the dimension missing from contemporary English life, feeling that has been dismissed in the recent past as an outmoded form of character and derided in the present as sentimentality.

The Death of the Heart begins with Anna Quayne's relation of how her mother-in-law banished her straying husband from his beloved home by forcing him to marry the young woman carrying his child, later named Portia. When the story is retold from the point of view of the old family servant, Matchett, it becomes a warning about an original replacement of feeling with performance. Each of Mrs Quayne's actions was carefully staged to promote the image of her generous sacrifice. But Matchett underscores the real suffering of the husband who was suddenly driven from "his place in the world" (78). A parallel phenomenon in the wider, common life of the nation underscores the synedochic significance of Mrs Quayne's action: the nation repudiates Major Brutt's World War I model of courage and patriotism; he too is driven from "his place in the world." (The putting away of sentiment and the putting on of performance, in turn, recall Bowen's own education at Downe House, where she was taught "how not to exhibit feeling.")[14]

In the next generation, Thomas Quayne and his wife, Anna, keep their distance from the exiled elder Quayne, denying the father and the messy embarrassment of his sentimental entanglement. Mr Quayne and Irene, his new wife, do not survive for long in the chilly atmosphere of exile, but before Mr Quayne dies he requests that his daughter, Portia, spend a year with the younger Quaynes, to get a taste of "normal" life. Portia arrives with no standard of manners recognizable to her sister-in-law, but with a significant capacity for feeling. Her installment in the household and her search for "normal, cheerful family life" set in motion first the Quaynes' self-defense: "Let's face it," Anna shrugs, "who ever is adequate? We all create situations each other can't live up to" (240). But ultimately Portia is a catalyst for the Quaynes' self-scrutiny. We ought to see Portia—in the third generation—not just as the protagonist of a novel of sensibility but as a snag in the Quaynes' plan to cut themselves off from their family and personal pasts; just as Major Brutt, described as a 1914-1918 car model for which "there was now no market" (90), foils the national wish to be cut adrift from an embarrassing—Anna would say sentimental—public past, whose byword was courage.

In focusing on individual lives in the Quayne circle, Bowen is not refusing to address larger issues of public concern, I want to emphasize, but tracing an allegorical pattern through which her readers can apprehend (and readily feel) British history in the recent past, in the immediate present, and (through Portia) in the near future. Like the experiment she describes in "Open to the Public," Bowen invites her readers to make personal and public histories interact.

According to this allegorical logic, then, specific characters are behind the pervasive changes in modern life, changes that reverberate outwards from Mrs. Quayne's *performance* of wifely love and self-sacrifice. In Bowen's nonfiction no such individual culprits can be identified. In a review entitled "Manners" (1937) she analyzes the real social circumstances behind her fictional characters' symptoms of unease: their defensive protection of their privacy, their fear of inadequacy in the face of hidden social norms. "The lives of most people now, say, in their thirties have changed inconceivably since childhood" she laments. For a variety of reasons she lists as "temperament, occupation, success or failure, marriage, or active nervous hostility to an original *milieu*" her readers have cut themselves off from "that first single world with its accepted currency" and, nomads, have elected to join not one "new world (or set)" but "half a dozen." Under these circumstances it is impossible to learn the set of rules by which each is governed. Moreover, each little world strives for homogeneity and is eager to root out "the person indelibly stamped with the stamp of another world" (68). Contemporary society thus puts an enormous strain on the individual to draw on a "private natural genius" to do what is expected (69).[15]

In dramatizing the social dynamic analyzed in "Manners," *The Death of the Heart* substitutes precise for imprecise agents of bourgeois unease; it structures with a series of defining moments the amorphous changes taking place in middle-class life over the first forty years of the century. In other words, Bowen has heeded her duty, as she understood it, to confer aesthetic shape on society, comprised of both private and public experiences. "Shape is possibly *the* important thing," Bowen declares in "Why Do I Write?" "I shouldn't wonder if it were the shape, essentially, that the reader, the mass, the public goes to the story for. ... Shapelessness, lack of meaning, and being without direction is most people's nightmare" (224). Although Anna and Thomas are only one generation removed from the "original cause"—the banishment of the home lover—their distance from Mrs Quayne's crucial action feels "historical," even remote: "something edited life in the Quaynes' house. ... At the same time, no one seemed clear quite *what* was being discarded, or whether anything vital was being let slip away" (171). This detail stretches subjective time so that the private failure to remember evokes a longer, more historical sweep in national life. Bowen's domestic characters are best understood not as *victims* of changes in national life but as its concrete representatives; they function both as individuals in a realistic narrative and as quasi-allegorical elements in what was in fact a diffuse modernity gradually changing the texture of material and social experience.

The story of Portia's birth is the story of the postwar era outlined in "Manners," for it is bound up with her father's loss of his "place in the world" and the "respect" that went with it (*DH* 78). Human relations, previously based on the clarity of each person's place in the world, are in the new era based on surface (the "mirrors and polish" of the Quaynes' Windsor

Terrace), on performance (a skill perfected by Eddie and responsible for his tenuous access to Windsor Terrace) and on the creation and satisfaction of consumer desire, best represented by Daphne and Mrs Heccomb in the Waikiki section of the novel.

Waikiki is the seaside home of Anna's former governess, Mrs Heccomb, and her two adult stepchildren, Dickie and Daphne. When Anna and Thomas decide to take a spring holiday, Portia is packed off for a four-weeks' sojourn in this Seale-on-Sea home. At first she is "stupefied by this entirely new world" (139), radically different in the semiotic system of its spaces, sounds, textures and smells, but only subtly different in its economy of manners. Like any class, it is fastidious about the observance of the tacit rules that place and define the group. Fear that "someone might be common" (189) demarcates the line between this middle-class and an amorphous group below it, while it is distinguished from the group above it by its relaxation of the upper middle-class restraint on feeling, bodily movement, and tones of voice (see 138).

The narrator humorously articulates the precision with which one class defines itself against the standards of the one nearest to it: Anna's movements are restrained, but she will, under tension, utter oaths; whereas Daphne's "person was sexy, her conversation irreproachably chaste" (146). But beneath these distinctions are fundamental similarities, and through them Bowen defines a society broadly infected with commercial values. In each micro-society a friendship is ruled by the dynamics of the marketplace. At Windsor Terrace, Eddie, estranged from his working class family, sells his cleverness to the Quaynes, who give him employment. At Waikiki, Daphne and Dickie sell their desirable company to the well-off Clara and allow her to buy their cinema tickets, and Daphne even trades on Clara's soft spot for Dickie by including him in social plans: "Daphne, by an unspoken arrangement, got her percentage on any fun Clara had" (166). Nowhere is Daphne's marketable appeal more in evidence than in the "Smoots" library where she works. The exchange of books does not connote the circulation of knowledge or culture; instead, Smoots is parodied as a site where a desirable standard of personality, taste, and upbringing is marketed, and for Seale-on-Sea, Daphne Heccomb is the epitome of that standard.

The Death of the Heart is concerned not with class conflict—moreover, Bowen restricts her canvas to the bourgeois classes—but with the emptiness of class identity unsupported by the links of feeling proper to stable familial and social milieus. The Waikiki section of the novel only reveals the standards of the decade more openly than Windsor Terrace. *The Death of the Heart* intricately details the life of two households, but paired in one novel, they comment on a widespread, national trend.

Like Elizabeth Bowen, E.H. Young uses an idiom of private life to depict a *national* climate of disillusionment and its psychological symptoms. The most public expressions of the culture of domesticity suggested that the home was continuous with the nation, that private virtues were also national ones. Drawing on the vocabulary of contemporary psychological theory, Young simply rounds out the picture by suggesting that the home might also cultivate private and national *vices*.

At a luncheon party after the war Virginia Woolf's persona in *A Room of One's Own*, Mary Beton, notices the absence of a confident, humming tone beneath the conversation, and identifies it as the loss of romantic illusion brought about by the first World War. *Celia* expresses that same loss for the generation whose coming of age coincided with the onset of the war and explores its consequences at middle-age. The loss of the saving illusion means, for example, that the crisis in each of the four marriages portrayed in the novel is resolved by the couple "just going on" (e.g. 312, 414). During her own marital troubles, Celia supplies in her imagination the romantic solution: "Nothing," she thinks, "would have been more romantic, more satisfactory and more convenient than discovering in [Gerald], at last, all she had always wanted and never found." But "none of these things happened" (374). Not enlightenment, but habit, fear, and inertia; or "the doggedness of middle-age taking the place of youth's high courage" (344) prompt the continuation of the partnerships.

The relatively broad scope of *Celia*—its portrayal of four families and three generations—implies that this pattern of scaled back hopes and ambitions is widespread and is learned in family life. *Celia* also affords a glimpse of the complex chain of psychological responses behind it. Going back twenty years to her life during World War I, Celia notes frustration in her personal life: "the emotions of her youth had never been properly released" (371). Then fear of change and strong emotion (282)—perhaps a response to uncertainty and dislocation—encouraged her to "drug" herself into "inertia" (282) by retreating into the romantic memory of her happiness with Richard; this retreat and inertia produce, in Celia's own words, a rather "unadventurous respectability" (383). Moreover, fear, uncertainty, and inertia lead each of the women in *Celia* to assume a mask that enables her to avoid confrontations, to hover between accepting and rebelling against the imposition of others' "oughts and ought nots" (110, 111). We can see in these qualities the roots of the national policy of appeasement, explicitly addressed in Young's last novel of 1947, *Chatterton Square*.

As they went inside flats and houses to illuminate family histories, personal relationships and the intricate workings of the mind, Young and Bowen articulated visions of national life twenty years after the war. But they did not only diagnose its ills; they also gestured towards its cure. Despite the extensive, sharp criticism in these novels of middle-class practices of privacy, both novelists outline a ground on which domestic life can legitimately reinvigorate a wider social life.

Celia suggests, for example, that the children of the postwar years, without the pressure of propaganda that comes with a nation at war, will be freer to determine their own lives. Thinking over the missteps in her own adulthood, Celia decides "that the best of [her son] Jimmy's generation must be the best there had ever been. With far more liberty of action and less force of public opinion, it was readier than hers to follow virtue for its own sake" (288). Like Bowen, Young outlines a model of "history" based on the generational patterns of a family. Young apparently shared something of Virginia Woolf's suspicion, in *Three Guineas*, that education in its then-current form would lead only to the young adopting the values of their elders and ultimately "joining the procession" headed for war. Celia admits that *detachment* from one's children might be the healthiest model: "Loving her children, she modestly believed, at least as much as most women loved theirs, she had been, in a sense, detached from them, their confidence and affection was not her first need and it was comfortable to think this might have been well for them. She took no credit for it" (407).

While Young placed her hope in a new generation unburdened by the woes of their elders, Bowen theorized a framework of civilization, hidden from the gaze of the turbulent present, but carrying on its essential work nonetheless. In *The Death of the Heart*, Bowen's conviction that private life concretely mirrors national life leads her to identify private experience as the best evidence of this abiding "civilization." Thus while the characters' aimlessness and unease arises within the 1930s climate, the narrator—presumably quite close to Bowen herself—provides a counterweight to what she evidently sees as an excessive pressure on the present. The solacing indications of civilization she offers include the management of individual suffering in "naïver, humbler, noble societies" (270) as well as our instinctive turn, when things go wrong in human relations, to the steadiness of "imperturbable [household] *things*" (207).

Stripped of class practices and the fashions of interwar England, domestic life remains the arena in which, through an essential and methodical process, human beings learn how to love. The "daily seeing or touching" of domestic objects and furniture "begins to become love. ... Habit is not mere subjugation, it is a tender tie" (139). The senses precede and determine the feelings of the heart, for, argues the narrator, they "bound our feeling world" (147-8). Thus no matter how much goes wrong in human relations, as it does for Portia with so little experience in the world, she can turn instinctively to the "guarantee" of "imperturbable *things*" that life is for the most part both orderly and seemly:

> Pictures would not be hung plumb over the centre of fireplaces or wallpapers pasted on with such precision that their seams make no break in the pattern if life were really not possible to adjudicate for. These things are what we mean when we speak of civilization: they remind us how exceedingly seldom the unseemly or unforeseeable rears its head. (207)

In pointing to this bedrock civilization, moreover, Bowen's narrator both restores the universal importance of the home (now based on its ability to nurture emotions rooted in elemental sensations) and rescues sentiment from its association, in the late nineteenth and early twentieth centuries, with the sensationalism and the vulgarity of a mass culture perceived as feminine.[16] The narrator restores sentiment to its ordinary, but fundamental and universal place in civilization, saying for example, "It is not our exalted feelings, it is our sentiments that build the necessary home" (140).

E.H. Young's and Elizabeth Bowen's choice to write domestic novels, far from demonstrating their fixation on an outmoded fictional form, was a strategy to make visible, concrete and immediate the diffuse forces of modernity encompassing both private and public realms. To account for their effort to re-envision the relation of public and private spheres, I have stressed their resistance to a national culture of domesticity reinforcing women's roles as housewives and mothers, a resistance shared by their more prominent feminist counterparts. A number of other factors clearly contributed to the widespread perception that private and public were no longer dichotomous realms: women's wartime work outside the home; their increased enrollment in institutions of higher education and their greater voice in forums for public discussion; the effect of radio news broadcasts penetrating the walls of the private home; and—as Alison Light has argued—an alignment of national life with domestic and formerly feminine qualities. In this paper I have outlined just one or two ways in which Young's and Bowen's domestic fiction reflects widespread contemporary recognition that private and public were reciprocally influential realms, different not in nature but in scale. I have asked how this prevalent concern might lead us to reassess the "important" literature of the Thirties. If we were to replace the dominant critical dichotomy—between a progressive poetry of moral responsibility and a retrogressive fiction of private sensibility—with a model of the Thirties portraying the many ways in which writers reopened the case of private vs. public, *Celia* and *The Death of the Heart* would be prominent texts in our canon.

Notes

1.   Janet Montefiore provides the most extensive review of critics from the 1930s to the present day who have excluded or marginalized women writers from discussions of Thirties' literature. 19-25. She also offers some reasons for such a lopsided critical legacy: sexual prejudice; acceptance of the consensus established in the Thirties by magazines and publishers' lists about which writers counted; confirmation of the Auden circle's own claim to represent the consciousness of their generation; and commentators' arbitrary practice of designating as Thirties' writers only those born after 1900. 21-2.
2.   For a discussion of Bowen's critical reception as a novelist of sensibility, see Maroula

Joannou 130-3. The assumption that domestic fiction refers only to private experience and personal relations is widespread. See, e.g, Randall Stevenson: "Like Jane Austen, Bowen concentrates upon the complicated interaction of motives, explicit and suppressed, which animate the relationships of a small, self-contained, group of refined people" (85).

In their own day women novelists of the Thirties were charged with writing novels "largely devoid of plot and without structure, ... displays of observation, sensibility, and sensitivity pinned to situations inside a family or among a group of friends." Anthony West furthered complained that in the work of these "lady novelists" "the private mind has a value equal to the universe and all it contains" (149). The controversy sparked by West's review continued for some months in *The New Statesman and Nation*. See especially a rebuttal by Mitchell and Nicol and C.E.M. Joad's corroboration of West's views.

Contemporary prejudice against "lady novelists" even extended to reviews of women's writing about social issues. See, for example, Q.D. Leavis's "Lady Novelists and the Lower Orders," reviewing Naomi Mitchison's *We Have Been Warned* and Amabel Williams-Ellis's *To Tell the Truth*. Leavis's title implies first, that the two novelists' attempt to portray the working class has failed: the working class is inadequately seen as "the lower orders"; and second, that this failure has its source in the novelists' gender and class. At the heart of Leavis's criticism is her contention that the middle-class female novelist is unable to transcend either in reality or imaginatively her limited sphere of experience.

3. See Nicola Beauman, A Very Great Profession: The Woman's Novel 1914-39; Hilary Radner, "Extra-Curricular Activities: Women Writers and the Readerly Text"; and Clare Hanson, *Hysterical Fictions: The "Woman's Novel" in the Twentieth Century*. Beauman describes the woman's novel between the wars as "written by middle-class women for middle-class women" (3) and as illuminating female attitudes to experience (5). Radner's essay in particular suggests that the woman's novel, by refusing to restrict itself to the conventions of either high art or popular culture, may be prone to exclusion from critical discussion of both "brow" levels of literature: "Thus the woman's novel has been ignored, or exiled, from the academic forum because academia has failed to generate an adequate methodology to represent this genre in its fullest sense" (256).

4. Samuel xxviii. Samuel Hynes dates this insularity a bit earlier, citing its connection to Britain's imperial expansion. It was G.J. Goschen, First Lord of the Admiralty, who first used the phrase "splendid isolation" in 1896. *The Edwardian Turn of Mind* 307.

5. Of the nearly three million new houses built in the Thirties, most were for private sale. John Stevenson 221.

6. Jeffery and McClelland 50.

7. I have information only about the first printing of *Celia* by Jonathan Cape: 12,500. It was published in the United States in 1938 by Harcourt Brace. Cape published most of E.H. Young's novels in England, and most were distributed in the United States as well. Several of her novels were adapted and broadcast for the BBC.

8. While *Celia* and *The Death of the Heart* can accurately be described as "women's novels," in this discussion I will prefer the term "domestic novels" to emphasize their portrayal of family life and of domestic space and to highlight their resistance to the ideological representations of domesticity in women's magazines of the period.

9. The reformulation of British domestic life between the wars included the overthrow of Victorian "indulgent sentimentality" in favor of a "modern domesticity which valued cheerful efficiency and robust 'common sense'" (Giles and Middleton 194). See also René Cutforth 43, 54.

10. Young's life and temperament laid the groundwork for this subsequent obscurity. She disliked publicity, and did not participate in any literary circle or supplement her novel

writing with journalism. Her private life too, was necessarily discreet: following the death of her husband in World War I, she shared her life with an already-married London schoolmaster.

11. As Lassner's chapter on *The Death of the Heart* suggests, Bowen similarly uses images of domestic space to convey the close association between character and inhabited space. But, Lassner demonstrates, such domestic imagery also points out structures and conventions more powerful than the individual.
12. For discussion of Bowen's critique of domestic privacy, see Hermione Lee, Phyllis Lassner, and John Coates.
13. "Virginia Woolf" 72.
14. "The Mulberry Tree" 21.
15. See John Coates for a full discussion of the relevance of "Manners" to *The Death of the Heart*.
16. In "Mass Culture as Woman: Modernism's Other," Andreas Huyssen details the process by which modernism both feminized and constructed itself in opposition to this mass culture.

References

Aldington, Richard. *The Colonel's Daughter*. Garden City, New York: Doubleday, 1931.

Beauman, Nicola. *A Very Great Profession: The Woman's Novel 1914-39*. London: Virago, 1983.

Bowen, Elizabeth. *The Death of the Heart*. 1938. New York: Penguin, 1962.

——. "Manners." Review of *Can I Help You?*, by Viola Tree. 1937; [in *The New Statesman and Nation*]. *Collected Impressions*. New York: Knopf, 1950. 67-71.

——. "The Mulberry Tree." 1934. *The Mulberry Tree: Writings of Elizabeth Bowen*. Ed. Hermione Lee. San Diego: Harcourt Brace Jovanovich, 1986. 13-21.

——. "Open to the Public." Review of *Helen's Tower*, by Harold Nicolson. 1937 [in *The New Statesman and Nation*]. *Collected Impressions*. New York: Knopf, 1950. 141-3.

——. "Virginia Woolf." Part I. Review of *Between the Acts* and *The Death of the Moth*, by Virginia Woolf. 1941 [in *The New Statesman and Nation*]. *Collected Impressions*. New York: Knopf, 1950. 71-5.

——. "Why Do I Write?" 1948. *The Mulberry Tree: Writings of Elizabeth Bowen*. Ed. Hermione Lee. San Diego: Harcourt, 1986. 221-9.

Brittain, Vera. "Peace and the Public Mind." *Challenge to Death*. Ed Storm Jameson. New York: E.P. Dutton, 1935. 58-66.

Coates, John. *Social Discontinuity in the Novels of Elizabeth Bowen*. Studies in British Literature 38. Lewiston: Edwin Mellen, 1998.

Cutforth, René. *Later Than We Thought: A Portrait of the Thirties*. Newton Abbot: David & Charles; New York: Crane, 1976.

Dowson, Jane, ed. *Women's Poetry of the 1930s: A Critical Anthology*. London and New York: Routledge, 1996.

Giles, Judy and Tim Middleton, eds. *Writing Englishness, 1900-1950*. London: Routledge, 1995.

Hanson, Clare. *Hysterical Fictions: The "Woman's Novel" in the Twentieth Century*. Houndmills and London: Macmillan; New York: St. Martin's, 2000.

Holtby, Winifred. "Black Words for Women Only." 1934. *History in Our Hands: A Critical*

Anthology of Writings on Literature, Culture and Politics from the 1930s. Ed. Patrick Deane. London and New York: Leicester University Press, 1998. 341-4.

Huyssen, Andreas. *After the Great Divide: Modernism, Mass Culture, Postmodernism*. Bloomington: Indiana University Press, 1986.

Hynes, Samuel. *The Edwardian Turn of Mind*. Princeton: Princeton University Press, 1968.

Jeffery, Tom, and Keith McClelland. "A World Fit to Live in: the *Daily Mail* and the Middle Classes 1918-39." *Impacts and Influences: Essays on Media Power in the Twentieth Century*. Ed. James Curran, Anthony Smith and Pauline Wingate. London and New York: Methuen, 1987. 27-52.

Joad, C.E.M. "Complaint Against Lady Novelists." *New Statesman and Nation* 19 August 1939: 275-6.

Joannou, Maroula. *"Ladies, Please Don't Smash These Windows": Women's Writing, Feminist Consciousness and Social Change 1918-38*. Oxford and Providence: Berg, 1995.

Lassner, Phyllis. *Elizabeth Bowen*. Women Writers. Savage, Maryland: Barnes & Noble, 1989.

Leavis, Q.D. "Lady Novelists and the Lower Orders." *Scrutiny* 4.2 (September 1935): 112-32.

Lee, Hermione. *Elizabeth Bowen: An Estimation*. London: Vision; Totowa, N.J.: Barnes, 1981.

Light, Alison. *Forever England: Femininity, Literature and Conservatism Between the Wars*. London: Routledge, 1991.

Mitchell, M.E. and Daphne Nicol. Letter. *New Statesman and Nation* 29 July 1939: 181.

Montefiore, Janet. *Men and Women Writers of the 1930s: The Dangerous Flood of History*. London and New York: Routledge, 1996.

Priestley, J.B. *English Journey*. 1934. London: Heinemann, 1968.

Radner, Hilary. "Extra-Curricular Activities: Women Writers and the Readerly Text." *Women's Writing in Exile*. Ed. Mary Lynn Broe and Angela Ingram. Chapel Hill: University of North Carolina Press, 1989. 251-67.

Samuel, Raphael. "Introduction: Exciting to Be English." *Patriotism: The Making and Unmaking of British National Identity*. Volume 1: History and Politics. London and New York: Routledge, 1989.

Stevenson, John. *British Society 1914-45*. 1984. London and New York: Penguin, 1990.

Stevenson, Randall. *The British Novel Since the Thirties: An Introduction*. Athens: University of Georgia Press, 1986.

Struther, Jan. *Mrs. Miniver*. New York: Harcourt Brace and Company, 1940.

West, Anthony. "New Novels." Review of *Dr. Norton's Wife*, by Mildred Walker, *Their Chimneys Into Spires*, by Kathleen Wallace, *Mary Cloud*, by Romilly Cavan, *Farewell Night; Welcome Day*, by Storm Jameson, *Care of "The Grand,"* by John Hampson, and *Lotus Blossom*, by George Lancing. *New Statesman and Nation* 22 July 1939: 149-50.

West, Rebecca. *Black Lamb and Grey Falcon*. 1940. New York: Penguin, 1982.

White, Cynthia. *Women's Magazines 1693-1968*. London: Michael Joseph, 1970.

Woolf, Virginia. *Between the Acts*. 1941. San Diego: Harvest-Harcourt Brace and Company, 1969.

——. *Three Guineas*. 1938. San Diego: Harvest-Harcourt Brace and Company, 1966.

Young, E.H. *Celia*. 1937. Virago Modern Classic Number 332. London: Virago-Penguin, 1990.

——. *Chatterton Square*. 1947. New York: Penguin; London: Virago, 1987.

6 *There's No Story There*: Inez Holden's Lost War Literature

Kristin Bluemel

The British writer Inez Holden (1904-1974) now exists as a footnote in the biographies of more famous artists like Evelyn Waugh, Augustus John, H.G. Wells, George Orwell, Anthony Powell, and Stevie Smith. Yet Holden deserves a chapter of her own in English literary history for her memorable contributions to Thirties' writing and the literature of World War II. Her novels, short stories, and diaries easily could have functioned as case studies illustrating the primary movements of these periods as they are described in Samuel Hynes's *The Auden Generation* and Valentine Cunningham's *British Writers of the Thirties*. Despite the representative qualities of Holden's work, discussion of her fiction had to wait for Jenny Hartley's feminist revisionary study, *Millions Like Us: British Women's Fiction of the Second World War*. This essay continues the work of recovery initiated by Hartley, analyzing a number of Holden's most important fictions and situating them in the contexts of the period's core debates about labor, art, and politics.

Holden was one of many middle-class writers who found the lives of workers on the home front compelling. Her narratives answer the ambitions that the scholar Constance Reaveley describes in her *Spectator* article of 7 April 1944:

> I watched the life of the factory. I thought a good deal went on that ought to be more widely known about and understood. I thought I would write to the Bishop, and urge that young men in training for Holy Orders should work for six months or so in a factory (or a mine or a shop) to get an insight for themselves into the way people live and work ... Again, it seemed to me that the girls I knew at the works needed a better literature to feed their minds. Fiction, like poetry, should be an interpretation and criticism of life ... I thought I would write to the head of a women's college, and suggest that a girl who wanted to write, and would work in a factory for a few months, could produce stories for factory girls about factory girls, which would give them a lot more interest than anything there is on the market for them at present. (Hartley, *Hearts* 148-9)

As Reaveley admits, she did none of these things. Holden, without the incentives or prospects of university students, took up where Reaveley left off, writing fictions that could appeal to working-class readers who wanted "stories for factory girls about factory girls." The narrative style of her fictions also would have appealed to readers of the *Times Literary Supplement*,

Spectator and other middlebrow journals that reviewed Holden's books. Holden's readers would have recognized in her representations of working-class people an invitation to work for the leftist ideals of the 1930s long after the most prominent writers of the Auden Generation had given up on them.

This essay will demonstrate how Holden's voice counted in the Auden Generation by analyzing relations between her later "heroic" wartime litera-ture and early "frivolous" society literature. In addition to recovering the lost work of a woman writer, it engages in the more theoretical project of ques-tioning the stories critics tell about British fiction of the Thirties and World War II. First, it asks how consideration of women novelists and short story writers breaks down the divide between the period's categories—"The Thir-ties," "World War II"—that still structure knowledge about English literature in the middle decades of the twentieth century. Second, it asks how Holden's fiction relates to the dominant aesthetic of the time, the documentary move-ment in English culture. Third, it asks how consideration of Holden's posi-tion as a middle-class woman writer who "went over" to the working class contributes to our understanding of the period's debates about relations of politics to form, political commitment to art. In the process of answering these questions, this essay points toward the larger meanings of Holden's radical border crossings: from glamour girl to socialist, adventuress to nov-elist, writer to worker and back.

To describe Holden's movements in terms of border crossing is to employ a metaphor that preoccupied many of the members of the "Auden Generation" and the critics who have written about them. In his book about the Thirties, for example, Cunningham uses this metaphor to figure his crit-ical enterprise as he attempts to provide a fuller account of the period by breaking down distinctions between literature and society, text and context. He frames his study with the following questions: "Admitting, then, the flu-idity of the '30s bounds, what of the decade's contents? How is one to decode the plurality of signs, to read the multiplicity of texts within, and compris-ing, the larger period text, how to map this terrain … ?" (16). Boundaries, signs, maps, terrain: Cunningham's journey in many ways takes its language from the poetry, plays, and memoirs of those writers it comments upon, repeating their enthusiasms and blind spots even as it claims to depart from the canonical story.

Cunningham's interrogation of the accepted bounds and contents of the 1930s leads him to conclude that, despite the "strong presence" of Auden, "It is even more obviously the case … that the '30s are greatly straitened when they are defined only with reference to Auden and his closest contempo-raries" (21). The writers he lists as "roughly the same age as Auden but not actually in the inner circles" include Orwell, V.S. Pritchett, Christopher Caudwell, and Samuel Beckett. These men he designates "maverick authors" who "attended neither Oxford or Cambridge" (21). It isn't until he discusses the critical bias against the 1930s novel that he mentions multiple names of women writers who, like the "mavericks" (and worker-writers) also didn't attend either Cambridge or Oxford. For some reason, however, the lack of an Oxbridge education does not earn any commentary in the cases of women who published fiction during the 1930s, and Cunningham rarely discusses their work in any detail. This inattention to a vital source of the period's "multiplicity of texts" belies his comment that, in addition to novelists like Rosamond Lehmann, Naomi Mitchison, and Winifred Holtby, "previously well-known women novelists like Virginia Woolf, Elizabeth Bowen, Jean Rhys, Ivy Compton-Burnett, and Dorothy Richardson ... cannot be simply left, as most books about the 1930s leave them, out of the account" (26). Cunningham's assertion that it is enough for him to identify "the gap that commonly denotes [women writers'] absence" (27) implies that only in the case of male writers will the contents of the map of the Thirties fundamentally alter once scholars look beyond the "Auden Generation." Women writers are presumed to have a single "place" that can be "marked on the '30s map for future reference" (27). This implies that the study of women's fiction may require a shift of a boundary here and there, but will not lead to startling discoveries about the underlying character of the Thirties terrain.

Several books on the Thirties published since Cunningham's report challenge this assumption. In addition to Hartley's study, they include Jane Dowson's *Women's Poetry of the 1930s*, Patrick Deane's *History in Our Hands*, Alison Light's *Forever England*, Janet Montefiore's *Men and Women Writers of the 1930s*, Patrick Quinn's *Recharting the Thirties*, James Gindin's *British Fiction in the 1930s*, Phyllis Lassner's *British Women Writers of World War II*, and Gill Plain's *Women's Fiction of the Second World War*. To a greater or lesser extent, each of these studies demonstrates that consideration of women writers actually matters to our configurations of 1930s literature and history. Yet to see most clearly how consideration of Inez Holden's fiction might impact what we see on the traditional 1930s map, readers should initially consult Andy Croft's *Red Letter Days*, the revisionist study of the period's fiction which provides the most direct challenge to Cunningham's vision of the connections between literature and politics.

Croft sees the Thirties as a "generous moment" and celebrates what he sees as the alliance between imaginative writing and leftist, socialist politics. He reviews more than 300 novels by working-class and bourgeois men and women to provide "a sense of the possibilities of a radical, critical, oppositional revolutionary literature" that goes well beyond the "staid, nineteenth-century tradition" or the typical list of "Red Novels" (8). His portrait of the decade invites Holden into the mainstream of literary activity insofar as it claims the 1930s as "The one moment in the twentieth century when ... the causes and concerns of the Left were genuinely popular, forward-looking and culturally dominant" and the "the novel the most popular literary form among readers of all ages and classes" (24, 25). In sharp contrast to Cunningham, Croft does not see the redness of the Red Decade as a false tint that represents either the transitory sympathies of "a small number of young upper-middle-class poets" for the Communist Party or the mind-numbing orthodoxy of a Marxist literary establishment. Instead, he describes leftist novels as "the characteristic achievement of a developing political and intellectual alliance, between the literary intelligentsia and the organized working class, between professional and amateur writers, metropolitan and provincial" (28-9).

One of the reasons an ambiguously-classed, non-activist writer like Holden can fit so comfortably in Croft's account is that his study disputes the accepted wisdom of Orwell and Spender that the Communist Party had a stranglehold on English letters in the decade before the war. Croft notes that most of the writers he discusses "belonged to no political party, few would have seen themselves belonging to a 'Red Decade,' some would not necessarily have described themselves as socialists" (27). Croft repudiates the belief that the Thirties was a decade of inhibiting leftist orthodoxy, passing it off as the legacy of exaggerated panic about the Communist Party inspired by Orwell's misguided comments in "Inside the Whale":

> Communists and near-Communists had a disproportionately large influence in the literary reviews. It was a time of labels, slogans and evasions. At the worst moments you were expected to lock yourself up in a constipating little cage of lies; at the best a sort of voluntary censorship ("Ought I to say this? Is it pro-Fascist?") It is almost inconceivable that good novels should be written in such an atmosphere. (40)

In contrast to this vision of Communist-dominated culture industry, Croft argues that even an overtly political journal like the *Left Review* avoided any single position and was crowded with talent—with established and experimental writers, working class and middle class, famous and new (26). This view of who matters for Thirties' writing demonstrates why Croft should be seen as making a new map of the 1930s rather than redrawing boundaries on the old one. He actually admits new materials into the decade's cast of writers, recognizing and prioritizing new names and identities, rather than simply reshuffling the same familiar figures. Holden might be one of the writers whose recovery Croft anticipated with his generous speculation about "how many more wondrous fictions are still lost, how many more unquestionably await rediscovery" (10).

Although Holden's fictions display her special talent for capturing the absurd pretensions and fixations of characters from the wealthier strata of English society, this essay argues for her rediscovery on the basis of her treatments of working-class characters in her short stories and her two novels of the war years, *Night Shift* (1941) and *There's No Story There* (1944). Like Orwell, Isherwood, Henry Green, and other celebrated bourgeois writers who wrote convincingly about the working class, Holden entered the worlds of the working-class people she wrote about, sharing the conditions of their lives before pushing for change through her documentary fictions. In Holden's case, however, participation was motivated as much by financial desperation as literary ambition or socialist commitment. She wanted the salary for her labors as well as the commissions that might come from writing about it. Without a family, profession, or education to fall back on, Holden's claim on middle-class privileges was unstable. Her experience living on the borders of conventional financial and sexual respectability may have enabled her to represent with more sensitivity than her celebrated contemporaries the frustrating contradictions and illuminating gaps in conventional ideologies about class, gender, ethnicity, and nation.

Holden's background makes her an unlikely candidate for the role of path-breaking author in English working-class and war literature. She was the daughter of an Edwardian beauty who was known as the second-best horsewoman in Britain (Spalding 103). When in her twenties, Holden herself was thought of as a bohemian society beauty, and the two novels she wrote during those years record the frivolous, absurd lives of privileged characters who could have stepped out of *Vile Bodies*. Yet Holden's life was marked by transformations of consciousness and circumstance, and her story complements the conversion stories about bourgeois socialist writers that Croft tells in his chapter, "Class War Across the Dinner Table: Tales of Middle-Class Life." One of Croft's stories is about Jack Lindsay, a young Australian poet and dealer in fine prints who roamed the circles of London's demimonde in 1927 hoping to meet the likes of Augustus John. Apparently, Lindsay was accompanied by Aldous Huxley on one of his trips and then appeared in caricature form in Huxley's *Point Counter Point*. Ten years later, Lindsay wrote *1649*, his most famous socialist novel (Croft 127). This thumbnail sketch leads Croft to ask, "What had happened in these ten years to turn a minor character in a late Bloomsbury novel of ideas into a major political novelist?" (128). With some alteration, we can ask Croft's question of Holden: "What had happened in ten years to turn a minor character in Bloomsbury artists' circles into an effective political novelist?" How could Holden—quintessential girl-about-town—be the author of *Night Shift*, a novel that impressed H.G. Wells as "First rate" and earned J.B. Priestley's jacket comment, "The most truthful and most exciting account of war-time industrial Britain"?

The answer may have something to do with the fact that when Holden was a child, her parents were utterly indifferent to her basic material and emotional needs. She remembered going barefoot in all seasons and being sent to a school for the children of poor tradespeople. Only when her rich uncle on her mother's side paid the overdue fees was she allowed to continue at the school. When she was fifteen, she went to Paris and then London, living on her wits and her exceptionally good looks (Goodman 29-30). Holden's first novels were published when she was in her twenties; *Born Old, Died Young* has an adventuress heroine whose cavalier approach to existence suggests something of the attitude Holden herself might have had at the time.

Despite her precarious economic position, Holden was notoriously generous and had a sense of drama and style. Her cousin and literary executrix, Celia Goodman, writes that Holden "simply found life endlessly amusing and interesting and was able to make it seem equally so to others. She was a keen and fascinated observer of human nature at all levels, but she was never malicious and she had a depth of compassion that prevented her from judging harshly any but the most odious characteristics" (35). As the biographer of Holden's friend and contemporary Stevie Smith notes, Holden grew increasingly bitter about gross social inequalities resulting from differences of wealth (Spalding 104). In reaction to these feelings, the leftward drift of literary culture, and, perhaps, her increasing intimacy with George Orwell, Holden developed a political consciousness and by the mid- to late-thirties identified herself as an anti-Communist socialist. The meaning of this identity for Holden is evident from her diary entry of many years later which reads, "It is strange the class consciousness of England, when through conversation two or three socialists find each other it is like the early Christians who were persecuted in Rome recognizing each other by some sign" (29 November 1949).

As much as scholars may want to use the evidence of Holden's personal experience to understand the causes and influences underlying the changes in her identity, the scarcity of biographical materials about her significantly limits the effectiveness of such lines of inquiry. However, if Holden's journals of the interwar and war years are ever made public (the published portions include only an excerpt in Schimanski and Treece's *Leaves in the Storm* and *It Was Different at the Time*), it may be possible to use Holden's words about her own experience—her relationships with Augustus John and Humphrey Slater, her friendships with George Orwell, H.G. Wells, and Mulk Raj Anand, her reflections on the experience of the Blitz, on poverty, on the BBC, on the Holocaust—to arrive at a fuller explanation of how she came to be a novelist of working-class life.

Holden's first such novel, *Night Shift*, is a fictional account of her wartime work at an aircraft factory in North London that was published in 1941. Documentary in form, its compassionate, humorous renderings of the workers' conversations amid the noise, danger, and routine of the factory demonstrate that for Holden the arrival of war did not diminish the importance of the 1930s political goals. Holden's choice of the popular forms and contents of the 1930s in her first novel of the 1940s is not a sign of her lack of imagination, but rather her commitment to a still unrealized social vision.

It is worth remembering that as late as 1937 Storm Jameson was writing in *Fact* that "The conditions for the growth of a socialist literature scarcely exist" and was calling for a "new literature" built on documents (Deane 314). Her description in "New Documents" of a realist fiction modeled after documentary film perfectly describes the aims and effects of *Night Shift*:

> As the photographer does, so must the writer keep himself out of the picture while working ceaselessly to present the fact from a striking (poignant, ironic, penetrating, significant) angle. The narrative must be sharp, compressed, concrete. Dialogue must be short—a seizing of the significant, the revealing word. The emotion should spring directly from the fact. It must not be squeezed from it by the writer ... His job is not to tell us what he felt, but to be coldly and industriously presenting, arranging, selecting, discarding from the mass of his material to get the significant detail which leaves no more to be said, and implies everything.
>
> And for goodness' sake let us get some fun out of it. (Deane 316)

Once Holden's war novel is read in terms of Jameson's call for a new literature, it becomes an interesting, "fun" book to consider in accounts of both 1930s and 1940s writing.

Night Shift invites obvious comparisons with other documentary accounts of factory life in wartime like Amabel Williams-Ellis's *Women in War Factories* (1943) or Mass-Observation's *War Factory* (1943), while its title also reminds us of its debt to peacetime documentaries such as Jack Common's volume of worker-writers' prose in *Seven Shifts*. Each of these four books shows a shared belief in the value of workers' lives and the ability of documentary prose to win for the workers their readers' support. However, it is worth noting that the wartime documentaries by Holden, Williams-Ellis, and Mass-Observation focus on exactly that which is omitted from Common's collection: descriptions of women workers. In fact, Common's book begins with an apology for "one serious omission: it does not include any contribution from the women's side of the world of work." The apology is followed by a promise, "to make good [the lack] in a subsequent volume, which the women will have to themselves." For whatever reasons, this promise went unfulfilled. Perhaps it required the social upheavals of World War II for women to feel empowered enough to document their experiences, to tell the story of their new position in public and private arenas. The difficulty for literary criticism is that the wartime socialist fictions of many women writers are invisible, buried beneath what Tom Harrison described in a December 1941 *Horizon* review as "right wing" productions of "lady novelists" (quoted in Hartley, *Millions* 7), or grouped with other wartime socialist fiction that was reviled as old fashioned and boring and was swept out of public view (Croft 340).

The six chapters of *Night Shift* are far from boring even though they represent six monotonous days in the lives of workers who are making camera parts for reconnaissance and bombing planes. The novel has an anonymous third person narrator who is described in the jacket copy as "having no very definite personality, acting rather as the lens of a moving camera." While jacket copy prose is rarely a trustworthy guide to literary influences, in this case the obvious attempt to link Holden with Isherwood by echoing the famous "camera" metaphor is accurate. A reviewer agreed with the jacket copy's implied grouping of *Night Shift* with Isherwood's *Goodbye to Berlin*, describing the novel in the 15 May 1942 *Spectator* as a documentary and praising it for having "the assured interest of good reportage" ("Shorter Notice"). More than Isherwood, Holden achieves the effect of creating objective journalism by displacing her middle-class origins and identity from the novel's first-person narrator to a character named Feather with whom middle-class readers would presumably identify.

Her narrator tells us that Feather is "the sort of girl who would have been 'ladying it' at a First Aid Post attached to some auxiliary service" and wonders if "something had happened to shake up her journey in the slow coach of security" (13). The narrator ends her speculations with the observation that "Anyway, her hair was still sleek and well brushed like the soft coat of a luxurious pet animal" (13). Holden treats her less fashionable characters with equal care, using a spare description and dialogue to bring to life the novel's more numerous working-class women such as Mabs, Nan, Mrs Lloyd, Mrs Chance, and Ma, or its managerial men, the Jewish foreman, Dick Strauss, or the engineers like old Sid or "Flash Jack."

Typical of Holden's style and concerns is a scene that records the reactions of the workers to an exchange between Mabs, who is humorously protesting the tedious demands of their work, and the unpopular Mrs Lloyd, who primly objects that "We have to work to produce the arms for the airplanes to fight the Nazis":

> "We know that," answered Mabs. "But it don't prevent you getting tired, do it? Besides, although it's war now, I worked in a factory very much the same as this, in peace-time, see." Everyone frowned on Mrs. Lloyd, there was a convention against easy heroical talk and pat-off patriotism in the workshop; that way of yapping-out was all right for people who did not work at all ... sitting well back in their arm-chairs and thought, "We are all in it together" because they listened to the radio news four times a day. "After all," said Mrs. Chance, "we work here to get away from thinking about the war, so what does she want to start in talking about it like that for?" (109-10)

This exchange, which characteristically honors the differences between working-class individuals as well as those individuals' differences from non-working patriots, takes place at the end of a shift on a Friday, the fifth day of the week. When nearly all the workers are killed in an air raid during the next night shift, the reader is shaken by the loss of a predominantly working-class community. The political meanings of this ending clearly create connections between *Night Shift* and other leftist novels of the period, but they appear to distance the novel from Holden's earlier work. To explain how Holden's heroic working-class war novels could have grown out of her early frivolous society novels, this essay looks next at the relationships between her first novel of 1929, *Sweet Charlatan*, her story of the 1930s, "Death in High Society," and her war novel of 1944, *There's No Story There*.

The most memorable innovation in the 1929 novel *Sweet Charlatan* is Holden's creation of a witch character named Rose Leaf, whose roles as hostess and murderess seem to demonically attract the young "hero," Cedric Dorn. The only sympathetic character in the book's cast of absurdities is Cedric's young wife, the bohemian waif, Autumn. Rose Leaf takes care of the various human impediments to her union with Cedric by magically killing them off. Only Autumn escapes because she has abandoned Cedric before Rose's evil spells can catch up with her. Although Autumn is herself abandoned by her author at the end of the book, we are able to imagine some positive fate for her given the following revelation:

> Once she [Autumn] had been enslaved by the frail affectations of Cedric, the belated Beardsley gesture, the sweet superficiality, ... the epigrammatic outlook on all that could be considered scholastically sound. ... The talented versatility that made of Cedric poet, painter and actor in parody; all this silly brilliance had ceased to hypnotise, and Autumn herself had returned to almost schoolgirlish simplicity of speech and thought and was even now considering the importance of doing what one liked. (181-2)

The language of this passage provides a taste of Holden's "socialite" style at its flippant best, with all its signs of a late modernist satire and sensibility. Yet the subdued earnestness of Autumn's escape from superficiality and the affirmation of her desires suggests that Holden might have maintained a latent sympathy for her young female character that arose from her own changing goals and identity.

Autumn's repudiation of the epigrams of the Bright Young Things in favor of simplicity of speech points towards Holden's movement in this same direction. The best examples of Holden's new style are the stories that she collected in a volume titled *Death in High Society* (1934). It is the language of these stories, rather than their contents, that sets them apart from other writings of the day. Each is written in "Basic English," C.K. Ogden's experimental language that was designed to facilitate communication between different classes and nations by limiting vocabulary to 850 words. The language was designed so it could be self-taught in thirty hours by anyone with a phonograph (Ogden 4). As Ogden explains in the foreword to *Death in High Society*, "[Basic English] is an all-round language for everyday use, which may be turned into a language for the expert by the addition of short special lists" (8). When it comes to literature "at its highest levels," Ogden acknowledges that Basic "is able to do little more than give an outline of what the writer said" (8), but he insists that it is still important for "the experts to see what sort of [imaginative] books go best into Basic and why" (9). Holden is Ogden's expert on the short story, and after noting that her stories or sketches appeared first in non-Basic English in such publications as *Harper's Bazaar*, *Nash's* and *The Evening Standard*, Ogden assures us that Holden's stories "are representative of an important part of the reading material on which the value of Basic for general purposes has to be tested" (9).

Holden's willingness to participate in Ogden's project, even translating previously published stories into his non-literary language, suggests that she was eager to contribute to a broader movement in leftist literary circles to develop an egalitarian, non-élitist language. Cunningham cites Michael Roberts's "Preface" to *New Country* as a characteristic leftist retort to T.S. Eliot's call for complexity and difficulty in modern poetry. Roberts declared that as the writer

> sees more and more clearly that his interests are bound up with those of the working class, so will his writing clear itself from the complexity and intro-spection, the doubt and cynicism of recent years, and become more and more intelligible to that class and so help in the evolution of a style which, coming partly from the "shirt-sleeve" workers and partly from the "intellectual", will make the revolutionary movement articulate. (Roberts 18)

Ogden, and presumably Holden, did not imagine that simple prose would necessarily facilitate a Marxist political program. Ogden's attempt to position his system as a conciliatory meeting ground between radicals who wanted to invent an entirely new language free of English vocabulary and syntax and conservatives who resisted all efforts to alter standard English is apparent in his "Introduction" to *The System of Basic English* (1934). Here he acknowledges Basic's potential to function as an unsettling force in society, but then indirectly reminds his more conservative readers about contemporary radical experiments that may gain ascendancy if moderate programs like his own are ignored: "Basic is admittedly a challenge to certain habits which have their roots very deep in our social behavior; but the moment is perhaps not altogether unfavorable to the demand for a new linguistic conscience in the new generation whose social experiments may otherwise be frustrated by outworn verbal formulae" (vi). Ogden soothes skeptics with the claim that "Basic represents an endeavor to preserve the essentials of a great tradition;

and it may even be regarded as conservative by those who advocate a complete break with the past" (vi). Cunningham conflates the move to simple prose with Marxism and Socialist Realism and scathingly writes that the latter, articulated as Party doctrine by Karl Radek at the 1934 Soviet Writers' Congress, "helped to slow down literary experiment and to smash up modernism especially in the novel, thus pushing the novel back beyond Henry James into the arms of nineteenth-century bourgeois naturalism" (299). Yet consideration of Holden's short stories in Basic suggests that Cunningham is simply blind to a new kind of postmodernist experiment, one that may have parallels to Socialist Realism and a potential leftist application, but is less politically doctrinaire than he would have readers believe.

The ambiguity of Basic's political uses parallels the ambiguity of Holden's literary course at this moment in her career. It is possible to regard Holden's contribution to Odgen's Basic English series as a transition piece between *Sweet Charlatan* and her later working-class war fictions. The language of Holden's stories, so different from *Sweet Charlatan*, parallels a shift in content as well; instead of focusing exclusively on the rich and foolish as she does in her 1920s novels, Holden introduces working-class characters who earn our sympathies and allegiance. While the limitations of Basic may preclude Holden's deployment of "the contrived colloquial vividness of an Orwell," her stories often flirt with a gothic or slightly violent subject matter that allows her to avoid what Cunningham sees as the worst danger of simple prose: dullness (302).

For example, the title story, "Death in High Society," begins with the departure of two nameless cleaning women from the London home of Esmee Earnshaw, who watches them secretly and vindictively from the comforts of her long, elegant gray sedan. Esmee's sense of entitlement and her distance from her employees is revealed by her belief that "the chance to go into [her house] at all was, even to her friends, a sort of special reward. For this reason it would have been natural if the brushing and cleaning of this house had been a special event, valued in the memory of such women" (113). "Such women," namely working class women, are vital to the story's plot, although the narrator concentrates on Esmee. We witness Esmee sneaking into her own house in order to check up on the thoroughness of her cleaning ladies and, as it so happens, her husband's letters, before she gets trapped mid-floor in the elevator that she'd installed in order to "get more work done in less time" (*Boating* 118). Since Esmee is cheap and mean, as well as rich, she has sent away her cleaners for the next three weeks to save on caretaking costs during the time she is supposedly down south relaxing in the sun. The story ends three weeks later with a satisfying, if macabre, form of retribution that gives the cleaning ladies the last word. "Well," says the first, "here we are again, dear. Where is she now, eh?" The second replies, "Keep your nose out of other cats' milk" while she makes her way with "slow, stiff feet … in the direction of the lift" (*Boating* 119).

Despite the sympathy for the working-class figures that this story inspires in its readers, one doesn't get a good sense of the cleaning ladies' characters or contexts. In contrast, the wartime novel *There's No Story There* provides a rich, detailed portrait of working class life amid the routine and danger of Statevale, a huge munitions factory. Holden's anonymous narrator follows a dozen or so men and women out of the 30,000 who keep the factory running, allowing her readers to imagine they know and could even be the workers. It is as though the working-class people who exit Esmee Earnshaw's house at the beginning of "Death in High Society" reenter *There's No Story There* and claim the next one hundred and eighty five pages for themselves. Unlike Holden's other wartime novel *Night Shift*, *There's No Story There* does not even have a wealthy character like Feather to guide its middle-class readers into its working-class world. Holden's careful concentration on diverse working-class lives and accomplishments, dialects and characters, represents the last important step in her movement toward writing working-class fiction. The fact that Holden deploys the techniques of documentary realism, using the camera eye of her female narrator to implicitly mount a leftist critique of the government while supporting the workers' bravery, contradicts the traditional notion that the war brought an end to Thirties-style political fiction.

Robert Hewison's account of literary life in London during the war describes this traditional notion by quoting Cyril Connolly's words in *Enemies of Promise* (1939). According to Connolly, by the late Thirties the primary enemy of literary promise was not the threat of bombs or Hitler but rather native politics (Connolly 127). Connolly's "Ivory Shelter" article in the *New Statesman* of October of 1939 notes that the one advantage for writers at work during this time was freedom "from the burden of anti-Fascist activities and the subtler burden of pro-Communist opinions" (quoted in Hewison 11). According to Hewison, the outbreak of war allowed Connolly to see "an opportunity, a justification, for the artist to withdraw to his ivory shelter" (11). Holden's engagement in the lives of others, her dedication in *There's No Story There* to earning for workers the understanding of middle-class readers who could advocate on the behalf of factory-bound citizens, contradicts this judgment. While she struggled as much or more than most writers to find alternative sources of income once paper shortages and bombings of publishing houses made publication very difficult, she did not abandon the political ideals from which Connolly sought freedom.

The limitation of Connolly's view and the critical history that echoes it is apparent as soon as women's and working-class interests are brought into critical conversations. Even if we set aside the political writing of government propaganda, writers' concerns with fair treatment of workers and the poor brought politics to the forefront of home front life and literature. The myth of the Blitz unity tends to obscure the history of class conflict early in the 1940s, when people in the East End were paying with their lives for the government's decision to shelter the rich rather than the poor. Journalists and diarists pointed out how quickly public shelters developed their own class systems. The rich and demimonde headed to steel-frame hotels while the East Enders had to settle for the few squalid, flimsy shelters in their neighborhoods (Hewison 33, 34). These inequities prompted the Communist MP Phil Piratin to lead East Enders on 15 September 1940 in a protest march to the Savoy's shelter where they all demanded access (Hewison 35). At the climax of the demonstration an all clear sounded and diffused the confrontation, but Piratin's action supports the notion, popular in the early 1940s, that "had the raids concentrated on the East End the workers there would have risen against the government" (Hewison 33).

Unfortunately for writers like Holden who perfected their Thirties-style documentary realism upon the subjects of wartime life, critics decided that public opinion was against war books by 1942 or 1943 (Hewison 44). When Kate O'Brien reviewed *There's No Story There* in the 24 November 1944 edition of the *Spectator*, she began with an admission that "it is difficult to guess how much the public wants to read about [the present war] ... in *imaginative* writing." O'Brien "wonders doubtfully how much appetite can be left for the novelists' view of actualities" since the war "is being so thoroughly reported to us, by straight journalism, by radio, and by pamphlets and volumes of short-range and eye-witness history. ..." Yet it is Holden's treatment of "actualities" that makes *There's No Story There* memorable and invites critics to reassess the accuracy of their 1930s and 1940s maps. As O'Brien notes at the end of the review, Holden captures "a very special quality" of lives lived in permanent danger, and if the book "makes sad, cold reading, it is indeed most edifying, too; it has a curious, plain dignity, and leaves many questions in the reader's mind."

If the British public was not interested in encountering difficult questions about war labor in 1944 because, as John Lehmann wrote in 1942, "The centre of balance has shifted from a rather extrovert, documentary type of realism to something more introvert," critics with the advantage of time and distance can retrospectively give Holden's novel the kind of attention it has always deserved (*New Writing* 14, quoted in Hewison 89). One of their motives for doing so is the feminist recognition that consideration of the sex of the writer can influence understanding of even gross patterns in literary production. As Hartley notes, "Women writers were moving in the opposite direction to their male contemporaries. Part of the 'public version' perhaps for the first time, these women were pleased to be participants and co-workers"—in other words, pleased to be "one of 'millions like us' with a willingness to join the collective enterprise" (*Millions* 9).

The words "Search, please," begin *There's No Story There* and establish the collective scene of workers submitting to their daily inspection by police before making their way into the secure areas of the factory. The disciplinary context of the inspection emphasizes from the outset the way the "unity" of the so-called "People's War" is fractured by class borders that are assumed and maintained by government institutions. The policy of arbitrary inquisition pursued by the proto-Fascist inspector Jameson is the most extreme form of government-supported class-division in *There's No Story There*. We first sense the way the factory's structures support Jameson's homebred dictatorial tendencies through the workers who begin to talk about him once they have distanced themselves from the inspection huts.

> "Morning, Bill."
> "Morning."
> "This new inspector Jameson's a bit of a bastard, isn't he?"
> "That's right, regular bastard he is."
> A man with tattooed arms and a black beret set far on the back of his head said, "Inspector Jameson, huh!" and spat to the ground. A sweat strand of hair fell forward over his face; looking out in hatred through the dark lock, he walked on towards the Danger Area. (8)

The alienation of the workers who are contributing to their county's defense from the security forces of that same country illustrates just one of the contradictions Holden's workers must negotiate on a regular basis. Even more numerous are the contradictions faced by the overlooker of Group IV, Section I, a Jewish man named Gluckstein who is known among the workers for his industrious work habits, health, and good nature.

The potentially tragic implications of the contradictions Gluckstein faces are most apparent in a scene that describes his reactions to one of Jameson's arbitrary inquisitions. Gluckstein, like all the workers whom Jameson interviews, mistakenly believes he has been specially selected for questioning. Only Jameson and the reader know that selections are random; Gluckstein, like every two-hundredth worker, is pulled aside based on his position in the line. The Inspector begins by asking Gluckstein if he has changed his address and prods him about the performance of two Irish workers under his supervision. When Gluckstein affirms loudly that the Irishmen are very good workers, Jameson says, "'Oh yes ... I believe they are good workers; I thought you might have some opinion on these subjects as you'd be likely to be more observant, wouldn't you, you being a foreigner?" (126). To Gluckstein's ears, this question must sound like a combined bribe and threat—a request that he spy on other "foreigners" precisely because he is regarded by the English policeman as himself a suspicious Other. After exclaiming, "I'm not a foreigner; I'm English" (127), Gluckstein is dismissed by the inspector, only to feel himself sinking back into painful memories of anti-

Semitic persecution in London's East End by the boys of his neighborhood and by Mosley's men.

Even if he could read Gluckstein's thoughts as we can, Jameson certainly wouldn't understand that his questions fall into a larger pattern of English governmental activity that anticipates and in some ways even mirrors Nazi activities. However, he would be gratified by the confirmation of his power that Gluckstein's well-disguised fear attests to:

> It was all beginning again, the persecutions which were always in [Gluckstein's] thoughts. It spread through him like a fever. All his life seemed to be like that: a recurring fever, an illness that localized itself and came out in some definite form, and after this he'd be better for a while; but at the back of his mind he knew that it would be there to happen again. It came back quite easily into his mind, the day he had asked his brother, "What are Jews? We are Jews, aren't we? Is everybody a Jew, or is it only us?" (128)

Gluckstein experiences his harassment by Jameson in unique ways because of his individual history, even though the questions that Jameson asks the arbitrarily selected workers are always identical. Jameson is well-aware of the more general terrifying effect his questions have on workers; we read that he "always liked to see a flicker of fear through men's eyes. You knew you were getting somewhere then" (134). The logic of class division as a governmental policy for home front citizens is simply made more obvious in Gluckstein's case through its intersection with the racial division marked by anti-Semitism.

The reality of England's history of anti-Semitism is emphasized, rather than discounted, by Gluckstein's misreadings of other characters' words and actions. For example, after leaving inspector Jameson, Gluckstein sees a terrifying mark chalked in white on the road that he had seen years earlier in the East End: "'P.J.'—Perish Judah" (136). The bitter twist to this vision is known only to the reader who has seen another worker, Phyllis Jenkins, scrawl her initials in the road as a sign to her boyfriend that she has passed along that way. What is a joke to Phyllis and her friends is experienced as a vicious assault by Gluckstein. Though an Englishman and patriot, he has been forced to see those categories as incompatible with his identity as a worker and a Jew. The narrator does not comment on the political lessons provided by the situation she has relayed, but readers are witness to the ways that individual citizens and England as a nation must suffer due to the erection of state-instituted and state-tolerated borders between different classes and races.

Holden imagines an alternative to such division at the end of *There's No Story There*. When a blizzard hits the factory, the workers who are on shift cannot return to their hostels. A new spirit of cooperation emerges between laborers on different shifts as everyone works together to keep production going. Even the distance between the workers and the college-educated supervisors breaks down amid the snow. We see this best through the last chapter of the novel, which takes the form of a letter that a newly transferred worker writes to her sister. Recalling the effects of the storm, the nineteen year old Mary Smith recounts an anecdote that Gluckstein told her about drying off in the boiler room with half a dozen other naked men after shoveling snow for hours. As Mary tells her sister, "He said it seemed like they were all equal and untroubled in their minds at the time, just sitting round the fire talking like kids at bedtime" (183).

Mary's recollection of the blizzard with its moments of laughter and harmony is the closest thing to a workers' utopia that Holden offers. Yet Holden is too much of a documentary realist to pretend such moments can be sustained. She is also too much of a humorist. The blizzard provides her with an opportunity to do what Storm Jameson advised and "get some fun" out of her documentary writing. In this case fun is bought at the expense of Tom Harrison and Charles Madge's Mass-Observation movement. Although Mass-Observation and Holden's version of documentary realism share common techniques and goals, Holden maliciously represents Mass-Observation in the form of the peculiar, horn-rimmed Geoffrey Doran who has been studiously recording the conversations and doings of the workers in a notebook (much the way we imagine Holden doing as she prepared to write *There's No Story There*). Doran loses his precious notebook in the blizzard and as he paws frantically through snowdrifts trying to find it, Holden enjoys a joke at Mass Observation's (and her own) expense when another worker comments, "There was a mass of workers observing him" (184).

In addition to providing Holden with opportunities for humor or for imagining more egalitarian ways of social organization and behavior, the blizzard sets the scene for her most explicit critique of the exclusion of workers' lives from serious literature. In the novel's last paragraphs Mary recalls for her sister another conversation in the factory, this time with a worker named Nordie who used to be a journalist. Mary had asked Nordie why she didn't write about the factory and Nordie had replied, "There's no story there." Mary comments to her sister: "I don't suppose there is, neither. The way you know people at work is different to ordinary life. It is jagged and uneven, not just straightforward like in a storybook" (185). Since Holden has just engrossed her readers with the very story that Mary has been conditioned to believe writers cannot tell, we are able to see the extent to which Holden believes stories themselves have been defined by the exclusion of workers from their pages.

A survey of Holden's fictions written during the 1930s and 1940s reveals how far she had to travel to arrive at this political-literary insight. Holden moves from a pre-war humorous cynicism that depends on middle-class readers' validation of the borders of privilege to a wartime empathetic realism that depends on readers imagining their way across borders of class. The publication of *There's No Story There* in 1944 marks an important event for those who are trying to create an alternative, more inclusive English literary tradition. It proves that readers can be moved by a "jagged and uneven" narrative, a story about workers told by a female narrator, one that unites the two alternative traditions of "red" and "women's" writing that scholars have recently begun to uncover.

The stakes of recognizing the strength of this kind of understudied fiction can be measured by divergent interpretations of the literary meaning of Labour's sweeping victory in July 1945. For example, Hewison questions whether books played any part in developing the nation's social conscience or even if a "diffuse" radical feeling was really influential in the election. He seems to doubt the strength of the connection between literature and politics at this point precisely because the "diffusion" of radical feeling makes the boundary between the two realms so hard to discern. For Croft, on the other hand, that election represents the triumph of the socialist ideals that novelists shared with the public in their fictions of the 1930s. He concludes that these ideals were maintained in "serious writing about the war" and that British literary culture was "dominated for nearly a decade by the heirs to the culture of the Popular Front campaigns, by Communists and their allies" (Croft 336). In contrast to Hewison's analysis, Croft's interpretation of literature's effect on the postwar political and cultural life of England helps us see Holden's wartime fictions as part of a larger body of literature that breaks down the divide between the decades. *Night Shift* and *There's No Story There* remind us of the importance of seeking and valuing "Thirties' novels" written in the 1940s, of looking to women's writing for our war literature.

There are other signs that Holden's dedication to a Thirties' materials of documentary realism, factory work, and women's lives was not out of step with the values of mainstream culture in the later war years. On a page of the *Spectator* immediately following O'Brien's review of *There's No Story There*, an ad in the left hand corner announces in large type that "The Hand that held the Hoover guides the Barge!" It continues in smaller font,

> A Woman Bargee? That's a man's job, you'd think, if ever there was one. Certainly it's hard work and heavy work. But there are very few men's jobs that the women of wartime Britain haven't learnt to tackle! It's because no job has daunted them, however hard or unusual it might be, that Britain today can claim the highest production per head of population of all the allied countries. (490)

These words are accompanied by an illustration of a woman in ruffled shirt, merrily poling her barge along. The ad concludes with a loud "Salute! from Hoover to the women war-workers of Britain" (490).

The Hoover ad suggests that as late as 1944 manufacturers were still confident that they could sell merchandise by declaring their pride in women who did "a man's job." It represents the way capitalist and national interests commonly joined in a celebration of the woman worker in order to promote consumerism and patriotism. Holden's novel of that same year celebrates workers, both male and female, in order to promote very different ends: the imaginative lives of readers and the interests of the workers themselves. The parallel contents in texts with such different aims suggests that the meaning of labor and the experience of the British working class was still being actively fought over in the popular and serious literature of the 1940s. While critics are certainly right to argue that the 1930s nurtured the nation's social conscience, they should also note that the entry of women into the "hard work and heavy work" of wartime industry sustained that conscience in the literature of the next decade, even as more dramatic horrors of active combat or Fascist terror preoccupied soldier-writers and publishers.

Holden always dedicated herself to entertaining readers with a good story and interesting language, but her fiction of the 1930s and 1940s often takes on subjects that tie it to the interests of the working class and simple, documentary forms that ally it with the literature of the Popular Front. The freedom of this vision from Party politics and its accessibility to people of all classes is evident from the end of *There's No Story There* as the damp, naked workers listen to the man in charge of the boiler-room telling stories about his youth. This nameless worker describes his travels to central Europe when he was trying to fulfill his ambition to be a painter and instead found himself involved in revolutionary workers' movements. After spinning tales about manning barricades, watching his friends die in street fighting, joining the International Brigade, being thrown in prison and losing his right hand (his painting hand, we assume) to blood poisoning, he tells the gathered men "I'm not interested in politics, never have been" (172).

The man in charge of the boiler-room believes that politics are what overtake people when they are living their lives, but he explains away his political choices with the words, "I always seem to have been in some place when there was a flare-up" (172). His comments start Gluckstein thinking about "his own attempt to get into the fight against everything he hated"— his attempts to be a hero on the side of the oppressed—and how "each time it was the same story, somehow he was kept out of it all" (172). Holden's novel suggests that both these men are blind to the political content of their lives because they see fragments or a vacant story of exclusion where there is actually connection, content, and even heroism. Holden may not have agonized in print about the appropriate political role for the leftist artist, but the ironic reverberations between the title of *There's No Story There* and its contents suggests that she did see herself as contributing to the decades' long fight for social justice in England. Her role was to find plot when others saw random events, see heroes when others saw workers, create stories when others saw no story there.

[This work was supported, in part, by a Grant-in-Aid-for-Creativity award from Monmouth University, for which I am very grateful.]

References

Common, Jack, ed. *Seven Shifts*. London: E.P. Dutton, 1938.

Connolly, Cyril. *Enemies of Promise*. Boston: Little, Brown, 1939.

Croft, Andy. *Red Letter Days: British Fiction in the 1930s*. London: Lawrence and Wishart, 1990.

Cunningham, Valentine. *British Writers of the Thirties*. New York: Oxford University Press, 1988.

Deane, Patrick, ed. *History in Our Hands: A Critical Anthology of Writings on Literature, Culture and Politics from the 1930s*. New York: Leicester University Press, 1998.

Dowson, Jane, ed. *Women's Poetry of the 1930s: A Critical Anthology*. London: Routledge, 1996.

Gindin, James. *British Fiction of the 1930s: The Dispiriting Decade*. New York: St. Martin's, 1992.

Goodman, Celia. "Inez Holden: A Memoir." *London Magazine* 33.9-10 (1993/94): 29-38.

"The Hand that held the Hoover guides the Barge!" *Spectator* 24 November 1944: 490.

Hartley, Jenny, ed. *Hearts Undefeated: Women's Writing of the Second World War*. London: Virago, 1994.

——. *Millions Like Us: British Women's Fiction of the Second World War*. London: Virago, 1997.

Hewison, Robert. *Under Siege: Literary Life in London, 1939-45*. London: Weidenfeld and Nicolson, 1977.

Holden, Inez. *Born Old, Died Young*. London: Duckworth, 1932.

——. *Death in High Society*. London: Kegan Paul, 1934.

——. *It Was Different At the Time*. London: John Lane, 1943.

——. *Night Shift*. London: John Lane, 1941.

——. *Sweet Charlatan*. London: Duckworth, 1929.

——. *There's No Story There*. London: John Lane, 1944.

——. *To the Boating and Other Stories*: London: John Lane, 1945.

Hynes, Samuel. *The Auden Generation: Literature and Politics in England in the 1930s*. Princeton: Princeton University Press, 1972.

Lassner, Phyllis. *British Women Writers of World War II: Battlegrounds of Their Own*. New York: St. Martin's, 1998.

Light, Alison. *Forever England: Femininity, Literature, and Conservatism between the Wars*. New York: Routledge, 1991.

Mass-Observation. *War Factory: A Report*. Ed. Tom Harrison. London: Gollancz, 1943.

Montefiore, Janet. *Men and Women Writers of the 1930s: The Dangerous Flood of History*. New York: Routledge, 1996.

O'Brien, Kate. "Fiction." *Spectator* 24 November 1944: 488.

Ogden, C.K. *The System of Basic English*. New York: Harcourt Brace, 1934.

Orwell, George. *Inside the Whale and Other Essays*. London: Penguin, 1957.

Plain, Gill. *Women's Fiction of the Second World War*. New York: St. Martin's, 1996.

Quinn, Patrick, ed. *Recharting the Thirties*. Selinsgrove: Susquehanna University Press, 1996.

Roberts, Michael, ed. *New Country: Prose and Poetry by the Authors of New Signatures*. London: Hogarth Press, 1933.

Schimanski, Stefan and Henry Treece, eds. *Leaves in the Storm: A Book of Diaries*. London: Lindsay Drummond, 1947.

"Shorter Notice" [Review of *Night Shift*]. *Spectator* 15 May 1942: 472.
Spalding, Frances. *Stevie Smith: A Biography*. New York: Norton, 1988.
Williams-Ellis, Amabel. *Women in War Factories*. London: Gollancz, 1943.

Part III—Revisiting Modernists

7 The Politics of Modernism in Kay Boyle's *Death of a Man*

Phoebe Stein Davis

"I feel that modernism still has a claim on our interest precisely because it does not make good sense, because we find in it more of the unfinished business of our time than in any other literature."

—Michael North *The Political Aesthetic of Yeats, Eliot, and Pound*

Many studies, conference panels, and journal articles published in the 1990s indicated a resurgence of interest in the politics of modernism.[1] On the brink of the twenty-first century, we returned to what literary critic Marianne DeKoven calls "the urgent question of whether or not we can attribute political efficacy to what many of us see as the most important formal modes of twentieth-century art" (675). I self-consciously portray this as a return, not in psychoanalytic terms—as a "return of the repressed" come back to haunt us once again—but to highlight the fact that the relationship between modernism and politics perhaps can only be fully excavated in hindsight. Certainly, the "urgent question" DeKoven identifies quite literally returns us to the formalist concern, as voiced by the New Critics, that "the most important formal modes of twentieth-century" literature must remain independent from politics, or risk being propaganda. The enduring impact of the formalist segregation of aesthetics and politics cannot be underestimated.[2]

At the same time, however, it is important to remember that the danger the New Critics posited in the power of politicizing aesthetics manifested itself openly for their generation. As Alice Kaplan explains: "we forget that fascism took hold in Europe partly as 'radical chic,' that it was gaily disseminated by poets and critics" (170). Nor can the concern about mixing politics and aesthetics be dismissed as the backward thinking of a few "straw men." Critics from New Critical to Marxist circles cautioned against it, albeit for different reasons. After witnessing the rise of fascism in Europe, Walter Benjamin drew a direct connection between the evils propagated there and the yoking of art and politics. In 1936, he explained this aestheticization of politics as an extension of fascism: the "logical result of Fascism is the introduction of aesthetics into political life" (241). For Benjamin, infusing politics with aesthetics led only to destruction: "All efforts to render politics aesthetic culminate in one thing: war. War and only war can set a goal for mass movements on the largest scale" (241). He explains that for fascists (he gives the Futurist Marinetti as his example), war provides an "artistic gratification" (242) like no other, an aesthetics that resulted in a terrifying appreciation of the beauty of war. However, as

137

Andrew Hewitt reminds us, it was not the integration of politics and aesthetics *per se* that troubled Benjamin. Unlike formalist critics, Benjamin is not highlighting the inherent dangers of letting aesthetics and politics influence one another, but recommends "politicizing art" (242), proposing a "politicization of aesthetics" (Hewitt 55), as opposed to an aestheticization of politics.

In her recent study, *Thinking Fascism*, Erin G. Carlston explains that it is precisely the desire to isolate political and aesthetic concerns from one another that must be examined in order to understand how modernist writers represent, interpret, explain, and reproduce the politics of fascism. She goes on to trace a history of literary criticism (from biographical to formalist) that has worked at "containing the far-reaching effects of fascist discourse" (15). According to Carlston, the problem with merely condemning fascism as evil and thus not a suitable topic for examination is that we have left no space for a "more self-critical approach" (15).[3] However, while Carlston identifies our resistance to examining modernist texts that treat fascism, there are a number of larger assumptions at work here that often lead readers and critics away from the politics of modernism. First, as Sara Blair has explained, there remains an enduring perception that the "unifying feature [of modernism] was the attempt to transcend the political altogether" (157). At the same time, the right-wing, reactionary nature of "high" modernism is often used as evidence to support the idea that when modernist writers did engage politically, they supported highly suspect political ideologies. While this fact is undeniable, the effect of this fact seems not only to be, as the New Critics maintained, that modernist literature should not engage political issues, but moreover, that it is incapable of doing so in any legitimate way.[4] However, the recent resurgence of interest in the political efficacy of modernist aesthetics allows us to examine how modernists used their experimental aesthetics and concern for language to explore the politics of fascism.

It is important to recognize that as part of the critical return Marianne DeKoven has mapped out in modernist studies, the work of male modernists has been scrutinized for its explicit and implicit fascist politics, while writing by female modernists about fascism is nearly uncharted territory.[5] Perhaps the central reason for this is that historically, writing by women has been read as inherently pacifist. Simply put, political movements and the wars they elicited were not considered within the purview of female modernist writers: "the 'reality' of the war and its authoritative representation were pinned to concepts of masculinity" (Higgonet 145).[6] While feminist criticism has done much to recognize the politics of women's writing, my goal here is to trace a different critical history of responses to writing by female modernists about politics. Through a reading of Kay Boyle's 1936 novel *Death of a Man*, I examine Boyle as a female modernist writer who was condemned in contemporary reviews of the novel for utilizing her mod-

ernist writing style to write about fascism. Boyle's novel about the relationship between a Nazi doctor, Prochaska, and his American lover, Pendennis
Jones, in the midst of the rise of the Nazi movement in Austria in the 1930s
offers an interesting case study in the ways one modernist writer became
embattled in New Critical circles for using her dual concerns with language
and politics to record political trauma.

More specifically, a discussion of Boyle's novel allows us to examine
how female modernist writers utilized their experimental writing style and
concern for aesthetics to engage fascism as an "intellectual problem" (Carlston 11), as well as an historical reality. According to historian Studs Terkel,
Kay Boyle held a unique position as a modernist writer who had "borne witness to the most traumatic and shattering events of our century. ... Both as a
creative artist as well as being there" (quoted in Spanier, "No Past Tense"
245). But while Terkel separates these two experiences—being a "creative
artist" and "being there"—*Death of a Man* represents a synthesis of "creating" and "witnessing." Boyle presented the personal trauma and its link to the
political events of the Austrian Tyrol region in the interwar period. *Death of
a Man* depicts the complexity of the personal reactions the citizens of this
region had, ranging from trauma, to ambivalence, to a desire to join the Nazi
party. Moreover, Boyle's novel does not take a clear "stand" for or against
fascism. Her project was far more complicated and daunting: according to
Boyle, she told this story from the Nazi point of view "... to find out, on a
human level, what the almost inexplicable fascination of Hitler was" (quoted
in Spanier 120).[7]

In order to explain the lure of fascism between the wars, Boyle uses a
lyrical and often surreal narrative style in *Death of a Man* to present a fictionalized account of the "almost inexplicable" political events Boyle herself
witnessed while living in the Austrian Tyrol of the mid-1930s. For Boyle,
how she "created" and what she "witnessed" could never be divorced
because, she explained "... language can never be a matter of merely literary concern because language and content, form and subject matter ... cannot be separated. They are one and the same thing" (*Talks* 216-17). The
inextricable relationship Boyle posits between "form and subject matter" is
at the heart of her concurrent concerns with capturing reality and experimenting with language, a goal central to her work as a modernist artist. "Revolution of the Word," the manifesto that appeared in the avant-garde journal
transition in 1926 signed by Boyle and other modernists, proclaimed that:
"narrative is not mere anecdote, but the projection of a metamorphosis of
reality ... the expression of these concepts can be achieved only through the
rhythmic 'hallucination of the word'" (13). Boyle was, in fact, a prominent
figure in what she called "the revolutionary army of the Left Bank" (quoted
in Spanier, "No Past Tense" 250), the movement in Paris in the 1920s that
called for "the revolution of the word" (other supporters included Hart Crane

and Eugene Jolas, to whom *Death of a Man* is dedicated).

Boyle's modernist concern with "the revolution of the word" in *Death of a Man* is significant to the novel's content in two ways: first, Boyle experiments with narrative form and temporality in the text, exploring the indeterminacy of language; and second, the inextricable connection between language and politics is one of the central subjects of the novel. It is Boyle's focus on the "hallucination of the word" as both a method *of* and subject *for* analysis that not only defines her as a modernist writer, but also allows her to capture the fear, despair, and fanaticism of the interwar period. However, because *Death of a Man* never completely abandons the norms of linear narration and syntax (as many modernist texts do), as I discuss below, Boyle's aesthetic experimentation in the novel has been overlooked, or dismissed as an inadequate tool to capture the political and historical reality she records.

While Boyle's writing remains lyrical and lucid, in significant passages throughout *Death of a Man* she experiments with temporality and linearity, forcing readers to suspend their narrative expectations. Despite the narrative's vivid descriptions, at these points in the novel it is almost impossible to distinguish the reality from the "hallucination" of the scene. In this way, the "hallucination" readers experience is often their own. For Boyle, this merging of "hallucination" and reality is central to her goal as an "historian" in the fiction she writes. She explains: "I think it's completely impossible to separate them [dream and reality], or to say where they are separated. They merge into each other and in every instance (I suppose I am really trying to be a historian) in every instance my stories are based very, very, very deeply in fact" (*Talks* 222). There is no contradiction for Boyle in not being able to distinguish dream from reality in a story based "very, very, very deeply in fact" (222). That is, this melding of dream and reality, the inability to "say where they are separated," reveals the very indeterminacy of language and is thus a necessary part of relating history.

Specifically, Boyle's text blurs the line between fantasy, reality, and memory at just the points in the novel when she is exploring the trauma she herself witnessed, and her characters experience, in 1930s Austria. In this way, Boyle is doing more than bringing her "fascination with the possibilities and failures of language" (Uehling 376) to describe Austria in the interwar period. Rather, Boyle uses her experimental narrative style to record, with a great deal of accuracy, the personal experiences and psychological effects of what historian F.L. Carsten explains as the political situation in Austria in 1933-1934: "within Austria, the National Socialists not only distributed leaflets and papers, burnt fireworks and painted swastikas in more or less inaccessible places, but they used high explosives to good effect and committed innumerable acts of sabotage" (249). But *Death of a Man* also makes it clear that these overtly political acts of "sabotage" were not the only violently disruptive effects of the rise of the Nazi party. While Austria was suffering in the early 1930s, as countries the world over were, from "the aftermath of the world depression" (Mellen 179), the poverty in Tyrol region was the direct result of the political struggle between Austria's chancellor, Dollfuss, and Adolf Hitler (Carsten 249). When Dollfuss's Christian Socialist government refused to commit to Hitler's regional fascist regime, Hitler responded by levying a tax of 1,000 marks for any Germans visiting Austria (Carsten 249). This was "a ruinous measure for a vital tourist industry of Austria which considerably aggravated the economic crisis" (Carsten 249).

The most striking example of Boyle's "hallucination of the word" comes in her description of the traumatized victims of this "aggravated ... economic crisis" wrought by the political situation in Austria: the children in the quarantined diphtheria unit where Dr. Prochaska works. These children are described very clearly as "the survivors of a great and universal disaster feeling their way slowly back to life again" (213). They come from "townfuls of starving beggars" (87), part of a populace Prochaska describes as, "not only children but men and women without shoes on their feet walking the streets of Vienna all winter" (87) who have experienced "the finality of despair" (87), the trauma of poverty and illness. In fact, the historical reality that Boyle interprets in these scenes in the hospital is based on her own experiences. While living in Austria in 1934, her own daughter Bobby contracted diphtheria and was treated at a local *Infektionhaus* by a Nazi doctor whom Boyle came to know quite well. When this personal experience is translated into the novel, the fact that the children's suffering arises from the political situation in Austria in the 1930s is clear.

In her recent study, *Unclaimed Experience: Trauma, Narrative, and History*, Cathy Caruth examines Sigmund Freud's use of literature in his psychoanalytic writings on trauma to argue that "literature, like psychoanalysis, is interested in the complex relation between knowing and not knowing" (3). Caruth helps us to understand why modernist concerns with language and referentiality become central to representing trauma. Caruth explains that it is "a central problem of listening, of knowing, and of representing that emerges from the actual experience of crisis" (5). If Boyle's novel presents a surreal, "almost inexplicable" (Boyle, quoted in Spanier, *Kay Boyle* 120) portrait of the political situation in Austria it is because the language that she uses to present "the actual experience of crisis" is, necessarily, what Caruth calls "a language that defies, even as it claims, our understanding" (Caruth 5). Furthermore, as Valerie Smith explains, the issue of how to represent the experience of trauma aesthetically quickly becomes politically charged:

> For if we acknowledge the inaccessibility of experience except representation, then we must admit that our best-intended attempts to understand another's (indeed our own) experience of suffering are always finally about language or other signifying systems. To recognize this then prompts its own series of

questions and considerations. We begin to ask how to articulate the relationship between "experience" and representations of that "experience." Experience cannot help but be mediated by narrative, then we begin to ask about politics of narrative interventions. (343)

Smith is explaining here what Boyle knew: "… language can never be a matter of merely literary concern because language and content, form and subject matter … cannot be separated. They are one and the same thing" (Boyle, *Talks* 216-17). In other words, the "subject matter" of *Death of a Man*, the "suffering" in the Tyrol in the 1930s, is "always finally about language" (Smith 343).

Boyle's novel repeatedly presents the experience of trauma as Caruth defines it: as "an experience that is not fully assimilated as it occurs" (5) and thus returns to haunt her characters. Boyle chooses the quarantine wing of the hospital, a place of silence and death, to describe what haunts the children in this novel. As the scene in the hospital begins and we peer voyeuristically (and perhaps reluctantly) into the beds of the diphtheria-stricken children, the deadly silence of the scene is broken only by the children's daily ritual: the story they tell to the youngest (and sickest child), in the ward, Cristabel, who awakens every morning with screams of "Mamma, Mamma" (99).

This cry prompts one of the older boys, Karli, to explain: "'she's not here, Cristl. You have to go downstairs and cross the garden and get out through the gate and walk into town and take the tram on the Andreas-Hofer-Strausse—'" (100). The narrator explains that "this was the way the farcical story began every day, or more than once a day, told in Karli's smart, piping, humorous voice to Cristabel who was three and had been there half her life" (100). The desperate impotence of this story (no one is going anywhere) seems clear until quite suddenly, like an incantation, Karli's directions home prompt the arrival of all the children's mothers:

> And without any warning but as if this were the signal for which they been waiting, the step and the murmur and haste of the absent women came into the room, the old women, the young women, their hair in braids or their hair cut short, and some in their peasant clothes for church with the gilt lace on their stiff-brimmed hats and others in their aprons; they came quickly into the place where the children were, Karli's mother, Helmut's mother, and Jochi's mother, and even Christabel's mother straight to the beds to which they had no right to come because of what they might bear away in affliction to others. They were poor women, all them, without the time to come …. (101)

The fact that these women do not have "the time to come" (101) does not ultimately reflect the sacrifices they make for their children, but presents another reading of this scene: the mothers are never actually there. As we read further, "the ghostly crowd of women *who were not there and could not come* pressed in between the children's beds. ... the tide of women rose and fell and rose. ... and there were no longer any women in the room" (103-4, emphasis mine). Like the traumatic effects of the hunger, poverty, and death these children experience every day, their mothers are both omnipresent and nowhere to be seen.[8]

It is important to note how realistically Boyle describes "the ghostly crowd of women who were not there," from their hair and dress to their demeanor. The narrator describes in detail how these mothers continue to blame their children for their hardship: "There she stood looking down in censure and blame on him, the snow from the long way she had come on skis still beading the cuff of her socks and her fingernails black from boot-grease and the kitchen" (103). That these mothers are more real in the children's (or narrator's) fantasies than in reality means that the borders between fantasy and reality in this part of the novel are completely erased and readers are left in a space that they must accept as *both* dream world and reality. While this passage seems more lyrical and lucid than experimental, with closer attention, the rhythmic tone of the passage masks the fact that what we are reading is not actually happening, or is happening only in the children's minds. In this way, readers are forced to accept what the children imagine *as* the reality of the scene.

In a later scene, *Death of a Man* makes clear the range of citizens personally affected by the political situation in Austria, from innocent, sick children to those who, like the Doctor, are attracted to fascism. Significantly, this scene too presents readers with a narrative that merges imagination and reality, one in which we are forced to accept, and at the same time question, the character's perception of the "reality" of the situation. This passage shuttles back and forth between a conversation Dr. Prochaska is having with Praxlmann, the local Nazi party boss, and Prochaska's memories of a meeting the two nuns with whom he worked at the *Infektionhaus*. Reality and memory merge into one another in this passage as Prochaska listens to Praxlmann lecture him:

> "Keep things where they belong now, women where ..." His laughter shaking out in rings, ring after illuminated expanding ring behind which his open mouth, the white moustaches, the face itself dwindled and the sound of laughing dwindled to a point as if he were fading backwards down the corridor of when that was, while up the passage he had bored through recognition came two women, both of them wearing long serge coats and both leaning to the weight of the suitcases they carried. (260-1)

Interestingly, it is at just the point when Praxlmann emphasizes women's static place in the Nazi movement that these "two women" appear, quite clearly not staying "where they belong." Prochaska creates a space, a "corridor," a "passage," through which he moves to his memory. However, once readers move through this space, they are immediately thrust into the scene in the present tense of the moment when Prochaska encountered the women. They are, in fact, no longer conscious of being only in Prochaska's mind. Although they have just read that Prochaska is sitting with Praxlmann in the *Gasthaus*, he is, at the same time, running "down the avenue through the dust that lay on the walk beneath the trees until the two women ... heard him calling and turned" (262).

To complicate matters further, readers are told very explicitly at the start of this scene that Prochaska goes to the Gasthaus, sees Praxlmann, but does not stay to speak to him: "Dr. Prochaska did not sit down at the old man's table before leaving and did not return directly to Infektionhaus but went further into the town to the *Weinstube* near the river to drink, and walked home late by the water in the darkness" (260). Although Boyle gives readers no determinate place to position themselves in order to understand what is actually happening in this scene in the *Gasthaus*, a central and important truth emerges from this melding of the real and the unreal. Quickly, it is made evident why this scene is important to Prochaska; he came upon the women as they left the hospital, purposefully avoiding a meeting with him. Prochaska jokingly chides them for avoiding him: "So this is the way you go off ... without a word to me, either of you ... not even saying .... We've been together a long time now and you go off without saying a word of good-bye to me. Is that any way to treat me, Sister Resi?" (262). At this moment, like a film put on pause, Prochaska's mind moves back to the "present" moment in his conversation with Praxlmann: "But suddenly what he was saying stopped and Praxlmann's face came into perfect and monstrous focus before him and Praxlmann's voice said: 'You know they've been making enquiries at the hospital. ... the Sisters of the Order reported your radio disturbed the patients, particularly between seven-thirty and eight-thirty in the evening, every evening'" (263). Immediately, Prochaska's mind returns to his conversation with the Sisters of the Order: "then Sister Marianna said: 'Ah, we couldn't find you so we were going to write a little letter, Herr Doktor!'" (263). What is revealed here is both a personal betrayal that makes Prochaska feel "he might have been talking to someone else entirely, saying this out of grief and mutilation with his eyes closed to who was there" (262) and a political reality: Hitler's speeches were broadcast in the evenings from Germany and listening to them was condemned as a criminal act in 1933.[9] Significantly, it is only through this oscillation between memory and present "reality" that Prochaska realizes that he has been implicated by the nuns and that he is in danger if he stays at the hospital.

Throughout *Death of a Man*, Boyle uses this oscillation between memory and present reality, this suspension of linear narrative, to demonstrate how her characters experience both political and personal trauma. As Pen unfolds the story of her childhood to Prochaska, we learn that she and her twin brother Gerald witnessed their mother's death in a horseback riding accident. For Pen, this memory is interjected daily into her present reality. This "return," Caruth explains, happens because this event has not yet been fully integrated: "what returns to haunt the victim ... is not only the reality of the violent event but also the reality of the way its violence has not yet been fully known" (6). When Pen tells Dr. Prochaska about these events she explains little of her mother's actual death, saying only, "we didn't see what happened or if he just went up on his hindlegs and shook her down backwards into the stream. The water wasn't deep and mother lay there on her back. ... and then in a minute we knew she was dead" (121). We also learn here that Pen has experienced trauma twice-over: her twin brother killed himself shortly after his mother's death.

Pen's traumatic experiences and her reactions to them directly raise the question that Caruth poses to her reader: "Is the trauma the encounter with death, or the ongoing experience of having survived it?" (7). For Pen, the trauma of survival haunts her daily; she explains that since the time of her brother's death she has felt a direct connection to Gerald, believing he speaks to her from the grave. Significantly, her brother can only talk to her after he is dead: "when Gerald killed himself he really began saying things to me for the first time" (122). Although in life, "words were absolutely no use to him" (123), through his suicide and in his death Gerald can communicate his feelings to Pen. Once again, in the world of the novel, readers are asked to accept a seemingly inconceivable idea (Gerald "speaking" from his grave) as the "reality" of the situation. The way Pen experiences these traumatic events directly supports what Caruth calls "the inextricability of the story of one's life from the story of death, an impossible and necessary double telling" (8). Pen explains her brother's suicide not as an ending, but specifically as the beginning of a repetition, an "impossible and necessary double telling": "when he hung himself it was just the beginning of what had happened to Gerald and me not once but over and over" (122). In this way, Pen experiences her trauma—her mother's death and her brother's suicide—not once, but "over and over" again.

The "inextricable" and repeated connections between life and death Caruth posits for those who experience trauma is not only a reality for Pen, but for the children who narrate "more than once a day" the "farcical story" (100) of their escape in the midst of the death that surrounds them. In fact, the novel directly parallels Pen's unassimilated experience of personal trauma with what I am calling the children's "political trauma." As Pen relates the story of her mother's death and her brother's suicide to Prochaska the narrator explains that: "her voice began speaking again and her face was turned from him, like the faces of the children lying ill, towards the open window with the trees standing in it" (121). Boyle demonstrates that Pen's experience of personal trauma is strikingly similar to the political trauma the children in the diphtheria ward experience. Furthermore, through Boyle's equation of the family trauma Pen repeatedly re-lives and the haunting images the children evoke every day of their absent mothers, *Death of a Man* not only demonstrates the role that the past plays in our present reality, but also the inextricable place the imaginary has in the production of the real.

Boyle's emphasis in *Death of a Man* on the role that language plays in creating the inextricable relationship between dream and reality was problematic for the novel's initial reviewers, who felt it was at odds with her political subject matter. Describing Boyle as in "over her head" (Ferguson 322, Canby 12), the majority of reviewers concluded that Boyle's narrative style masked the political realities of the situation she described.[10] Perhaps because Boyle was firmly allied with the Left throughout her life,[11] reviewers were appalled by what they perceived to be her sympathetic portrait of the Nazi Dr. Prochaska and the apathy of his American lover, Pendennis Jones. Many reviews mentioned the mysticism with which Boyle shrouds the Nazi party and attributed the moral failings of the novel to her "rather impressionistic method" (Canby 12). Clearly, for these reviewers, it was Boyle's aesthetic concerns that undermined the political efficacy of her novel. As one reviewer concluded: "you can't see the forest for the prose" (Ferguson 322).

Literary critics on both sides of the Atlantic agreed. The legendary British literary magazine the *Spectator* described Boyle's style as "an obstacle" which, despite "its great strength and charm, draws our attention at present too consciously to itself instead of to its subject" (Burra 560). More specifically, reviewers felt that Boyle's style prevented a purely anti-Nazi reading of the novel. Mark Van Doren's infamous claim in the *Nation* that "there is the attempt on the part of Miss Boyle to hypnotize the reader into a state of what may be called mystical fascism" (494), was in keeping with the general sentiment of these reviews: that the novel—what one reviewer called, "Kay Boyle's Sketch of a Likable Nazi" (Canby 12)—failed to make a case against the fascism it described. *Time* magazine summed up the general consensus about Boyle's book, calling the novel a "Nazi Idyll" (87).

Critical examinations of *Death of a Man* today, much like the reviews that appeared in 1936, center on the question of whether Boyle's portrait of Prochaska and his clandestine struggle with the National Socialists against the Christian Socialist government of Chancellor Dollfuss reflect pro-Nazi sympathies on Boyle's part. It is important to note that this debate stems, at least in part, not from the text of the novel itself, but from the events that surrounded Boyle's publication of *Death of a Man*. In 1935, Boyle published "The White Horses of Vienna," a short story about a Nazi doctor. Although the story won the O. Henry award, it was condemned as pro-Nazi both by a judge on the award committee and Boyle's own family. This episode, coupled with the fact that in *Death of a Man* Boyle draws on her own experiences living in Austria with her husband and three children from 1933 to 1935, slated Boyle's novel for controversy. The debate over Boyle's political allegiances often turns on another bit of biographical information: that while living in the Austrian Tyrol region, Boyle listened ("in secret" against local laws that prohibited it) to Hitler's radio broadcasts and described to friends the "strangely thrilling," "really moving appeal of Hitler" (quoted in Spanier, *Kay Boyle* 121).[12] Boyle biographer Joan Mellen concludes from this that *Death of a Man* reflects the appeal Kay Boyle found in the Nazi party (Mellen 190) and that this accounts for the novel's "limited political and historical understanding of what was happening in Austria" (Mellen 193).

Other contemporary critics disagree. Sandra Whipple Spanier, for example, explains that although " it does appear that Kay Boyle ... might have been momentarily moved by the passionate intensity and promise of early Nazis" (*Kay Boyle* 121), she concludes that Boyle "most definitely is not pro-Nazi or pro-war in this novel [*Death of a Man*]" (Spanier, *Kay Boyle* 122). Burton Hatlen and Marilyn Elkins insist that the novel provides "a negative judgment" of the Nazi movement (Hatlen vi), and that the novel represents "an early indictment of Nazism" (Elkins 6). It is significant to note that although there is little consensus on the novel's pro-or-anti-Nazi sympathies, all critics (even those who believe that Boyle chose to write the novel as she did in order to show the complex reasons why people joined the Nazi cause) agree that it was Boyle's "literary decision[s]" that proved most "fateful" to the success of the novel (Mellen 187).

What is lost in these readings, however, is the fact that through its modernist concern for aesthetics and language, *Death of a Man* demonstrates the inextricable bonds between language and fascism. Even these most recent readings of the novel, those that clearly want to rescue Boyle from accusations of pro-Nazi sympathies by virulently defending her novel as anti-fascist, lead readers away from the central point Boyle is making about the role that language itself played in the rise of fascism in Austria in the 1930s. Boyle's novel makes it clear that this connection between language and fascism works in two different ways: first, fascism in the form of the rise of the Nazi movement and the production of its fascist subjects was accomplished through language, and second, as a text, *Death of a Man* reproduces the fascism it depicts. As Erin G. Carlston explains, it "was not [possible] in the inter war period ... to produce texts that treat fascism while remaining wholly Other to it, outside the terms of fascist thought" (17). It is precisely this fear that literature and fascism have a direct relationship to one another that causes the majority of today's critics to defend Boyle: "The fear that literary texts might ... stand in a direct causal relation to political events, and particularly to the Holocaust, tends to provoke a mad rush by critics to try to rescue their favorite authors from charges of collaboration, by showing some profound divergence from the fascist program in their texts, or pointing to the writers' actual persecution by fascist regimes" (Carlston 12).

Because of the feared causal linkage between literature and politics, Boyle's modernist insistence on the multiplicity of meanings, on producing a reality through the "hallucination of the word" (13) is often seen as having no place in writing that captures events—the rise and power of the Nazi party—that had such personally and politically catastrophic consequences for so many. Responding to critics who lambaste Sylvia Plath for utilizing (and in their view appropriating) the Holocaust in her poetry, Jacqueline Rose understands that many people believe that "faced with the reality of the Holocaust, the idea that there is an irreducibly figurative dimension to all language is an evasion, or denial, of the reality of history itself" (207). But, Rose argues, our response should not be to reject Plath's poetry but to realize that "the issue then becomes not whether Plath has a right to present the Holocaust, but what the presence of the Holocaust in her poetry unleashes, or obliges us to focus, about representation as such" (207). Ultimately, then, writing about fascism becomes an issue of representation: "speech itself is the problem" (Rose 208). However, as Rose explains, the "figurative" aspect of language is undeniable in any language system, even in the face of fascism and the Holocaust. Denying the role (and power) of figurative language in politics only denies an examination of it. Rather, as *Death of a Man* demonstrates, one must mine the complexity, what "does not make good sense" (North viii), in order to explain the role that language itself played in the production of, and the desire for, fascism.

Death of a Man most clearly reproduces "fascist thought" in the novel's most controversial scene. On their way to a ski meet in the mountain town of Kirchstadt, where Prochaska has come to compete and secretly to meet fellow Nazis in the mountains to light swastika fires, he and Pen meet "two Jewesses" on a crowded train (142). As they argue as to whether Pen will be allowed, as she wishes, to accompany Prochaska on the very dangerous mission to light the fires, Pen repeatedly tries to force Prochaska into a conversation with the two women: "'This young man comes from Vienna, said the girl [Pen] and she made a gesture, without turning towards the doctor. ... 'This young man's in the races tomorrow,' said the girl, making the movement again with her hand and the cigarette in it towards the doctor" (141). Boyle's manipulation of point-of-view in this scene through the narrator's repeated use of the words "the girl" and Pen's use of term "this young man" for Prochaska makes the reader an outsider, a spectator to this scene. Although Pen seems at one level to be challenging the Doctor's perspective on these women, perhaps in an effort to humanize them, the use of impersonal nouns like "young man" and "girl" by both Pen and the narrator underscore the reader's inability to maintain one perspective on this scene (Pen's, the women's, the Doctor's).

However, almost immediately after this scene begins, readers are denied this comfortable distance by Boyle's narrator, who weaves a persistent string of virulent anti-Semitic remarks about these two women throughout these passages. The women are described, in no uncertain terms, as alien, animalistic, dirty, promiscuous, sexual, fat, and lazy: "both with the rich Oriental mouths and noses of another people, both with the heavy flesh and slow eyes of creatures of another species among these hollow-cheeked athletic women and men. ... their tapering feline fingers sharply and ornate nailed. ... harem-soft and harem-seductive" (137, 138, 139). The women are not only different from the others, but physically revolting for the difference in their dress and general physicality. They "wore heavy woolen socks like all the others but they had added little scarlet tassels at the ankles of their soft-fleshed shapeless legs and instead of traveling bare-headed they wore red and yellow stocking-caps pulled down in incongruous coquettishness over the rich oily undulations of their hair" (137).

But while these women are clearly out of place and identifiable as Jews, the Doctor's identity as a Nazi remains hidden as the two women lament the prejudice they have experienced in the region: "'The people are so intolerant in Tirol,' said the other sister and her dark bovine eyes rolled heavily from side to side in her thickly powdered face" (140). Readers might assume that these are Pen's thoughts as she "was looking at the two women seated opposite them," (137), or Prochaska's, who speaks only once to the women to kindly advise them that the hotels will most likely all be "full" upon their arrival in Kirchstadt. But the anti-Semitic thoughts about the women are never attributed to Pen or Prochaska. Rather, they are presented as the matter-of-fact descriptions from an omniscient narrator, whose point of view the reader has come to accept. (Who, after all, would refer to Pen as "the girl," save for the two women, who of course would not describe themselves in these anti-Semitic terms?) The effect for the reader is the reproduction of an insistent anti-Semitism that is all the more pervasive because we cannot safely distance ourselves from it by attributing it to the Nazis in the novel.

Left just with that, one would certainly question Boyle's motives, but the scene on the train is immediately followed by an important scene on the mountain top as Prochaska lights the fires and Pen looks on. As Pen and Prochaska attempt to climb to safety from those who would imprison them for this prohibited act, "their two hearts spoke the same inexplicably youthful and inexplicably terrible words, saying":

Nothing having brought us here or together except the flesh of our bodies, the intoxication of movement, the mystery of the darkness together, nothing having any significance except those things we have not done before, our own knowledge of those things to be seized with the hands, the eyes, the lips, the limbs even while the mind is shed as cowardice is shed, disdained like caution, the mind cast off and even the reason for it cast aside .... (174)

As Pen and Prochaska explain the motivation that drives them to light these fires, they use the language of physical desire to describe what they feel, but cannot speak, as they watch the swastikas burn on the mountainside. But although the immediacy and physicality of this moment is highlighted, there is equal emphasis in this passage on all that is absent from their minds and hearts as they make this symbolic statement of support for the Nazis. "Nothing" is important save for "every instant, every breath that's taken, NOW" (174). The "inexplicably terrible" lure of this moment is clear, and so is the loss; implicit in this passage is the idea that this political activity is simply about the thrill of doing something one has never done before, jettisoning the "mind" and "reason" and calling that the ability to "shed cowardice."

In Boyle's case, the danger in bringing together politics and literature in 1936 is that *Death of a Man* may not only reproduce fascist thinking, but reproduce the desire for it.[13] But Boyle takes that risk in order to capture the complex role that desire plays in the rise of the Nazi party in Austria. *Death of a Man* is about the desire for fascism itself, what Jacqueline Rose, in her reading of Sylvia Plath's controversial poem, "Daddy," calls "the mark of a desire that should not speak its name" (232). Thus, while most critics conclude that Boyle uses the love affair between Pen and Prochaska to personalize the political, as a way to humanize her characters, Boyle is making a direct connection between Pen's desire for the Nazi Doctor Prochaska and Prochaska's desire to be a part of the Nazi party.[14] To say that Boyle uses a romantic relationship to make the political personal would be, after all, to rest in that dichotomy between the personal and the political. Rather, *Death of a Man* explores the complexity of the personal human attraction to fascism, what Boyle calls, the "almost inexplicable fascination of Hitler" (quoted in Spanier, *Kay Boyle* 120).

To this end, Boyle's novel represents the ambivalence of desire, the simultaneous attraction and repulsion that makes up the complexity of this human emotion. Never is this doubleness of desire more clear than in the scene described above on the mountaintop. Just moments earlier, Pen is described as thoroughly seduced by the power of "their own supremely shining cross. … They stood like children staring, their eyes fixed raptly on it, their lips parted, watching the separate living worms of flames moving tenderly, vulnerably in the balloons that cupped and magnified their light" (173). At the same time, however, Pen is clearly troubled by the fact that the officials at the ski competition did not allow a Jewish man (significantly, the brother of the two women on the train) to compete in the ski meet. As they hike away from the fires, Pen explains: "There was something I wanted to ask you," to which the doctor responds that Pen should save her breath, focus on her body, not her thoughts (176). But Pen is persistent, if a bit reticent: "'That Jew, she said, working her way up hand over hand by the sticks with the leather straps over her wrists. 'Why can't they let a man jump—'" (176). But at just the moment when it seems that the novel will disrupt the xenophobic frenzy these fires seem to provoke in Pen and Prochaska, Pen oscillates back to an unthinking, unquestioning allegiance to what the fires represent. The Doctor does not respond to Pen's question, and Pen suddenly focuses her attention and childish hatred on the men in the distance who have found their fires and begin to stamp them out with their feet: "Damn them, damn them, oh God damn them. ... She stood holding hard to her sticks, crying almost, watching them with anger as they did what they had climbed to do" (176).

In reviewing the history of the critical responses to *Death of a Man*, it is important to note that the way Boyle chose to write the story of the political events she saw first hand in Austria—emphasizing the ambivalence of her characters and the indeterminacy of language itself—has remained the central point of contention in critical discussions of this novel for more than fifty years. However, despite the consensus that *Death of a Man* represents "a synthesis of Kay Boyle's aesthetic and social concerns" (Spanier, *Kay Boyle* 116), examinations of Boyle's aesthetic and political concerns in the novel have been kept almost entirely separate. For example, while critics Burton Hatlen and Marilyn Elkins explain that Boyle integrates discussions of gender and "the personal" into her treatment of the politics of war by setting her tale of the love affair between Prochaska and Pen in the Tyrol region just before World War II, the aesthetics of the text are treated as an entirely separate issue. For the most part, critics have seen Boyle's experimentation with language in the novel, her use of an often surrealistic narrative style, as a reflection of her lingering concern with modernist aesthetics, rather than a deliberate choice on her part.[15]

However, as Suzanne Clark argues, rather than working from aesthetically experimental to socially engaged, Boyle is "working instead at multiple and complex borders" (129). While Sandra Whipple Spanier sees *Death of a Man* as a text in which Boyle "continue[s] to experiment with language" (*Kay Boyle* 123) just before she jettisons her aesthetic concerns altogether in order to fully address social issues, I want to argue that Boyle's "hallucination of the word," her concern for the indeterminacy and power of language in this novel, is precisely what enables her to present the realities of the political and historical moment she writes about. To this end, I want to close my essay with an examination of the ways in which *Death of a Man* blurs not only the borders we construct between the personal and the political, but also those we construct between the aesthetic and the political. For Boyle, the blurring of these borders is inevitable, as she makes clear in a novel that highlights the direct connection between modernist aesthetics and modern politics.

From the first pages of the text, *Death of a Man* demonstrates the inextricable bonds between language and fascism. In the opening scene of the novel, as Prochaska climbs in the mountains around Feldbruck on his day off from the hospital, he describes his political struggle in linguistic terms: "Here was his country, small enough now almost to be held in the palm of his hand, but this was only for a little. The shape of his country would be altered, as the shape of his own life would be altered, and this was a little time of silence to be passed before the articulation of the end" (5). As the novel progresses, Boyle presents a community enveloped in this "little time of silence," made up of citizens whose distrust and fury lead them to communicate by whispering in beer halls, lighting swastika fires, and throwing bombs. As the narrator explains, the political situation in Austria "had come to be known now throughout their country without the communication of speech" (72). Significantly, the only person with the ability to speak strongly and freely in this novel is "A," Boyle's thinly veiled portrait of Adolf Hitler, the man whose name his followers cannot yet fully "articulate."

But while *Death of a Man* highlights the necessary silence of the Nazi party in Austria at the time, the novel also reflects the fact that the real danger seems to be, ironically, in successful communication. The success of fascism, "the end" Prochaska fantasizes about, will come only through "articulation." The novel explains that "articulation" by the Nazi characters is both an explicitly "modern" phenomenon, and a dangerous one. We learn early on in the novel that: "Dr. Prochaska's speech was different from the others for he belonged to Vienna, to the intellect, to the relentless, modern, scientific thing. ... He was not at all in doubt ... for he knew he was part of the unconfused and virile youth of his country, of the new manhood that was stirring" (19). This "new manhood" is, of course, the rising Nazi Party in Austria. Alice Kaplan explains the direct connection between this political movement and the newness, the "difference" of the language of fascism. Fascism in Europe between the two World Wars was, Kaplan explains, "a new poetic language, an immediate vocal presence, an entirely new way of writing and speaking about the state and the world" (3). *Death of a Man* demonstrates the direct connection between "the unconfused and virile youth" Prochaska is a part of and this "entirely new way of writing and speaking about the state and the world" (3): "Fascist subjects are virile, phallic, their devotion to the language they learn is total, boundary-less" (Kaplan 10).

In *Death of a Man,* the "relentless," "unconfused," and "virile" language of those who support the Nazi cause is portrayed as both frightening and dangerous. In this way, the novel reflects Boyle's belief that "the linguists of the Nazi states, as we know, made a political weapon of the German language; a weapon more effective than any history had ever known before—a total weapon—that degraded the dignity of human speech to the level of baying wolves" (*Talks* 217). Clearly, for Boyle, this language of modernity is not a purely aesthetic concern, but a force that can wield destructive political power. The ways in which the Nazis have transformed the German language and those who speak it is central in the novel. When Dr. Prochaska retreats to the lavish apartment he lives in below the hospital ward he sits "listening to … the words of the men speaking the German tongue from Germany, serene, powerful and certain" (21). Ironically, it is the "relentless[ly]" "unconfused" and "certain" nature of Nazi speech that makes it both so powerful and so barbaric for Boyle. As the novel explains, language becomes destructive when it loses its ambiguity, its multiplicity of meanings.

The dangerous and intoxicating power with which the Nazis have infused language is clear later, in one of the final and pivotal scenes of the novel, when Dr. Prochaska meets another Party member in the mountains to deliver some money and papers. As the courier describes one of Hitler's recent radio speeches and "the voice speaking it, like great music, like a great poem being sung!" (297) the Doctor thinks to himself that "Like all of them … he was drunk, stupefied, on the thought of death and the rapture of his own fearlessness to meet it" (298). It is not only the disregard this young Nazi has for his own life, but the scripted quality of his speech that awakens the doctor to the humanity his political beliefs undermine. The novel continuously highlights the way in which such precise and controlled language has the power to enthrall a nation to the point of its own destruction. As the narrator explains: "The prescribed lines were recited, the indicated gestures made in observance of that mysteriously learned and never-written script which their own caution had conceived for them, actors in perpetual rehearsal of a play in which the entire nation was cast" (155).

Thus, the narrator also demonstrates that this intoxication stems, oddly enough, from the dehumanizing power of language. In an earlier scene in a local beer-hall, Prochaska listens to a Nazi informant and his words seem to take on a life of their own, overshadowing the individuality and humanity of both the men: "[he] had not the shape of one man but many, listening for this message as it came, impersonal as a gramophone disk being played, through the dispensable human mouth piece that was for the moment the musician, and would be at another time the hotel-keeper, and at another a voice speaking on the radio" (112).[16] The idea that what the Nazi party has done through language is to make the human being "dispensable" is driven home for Prochaska as he listens to the "rapture" of the courier "on the thought of death" (298). This Nazi courier is elated, made "drunk" by the fact that he is just a "dispensable human mouth piece" in a crowd; he even feels empowered by his anonymity and lack of individuality. This is just the ominous power of fascism according to Benjamin: "Its [Mankind's] self-alienation has reached such a degree that it can experience its own destruction as an aesthetic pleasure of the first order" (242). As Alice Kaplan explains, this "imagined imperviousness to destruction" stems from an "elation" associated with "alienation"— in a "bizarre" and simultaneous "introjection and projection … a man rejoices as he disappears into a crowd, deems himself uniquely privileged for doing so" (6).

While Prochaska seems both chilled by and attracted to this quality of fascism, it is just this quality that Pen finds problematic in his blind belief in the Party. At one level, Pen is drawn to Prochaska because he is, unlike herself, so sure of what he will become. At the same time, she leaves him for his ability to embrace the Nazi cause without question, for "believing what they tell you just as its told to you" (209). She demands: "how can you go on swallowing it and swallowing it, why doesn't something start choking you in the middle of every speech they're roaring at you, each one a little bit louder than the other so you won't have the peace and quiet to put two and two together?" (209).[17]

The answer to Pen's question, the novel tells us, lies in the fact that Prochaska no longer thinks of himself as human, but as a "sign" in a language system devoted completely to composing the future out of words. He explains: "I am no longer a man, do you understand? I am no longer myself even, believing as I do in the future. I am a signal, a sign of what is about to happen" (91). Significantly, Prochaska uses the same language to describe himself and the fires he sets on the mountaintops: these fires are "a sign of what is going to happen ... and to maintain we are ready for it" (114). He and the fires are part of a political movement, one that manifests itself in the form of a new linguistic system. In his discussion of Italian fascism, Andrew Hewitt explains that this double move, the "virtual effacement of the body" coupled with a reformulation of the body as "signifying machine" (49), was an integral part of the Futurist movement.[18] In much the same way, Boyle explains that although Prochaska's "death" was not a literal one in the novel, he effectively dies through this transformation from body to "signifying machine": "Death in Prochaska's case was not necessarily of the flesh, but of the free will, because of the ideological choice he had made" ("A Note" 324). Thus, *Death of a Man* explores both Prochaska's attraction to the loss of humanity that fascism brings about, and the concomitant power Nazi subjects felt as part of a new system of language.

But while Prochaska draws his strength from the "serene, powerful and certain" (21) language of the Nazis, Boyle offers a critique of fascism by repeatedly highlighting the difficulty and uncertainty inherent in language itself. Although Pen wants Prochaska to find his own language, separate from the dogma of the Party he embraces, their relationship is based on all they do not, and cannot, talk about. In fact, their relationship is one born out of silence. For example, the narrator describes the moment when the doctor realizes his desire for the bitter and wounded young American woman as one of literal silencing: "then his eyes met hers again and his breath came suddenly short as if she had laid her hand for silence and in caution on his mouth" (46). Later, after Pen and Prochaska have gone their separate ways, the same image of Prochaska's mouth (this time in successful articulation of language), becomes central to his understanding that he must be with her again: "he saw his own mouth shape a word, shape a name in anguish and wonder, and his heart filled up with joy as if he had been given speech again at last. 'Pendennis, Pendennis,' he said" (268).

This moment of language acquisition—"as if he had been given speech again at last"—is, significantly, one of self-actualization for Prochaska: "he saw his own face in a mirror in the station restaurant and suddenly stopped short, as if for the first time knowing he was the man watching behind those eyes" (268). Although this scene seems to offer some hope that after at last seeing himself for who he is, Prochaska can be with Pen, the two lovers never see each other again. As Prochaska goes to Vienna to find Pen, she boards a train to Feldbruck and their trains pass in the night. It is important to note that although Prochaska does finally speak again, in a language very different from the Nazi rhetoric he has been spouting, he never actually speaks Pen's name *to* Pen, and thus does not successfully communicate with her.

The novel not only underscores all that Prochaska and Pen do not say to one another, but demonstrates that the frustrated communication between them stems from nationalist allegiances. Prochaska's first thought when he sees (and hears) Pen and her British husband on the hiking trails in the opening scene of the novel is that they literally don't speak the same language: "The strangeness of the foreigner's language was what drove him off, he thought: he had no ear for people who spoke with an accent, and he could not speak the English tongue" (8). Later, when Pen comes to tell Prochaska that she has sent her husband home to England so that she and the doctor can be together, he experiences this moment as one of language acquisition, not romance. She explains, "I've sent Wagtail or whatever his name is home—" "Home—? said Dr. Prochaska, pronouncing it slowly, carefully, as if this might be the word of some new language he was learning, and he wanted to be sure" (78).

Although the novel points to the possibility that through their relationship Prochaska and Pen might somehow find a "new language" with which to communicate, we quickly learn that this is impossible because of the national and political realities of their situation. Prochaska seems to know that unless Pen can fully understand his allegiance to the Nazi Party, their communication, and thus their relationship, will fail. He implores her to look at pictures of his family and hear about his upbringing in Vienna: "I want you to see the photographs of my family … you do not know anything about me. I wish to make it possible for you to comprehend. … I want you to believe in what I am doing" (83, 92). For Prochaska, the political and the personal are inevitably intertwined. He explains his political allegiances as "these things that cannot be separated from myself—" (84). Pen too sees that their relationship is doomed by national and political forces. Certainly, their differences make their ability to communicate awkward, if not impossible. Pen explains, "my father's in Florida playing golf, yours is lying flat on his face [in a frame] on the rug over there" (93). But this personal difference is clearly a reflection of their different political allegiances for Pen: "God damn my speechless little country, Herr Doktor, it hasn't a word to say to yours" (93).

The fact that the political is, most importantly, experienced at the personal level is further manifested in *Death of a Man* as Boyle's own traumatic experience in Austria in the 1930s is explicitly depicted in various scenes throughout the novel. One particularly riveting scene recounts, nearly verbatim, Boyle's experience of being in a hotel in Innsbruck in 1934 when it was bombed. Pregnant and awaiting the birth of their first son, Boyle and her husband checked into a room in the hotel above the beer garden. Just after midnight a bomb was thrown at the anti-Nazi printing press next door, detected by a guard, and thrown into the beer garden of the hotel, where it exploded. Boyle underscores the connection between the personal and the political in *Death of a Man* by introducing this bombing in the midst of a mother/daughter conflict in the bathroom. In the novel, the bomb explodes in the hotel that the Nazi party boss Praxlmann owns. At the time of the bombing, Praxlmann's wife is lecturing their daughter (who sits in the bathtub) on marriage. When Cilli explains that she perhaps would like to marry a doctor like Prochaska, her mother flies into a rage and "twisting her head back she forced the soap between the jaws, the slithering, teeth-scarred and foaming substance in and wiped it across Cilli's tongue" (230). Immediately after this moment, with the explosive force of her mother's rage still hanging in the air, a bomb explodes outside in the beer garden and the mother leaves the bathroom, abandoning her daughter who stands naked among broken shards of window glass. Here, the personal and the political become indistinguishable from one another. Boyle takes her personal experience of a political act (the bombing) and sets it in the most personal of moments (the fight between a mother and her naked daughter), while highlighting the irony of the bombing as a political act (the bomb intended for the anti-Nazi press explodes in the beer garden where Nazi party members meet each night to plan their political takeover). Moreover, even the conflict here between mother and daughter cannot be construed as strictly "personal"—Muti Praxlmann's rage stems from her reaction to Prochaska, a highly politicized figure in this novel.

In the end, it was Boyle's emphasis on the personal experience of political trauma that presented the largest problem for her readers. Many critics believed that Boyle's personal experiences in Austria in the 1930s clouded her political allegiances and even served as a source of sympathy for her Nazi characters. However, *Death of a Man* highlights the inextricable relationship between the personal and the political in order to explore, "on a human level," why people in the Austrian Tyrol joined the Nazi cause. Moreover, *Death of a Man* demonstrates that only through "the revolution of the word" can writers portray the "human level" at which people experienced the trauma of the rise of fascism. Boyle insists on the central role that language played in creating fascism and reproduces the reality of political trauma through the "hallucination of the word" (13). It is just this insistence that aesthetic practice and political meaning cannot be separated from one another that makes Boyle an important figure in our reexamination of the relationship between modernism and politics.

Notes

1. These studies approach this issue from a variety of perspectives. Allyson Booth's *Postcards from the Trenches: Negotiating the Space between Modernism and the First World War*; Susan Schweik's examination of American women poets and the Second World War, *A Gulf So Deeply Cut*; and the recent Special Issue of *Modern Fiction Studies* devoted to "Modernisms and Modern Wars," examine how "high" modernists Virginia Woolf, Gertrude Stein, H.D., Marianne Moore, and William Faulkner (among others) address the political realities of war. Lisa Rado's collection, *Re-Reading Modernism: New Directions in Feminist Criticism*, is only one of the many recent studies that reassess the political implications of "high" modernism's relationship to mass culture between the two world wars. I am thinking here of influential books by Michael Tratner, Rita Barnard, Walter Kalaidjian, Cary Nelson, Barbara Foley, Laura Hapke, and Paula Rabinowitz. The 1990s has also seen the publication of a number of works that focus on the politics of individual modernist artists, among them, Alan Filreis's recent book on Wallace Stevens.
2. In the 1990s, critics have debated the origins and resilience of this formalist division of aesthetics and politics. Andrew Hewitt traces this "dissociation" of aesthetics and politics (38) in two 1968 texts which exclude the avant-garde art of Futurism from the modernist canon. Hewitt explains that this exclusion was based on the claim that Futurism was either not fascist because it was modernist, or could not be called "modernist" because of its fascist politics. He argues that Fredric Jameson's study of Wyndham Lewis is the text that, by bringing together a discussion of fascism and modernism, began the study of "fascist modernism" (41). While Hewitt traces a specific historical moment when aesthetic and political aims of art were polarized (and reunited, in Jameson's case), Barbara Eckstein explains that there is a new generation of literary critics ("the descendants of the New Critics") who adamantly "maintain the separation of art and politics" (4).
3. Carlston draws here on the work of Cairns Craig, who explains that we "refuse" to spell out the complexities of fascism "in order to preserve in ourselves the emotional recoil upon which our disgust for it is based, an emotional recoil which may prevent us recognizing elements in our thought which we share with Fascism" (262).
4. The idea that modernist aesthetics could not capture political realities stemmed, at least in part, from the fact that the modernist project of the 1930s and 1940s stood in contradistinction to the overtly political work of radical writers of the same period (e.g., Mike Gold, Tillie Olsen, Meridel LeSueur, and Harlem Renaissance writers Langston Hughes and Claude McKay). For an in-depth study of the radical writers of the 1930s, see Mullen and Linkon's *Radical Revisions: Rereading 1930s Culture*.
5. Studies of male modernists and fascism include books by Robert Casillo, Cairns Craig, Peter Nicholls, Michael North, and Tim Redman. Ground breaking work by Jane Marcus on Djuna Barnes's treatment of fascism has only recently been followed by Erin G. Carlston's 1998 study, *Thinking Fascism*, which has shaped much of my thinking in this essay. One other recent text, Jean Gallagher's fascinating 1998 study, *The World Wars Through the Female Gaze*, includes a chapter on the relationship between vision, visual

culture and fascism.

6.   Erin G. Carlston's study of texts by female modernists that take fascism as their subject is a direct response to the fact that there has been "considerable discussion about the relation between men modernists and fascist politics, [but that] much of this critical work has tended to overlook both women writers and questions of gender and sexuality in the political movements of the modernist period" (4). Carlston is more specifically responding to the fact that "readers who *have* addressed these questions have frequently assumed women writers were necessarily antagonistic to fascist ideologies" (4). Margaret Higgonet links this assumption to a larger cultural "belief that men are naturally fierce and warlike, while women, as mothers, have an affinity for peace" (1). I trace this assumption in the reception of Gertrude Stein's war writings in my article in the special issue of *Modern Fiction Studies* on Modernisms and Modern Wars.

7.   I want to make it clear that I am not equating fascism and Nazism, but looking at the rise of the Nazi party in Austria as one facet of fascism in Europe. I also recognize the trend that Erin G. Carlston defines: "One dominant approach [to defining fascism] ever since the war, both in scholarship and in the popular media, has been to subsume all fascist phenomena under the history of the Nazi regime" (9).

8.   I want to thank Chris Castiglia for his invaluable insight into the simultaneous absence and presence of both trauma and mothers in this scene. For further discussion of fascism and mothering, see Alice Kaplan, pages 10-11, and Virginia Woolf's *A Room of One's Own* 107. Interestingly, while Kaplan argues for the "need to realize how dependent the phallic fascist is on the mother-nation, mother-machine, mother-war" (11), Woolf sees fascism as a movement that depends on a motherless state, doomed because it wants to give birth to art and artists through "incubators," bypassing the female body (107).

9.   According to F.L. Carsten: "In June 1933 the National Socialist Party and its subordinate organization were dissolved by the Austrian government and any activity for them became an offence" (249).

10. Interestingly, Alice Kaplan uses the same language these reviewers did to describe her own struggle to stay afloat in the sea of fascist rhetoric: "Even from within my struggle to historicize, fascism makes me feel 'way in over my head'" (7).

11. The fact that Boyle's politics were consistently Leftist and that she was "a revolutionary of lyric language" (Clark 128) is seldom debated. Kay Boyle's mother was a leader in the Farmer-Labor Party who served as the honorary chairperson of the World Women's Party in 1930s, and Boyle herself was a self-described expatriate who wrote for avantgarde "little magazines" (among them *Broom, Poetry, transition*).

12. I agree with Carlston that a "more self-critical approach [is] . . . endangered by an overemphasis on individual biographies . . . biographically based criticism is one way of containing the far-reaching effects of fascist discourse" (15). I provide this biographical information as a way to contextualize the debate over Boyle's pro-Nazi sympathies, not as a basis for her condemnation.

13. Carlston asks readers to focus specifically on the desire that fascist texts produce in their readers: "we must ask what part our own illegitimate desire plays in our fear, and consider the possibility that the real anxiety underlying the criticism of a broad definition of fascism is that such an approach might reveal the fascist elements of texts that we have read with 'innocent' pleasure, and even force us to acknowledge the seductiveness of more clearly fascist texts we would love to hate" (16).

14. Pen's rageful desire for the approval of her own father, a tyrannical toothpaste manufacturer who looms in the distant American resorts of Florida, also fits nicely into this paradigm. Immediately after Prochaska tries to explain the way that Austrians feel about Hitler, as "the Saviour" (88), Pen announces: "there was my father" (89). She goes on to describe his complete control over her life: "He used to make me do everything I didn't

want to do" (90). As Jacqueline Rose explains: "victimization by this feared and desired father is one of the fantasies at the heart of fascism, one of the universal attractions for women of fascism itself" (232). For further discussion of the "erotic dimension of fascism" (14), see Kaplan.

15. Sandra Whipple Spanier explains that *Death of a Man* holds an important place in Boyle's *oeuvre* because it marks her "growing tendency to treat matters of the contemporary social world that in the next decade would come to supersede her commitment to aesthetic revolution" (*Kay Boyle* 123-4). However, Suzanne Clark explains why attempts to map out a continuum in Boyle's work from experimental to historically and politically engaged is problematic. She writes: "Boyle's early fiction seems experimental but not political, and as her later fiction becomes less experimental, it also seems more involved in the context of history, more firmly embedded in historical time. ... But this is misleading. ... As the novels become 'clearer,' and more clearly lodged in a sense of political history that defies dominant positions, they also become more rhetorically challenging to familiar (family) ideologies of human relationship and more clearly *different* from familiar male narratives" (Clark 145). But as Jacqueline Rose explains, a text that is anti-patriarchal is not necessarily pacifist, because "fascism must surely be distinguished from patriarchy, even if in some sense it can be seen as its effect" (235).

16. Alice Kaplan argues that radio played an integral part in the rise of fascism in Europe between the wars. Explaining that "the work of the dictator, the one who speaks" is literally "dictating" over the radio (8), Kaplan describes the effect of the "fragmentation of perception" (4) that radio elicits as a necessary component of the "worship of ... the recorded, amplified voice" (5).

17. Kaplan explains that simultaneous introjection and projection are the dual movement of the Nazi: "the fascist subject incorporates the state, experiences the state within himself: he *swallows* what he wants and spits out the rest in angry talk" (6, emphasis mine).

18. Hewitt makes an important distinction between how the Futurists and the Nazis conceptualized the Jewish body. For Futurists like Marinetti, Hewitt argues, the body was "simply a fetish" (50), but for the Nazis, Jews were literally the "*embodiment* of the *abstract*" (52).

References

Barnard, Rita. *The Great Depression and the Culture of Abundance: Kenneth Fearing, Nathanael West, and Mass Culture in the 1930s*. New York: Cambridge University Press, 1995.

Benjamin, Walter. "The Work of Art in the Age of Mechanical Reproduction." *Illuminations*. New York: Harcourt, Brace & World, 1968; New York: Schocken, 1969. 217-42.

Blair, Sara. "Modernism and the Politics of Culture." *The Cambridge Companion to Modernism*. Ed. Michael Levenson. Cambridge: Cambridge University Press, 1999. 157-73.

Booth, Allyson. *Postcards from the Trenches: Negotiating the Space between Modernism and the First World War*. New York: Oxford University Press, 1996.

Boyle, Kay. "A Note from the Author." *Death of a Man*. New York: New Directions, 1989.

Burra, Peter. Review of *Death of a Man*, by Kay Boyle. *Spectator* 2 October 1936: 560.

——. *Death of a Man*. 1936. New York: New Directions, 1989.

——. Interview. *Talks With Authors*. Ed. Charles F. Madden. Carbondale: Southern Illinois University Press, 1968. 215-35.

Canby, Henry Seidel. "Kay Boyle's Sketch of a Likable Nazi." Review of *Death of a Man*, by Kay Boyle. *The Saturday Evening Review* 10 October 1936: 12.

Carlston, Erin G. *Thinking Fascism: Sapphic Modernism and Fascist Modernity*. Stanford: Stanford University Press, 1998.

Carsten, F.L. *Fascist Movements in Austria: From Schonerer to Hitler*. London: Sage Publications, 1977.

Caruth, Cathy. *Unclaimed Experience: Trauma, Narrative, and History*. Baltimore: Johns Hopkins University Press, 1996.

Casillo, Robert. *The Genealogy of Demons: Anti-Semitism, Fascism, and the Myths of Ezra Pound*. Evanston: Northwestern University Press, 1988.

Clark, Suzanne. *Sentimental Modernism: Women Writers and the Revolution of the Word*. Bloomington: Indiana University Press, 1991.

Craig, Cairns. *Yeats, Eliot, Pound and the Politics of Poetry*. Pittsburgh: University of Pittsburgh Press, 1982.

Davis, Phoebe Stein. "'Even cake gets to have another meaning': History, Narrative, and 'Daily Living' in Gertrude Stein's World War II Writings." *Modern Fiction Studies* 44.3 (Fall 1998): 568-607.

DeKoven, Marianne. "The Politics of Modernist Form." *New Literary History* 23 (1992): 675-90.

Eckstein, Barbara J. *The Language of Fiction in a World of Pain: Reading Politics as Paradox*. Philadelphia: University of Pennsylvania Press, 1990.

Elkins, Marilyn. *Metamorphosizing the Novel: Kay Boyle's Narrative Innovations*. New York: Peter Lang, 1993.

Ferguson, Otis. "The Brown Blouses of Vienna." Review of *Death of a Man*, by Kay Boyle. *New Republic* 21 October 1936: 322.

Filreis, Alan. *Modernism From Right to Left : Wallace Stevens, The Thirties, and Literary Radicalism*. New York: Cambridge University Press, 1994.

Foley, Barbara. *Radical Representations: Politics and Form in U.S. Proletarian Fiction: 1929-1941*. Durham: Duke University Press, 1993.

Gallagher, Jean. *World Wars Through the Female Gaze*. Carbondale: Southern Illinois University Press, 1998.

Hapke, Laura. *Daughters of the Great Depression: Women, Work, and Fiction in the American 1930s*. Athens: The University of Georgia Press, 1995.

Hatlen, Burton. "Introduction." *Death of a Man*. New York: New Directions, 1989. v-xii.

Hewitt, Andrew. "Fascist Modernism, Futurism, and Post-Modernity." *Fascism, Aesthetics, and Culture*. Ed. Richard J. Golsan. Hanover: University Press of New England, 1992.

Higgonet, Margaret R. "Cassandra's Question: Do Women Write War Novels?" *Borderwork: Feminist Engagement With Comparative Literature*. Ed. Margaret R. Higgonet. Ithaca: Cornell University Press, 1994. 144-61.

Jolas, Eugene. "Revolution of the Word." *transition* 16-17 (June 1929): 13.

Kalaidjian, Walter. *American Culture Between the Wars: Revisionary Modernism and Postmodern Critique*. New York: Columbia University Press, 1993.

Kaplan, Alice Yaeger. *Reproductions of Banality: Fascism, Literature, and French Intellectual Life*. Minneapolis: University of Minnesota Press, 1986.

"Nazi Idyll." Review of *Death of a Man*, by Kay Boyle. *Time* 12 October 1936: 87.

Marcus, Jane. "Laughing at Leviticus: *Nightwood* as Woman's Circus Epic." *Silence and Power: A Reevaluation of Djuna Barnes*. Ed. Mary Lynn Broe. Carbondale: Southern Illinois University Press, 1991. 221-51.

Mellen, Joan. *Kay Boyle: Author of Herself*. New York: Farrar, Straus & Giroux, 1994.

"Modernisms and Modern Wars." Special Issue of *Modern Fiction Studies*. Ed. Margot Norris. 44.3 (Fall 1998).

Mullen, Bill, and Sherry Lee Linkon, eds. *Radical Revisions: Rereading 1930s Culture*. Urbana: University of Illinois Press, 1996.

Nelson, Cary. *Repression and Recovery: Modern American Poetry and the Politics of Cultural Memory, 1910-1945*. Madison: University of Wisconsin Press, 1989.

Nicholls, Peter. *Ezra Pound: Politics, Economics, Writing*. New York: Macmillan, 1984.

North, Michael. *The Political Aesthetic of Yeats, Eliot, and Pound*. Cambridge: Cambridge University Press, 1991.

Rabinowitz, Paula. *Labor and Desire: Women's Revolutionary Fiction in Depression America*. Chapel Hill: University of North Carolina Press, 1991.

Rado, Lisa, ed. *Re-Reading Modernism: New Directions in Feminist Criticism*. New York: Garland, 1994.

Redman, Tim. *Ezra Pound and Italian Fascism*. Cambridge: Cambridge University Press, 1991.

Rose, Jacqueline. *The Haunting of Sylvia Plath*. London: Virago, 1991.

Schweik, Susan. *A Gulf So Deeply Cut*. Madison: University of Wisconsin Press, 1991.

Smith, Valerie. "'Circling the Subject': History and Narrative in *Beloved*." *Approaches to Teaching the Novels of Toni Morrison*. Ed. Nellie McKay and Kathryn Earle. New York: Modern Language Association, 1997. 342-55.

Spanier, Sandra Whipple. *Kay Boyle: Artist and Activist*. Carbondale: Southern Illinois University Press, 1986.

——. "Kay Boyle: No Past Tense Permitted." *Twentieth Century Literature* 34.3 (1988): 245-57.

Tratner, Michael. *Modernism and Mass Politics: Joyce, Woolf, Eliot, Yeats*. Stanford: Stanford University Press, 1995.

Uehling, Edward M. "Tails You Lose: Kay Boyle's War Fiction." *Twentieth Century Literature* 34.3 (1988): 375-83.

Van Doren, Mark. "Under the Swastika." *Nation* 24 October 1936: 494.

Woolf, Virginia. *A Room of One's Own*. New York: Harcourt Brace Jovanovich, 1929.

8 Eating the Maid: Leonora Carrington's "The Debutante"[1]
Natalya Lusty

"Nanny do lets pretend that I'm a hungry hyena and you're a bone!"
—*Through the Looking Glass*

The role and representation of women within the Surrealist movement has continued to be one of the most contested and difficult sites of modernism. Whilst women functioned as muses, scribes and emblems of and for the revolutionary cause of Surrealism, especially within the early part of the movement, the large number of women writers, artists, intellectuals and political activists who became associated with the movement during the 1930s and 40s,[2] and who have only more recently become objects of intellectual inquiry and evaluation, have inevitably shifted the contours of the movement and its relationship to the wider cultural and historical zone of modernism. For if, as Walter Benjamin suggested, Surrealism functioned as the radical other of modernism, women were the figurative and literal embodiment of that alterity. In his astute reading of Breton's *Nadja*, Benjamin defines the relationship between Breton and Nadja as akin to the relationship of the gentleman and his beloved in courtly love poetry. He writes that "The Lady, in esoteric love, matters least. So, too for Breton. He is closer to the things that Nadja is close to than to her" (181). Benjamin's analysis draws attention to the essentially traditional basis of Breton's emancipatory vocabulary, reminding us of the problematic tension between Nadja as the inspired crazy muse and Nadja as embodied historical subject, who, because of her eccentricity or poverty, or both, is eventually institutionalized. Benjamin's comments also reflect the ways in which Surrealism mined the experience of the Other—"the mad," "the criminal," "the primitive"[3]—in order to unleash "the socially transformative potential of repressed libidinal forces" (Cohen 110), and which served to substantiate its anti-bourgeois political and aesthetic rhetoric. It is during this second wave (from the 1930s to the early 1940s), a period in which Breton occupied an increasingly entrepreneurial role, that Leonora Carrington made her debut into the Surrealist movement.[4] Only twenty years of age, and striking because of her dark Irish beauty and eccentric humor, Carrington soon won Breton's ardent admiration and support, and he promoted her as an "authentic" surrealist heroine.[5] His inclusion of Carrington's "The Debutante" in the important and canonical *Anthology of Black Humour* reinforced his admiration for her work and particular brand of transgressive independence.

British born and raised, Carrington was introduced to Max Ernst at the International Surrealist exhibition in London in 1937. After a trip to Cornwall

163

with members and associates of the Surrealist group, including Max Ernst, Man Ray, Nusch and Paul Eluard, Lee Miller and Roland Penrose, Carrington decided to move to Paris and resumed the intimate and collaborative relationship begun with Ernst in England. However, as tensions within the Surrealist group intensified and the animosity between Ernst's wife, Marie-Berthe, and Carrington became intolerable, Ernst and Carrington relocated to St Martin-d'Ardéche in the South of France. Here, in the final years before the war, they began working and living together and playing host to a string of visitors. They collaborated on publications, paintings and sculptures and exhibited in the two important Surrealist shows in Paris in 1938 and in Amsterdam in 1939. In this period Carrington wrote what would become her most anthologized work—the masterfully macabre "The Debutante." In this story the image of the debutante as both child and woman, caught in the transitory and difficult space of adolescence, evokes the surrealist category of the *femme-enfant* and records the cross-class commodification and cultural exchange of women's bodies.

The theme of unruly adolescence evoked by the debutante's violent resistance to her "coming out" also recalls two notorious criminal cases involving women in Paris in the mid 1930s, that of the Papin Sisters and Violette Nozière. Like Nadja, these women were close to the things that Surrealism wanted to be close to—psychosis and criminality—and were championed as emblems of Surrealism's anti-bourgeois aesthetic and social revolt. Their crimes were read as evidence of a backlash against an increasingly corrupt and hypocritical social and political post-war France. But in paying homage to the crimes of both the Papin sisters and Violette Nozière, the Surrealists seemed to overlook the real sense of trauma suffered by these women, illustrating the degree to which the figure of the "ruined" woman is problematic as a metaphor for and embodiment of surrealist ideology.

Originally written in French and published as part of the collection *La Dame Ovale* in Paris in 1939, "The Debutante" addresses the question of feminine and sexual identity within the sociocultural and political world of the late 1930s, including the changing role of the debutante during this period and the increasingly prevalent participation of women within the Surrealist movement. Throughout the course of this short narrative the body of the debutante, traditionally the commodified emblem of heterosexual and heterosocial ritual, becomes tropologically marked by the disruptive logic of hybridity, effected through the representation of a violent masking. In exploring the themes of masking, passing and transformation, Carrington's text registers the cultural shaping of the feminine body as well as the codes of violence inherent to surrealist aesthetic practice. Presented as an adolescent scene of rebellion, Carrington's debutante experience in "The Debutante," as in other autobiographical commentaries, conjures the racial, sexual and class narratives of violence in the 1930s. Carrington's personal experience of power, resistance and complicity, growing out of her involvement with the Surrealist group, provides the context for these wider social conditions.[6]

Carrington's repeated autobiographical discussion of her experience as a debutante in 1935 thus elliptically signals her other momentous "introduction" shortly afterwards—to the Surrealist group in 1937. In two of Carrington's early Surrealist publications, "The House of Fear" and "The Debutante," Max Ernst and André Breton,[7] respectively, provided introductions which placed Carrington within the dynamic of an erotically charged and entrepreneurial relationship. These texts resonate with a culture of patronage and introduction intrinsic to the operation of Surrealist coterie politics and artistic production and which resembles in part the rituals of debutante culture and its own system of patronage, hierarchy and authenticity. Moreover, in choosing to write her first published stories in French, Carrington signals her rejection of her upper-class English family, at the same time augmenting her affiliation with the Surrealist movement. Carrington's narrative exploration of the commodified body of the debutante in the rite-of-passage rituals of the English upper-class therefore addresses a wider cultural and aesthetic exchange of women, including the exchange of women's literal and figurative bodies within the Surrealist movement. The narrative employs a surrealist aesthetic economy of violence, rebellion and hybridity to offer a satirical account of the world of Edwardian manners. However, it critiques this economy by foregrounding gender and class in a way that disrupts the "revolutionary" rhetoric of canonical Surrealist aesthetic and political ideology.[8] While the violence performed in the narrative reinforces a canonical surrealist taxonomy of violence, through its themes of masking and passing, it also unfolds the dynamics of power inherent in a Surrealist celebration of female violence.

I begin examining the themes of masking and feminine identity in "The Debutante" by turning to Joan Riviere's 1929 essay "Womanliness as a Masquerade" and the personal and public context in which it emerged in order to disclose some of the complexities and contradictions for modernist women writers, artists and intellectuals. As I will show, Riviere's delineation of femininity as masquerade in terms of a theory of aggression and conflict resolution, one that is inflected by the boundaries of race and class, shares certain salient features with Carrington's attempts to represent an epistemology of the self more complex than the conventional Surrealist dichotomization of woman as pure and impure, idealized and debased. Riviere's article is important precisely for the way in which it delineates the politics of praxis for modernist women intellectuals and writers as well as for its tracing of the violence of gendered masking strategies. While I have no evidence of Carrington's familiarity with this piece, I hope that a brief analysis of "Womanliness as a Masquerade" will demonstrate its relevance. Her article opens up a series of questions around masking and performance rituals which become important for my reading of Carrington's aesthetic use of violence and transgression.

First published in the *International Journal of Psychoanalysis* in 1929, Riviere's article contributed to the important work on sexual difference, in particular female sexuality, begun by analysts such as Sigmund Freud and Ernest Jones, Freud's biographer. At the time of the paper's publication, Riviere had been seeing patients of her own for over a decade, having initially been in analysis herself for four years with Jones. She was subsequently analyzed by both Freud and Melanie Klein, with whom she worked for many years helping to develop child analysis. Despite her closeness to two of the most important figures working on female sexuality within psychoanalysis at this time, it is uncanny that neither Jones nor Freud ever responded to her paper. This lack of response almost begs us to assume that the immediate context for the masquerade is a defense against the oppressiveness of sexual identities constructed by a masculinist psychoanalytical tradition.

Riviere begins her essay by analyzing feminine identity within the context of the newly participating intellectual and professional woman. At the center of "Womanliness as a Masquerade" an intellectual woman moves between a "masculine" intellectual professional performance that includes public speaking and writing and a "hyper-feminine" display of flirtatious and coquettish behavior adopted upon completion of her public performance. Under analysis it is revealed that Riviere's subject has "quite conscious feelings of rivalry and superiority" toward many of her male colleagues and that her coquettish behavior toward them "was an unconscious attempt to ward off the anxiety which would ensue on account of the reprisals she anticipated … after her intellectual performance" (137). The subject's masquerade of the "guiltless and innocent" unknowing woman, represented by her display of hyper-femininity, is a strategy that diminishes the success of her intellectual performance. According to both analysand and analyst, this behavior is inappropriate, reflecting the ambivalent cultural position of the intellectual woman in this period: she is damned for performing as a man and damned for performing as a woman to hide her performance as a man.

Riviere concludes that "womanliness … could be assumed and worn as a mask, both to hide the possession of masculinity and to avert the reprisals expected if she were found to possess it" (36). Up to this point Riviere's paper is straightforward, but in a move that posits the radical nature of her anti-essentialist position, she declares that there is no difference between "womanliness," which, by nature of woman's "lack" is only a dissimulation of masculinity; and the masquerade, a dissimulation of dissimulated "masculinity."[9] Thus, the reassurance that the masquerade is just that quickly spills over into the disturbing awareness that there is only ever the mask—a disturbance which constitutes the alienation (and rebellion) of woman's being. Further investigating the analysand's performance of the gender masquerade, Riviere uncovers a series of daydreams and fantasies which are marked by both race and class. The fantasies, originating from the analysand's childhood in the American South, revolve around a fear of attack from a Negro man. These are dealt with by the analysand offering herself sexually to him, to delay and hopefully thwart the imagined attack. In a variation of this scenario the subject under analysis reports that she assumes the menial role of washing clothes so as to disguise both her power and privilege.

It becomes clear, then, that Riviere's analytical development of the "masquerade" has its origin in racialized fantasies of violence and sexualized fantasies of race; scenarios that display the subject's cross-class and cross-race identifications as well as her transgressive sexual desires, and which may serve, according to Ann Pellegrini to "undercut the powerlessness the white woman experiences *vis à vis* the law of the father" (138). In Riviere's narrative the threat of what lies behind the mask is the "darkness" and "danger" that the subject herself imagines: a sexual and racial taboo which has been culturally transferred and which if crossed threatens to unleash the retributive paternal fear of miscegenation. And yet clearly the masking strategy is a performance that stages a rebellion as well as an attempt at mastery and control. Pellegrini argues: "Putting herself in the place of a lower-class woman, black or white, or a black man, the white woman can look back at and down on her other(ed) self. Because Riviere nowhere explicitly addresses the social conditions or historical context in which the woman's psychical defenses against anxiety are negotiated, she leaves out of consideration an explicit engagement with questions of power, resistance, and complicity" (138). It is precisely these ("left-out") questions of power, resistance and complicity, which I want to explore in my reading of "The Debutante." First, however, I want to signal why I think Riviere's essay provides a useful frame for examining Leonora Carrington's own disciplinary relationship to Surrealism.

In focusing on a very specific type of woman—the intellectual woman newly competing within the male-defined institution or discipline—Riviere's piece is poignantly self-reflective. In a letter of introduction to Freud, Ernest Jones, Riviere's analyst for many years, describes Riviere as "a case of typical hysteria" and having "a strong masculine identification" (Heath 46). He also notes, however, that she is extremely useful to the cause (of psychoanalysis) primarily because of her fluency in German and English; Riviere would eventually become an important mediator between Freud and the English-speaking world as well as between Freud and Jones. The tension between the subject under analysis in Riviere's piece and her own position within the psychoanalytic coterie uncovers a more general problem of the relationship between modernist women intellectuals and artists and the disciplinary fields in which they worked. On this relationship Heath asks:

> What did it mean to be an intellectual and a woman, an intellectual woman? The question for Riviere's patient in the paper can hardly but have been a question for her too (as it was widely in the writing of the period, the question of identity as a woman ...). (46-7)

The question of identity as a woman became increasingly important in the years between the wars and was exemplified by Freud's famous question: "What does a woman want?," which has guided the direction and nature of contemporary feminist analysis on subjectivity and desire. Indicative of the influence of Freud on the early stages of the Surrealist movement is Breton's own declaration that women constitute the most "marvellous and disturbing problem in all the world." Breton rejected the model of the professional "new woman" as too hard and entrenched within the modernist bourgeois literary establishment. Instead Surrealism relied on the rhetorical paradox of the idealized and transgressive woman as the emblem of Surrealist poetics, revealing both the Romantic and Symbolist influences on literary Surrealism.[10] Reading Riviere's analysis of her subject as a mask for her own relationship to psychoanalysis suggests the encoded ways in which women modernists might illustrate the complexity of their disciplinary affiliation. The question of Riviere's position within this piece and within a male dominated psychoanalytic coterie is masked by her analysis of the "other" woman, the intellectual woman who is both the subject and object of her analysis. As an object of analytical exchange herself, between Jones and Freud, as well as a significant contributor to the field of psychoanalysis, translating into English many of Freud's most significant essays, Riviere's life and work reveal the at once resistant and often complicit nature of modernist women's intellectual and artistic production at the same time that her analysis of the violence of gendered masking strategies attempts to describe its etiology. If Riviere's article describes the symptoms of this experience, Leonora Carrington's "The Debutante" explores the political, cultural and aesthetic structures inimical to it, through the performance of a violent masking ritual and the representation of the cross-class commodification of the female body.

The surreal narrative of "The Debutante" begins with an early morning visit to the zoo by the protagonist of the story, the debutante. The zoo is a place she visits frequently, preferring the company of the animals at the zoo to friendship with girls her own age. The debutante manages to persuade her friend the hyena to attend her coming out ball in her place. Smuggling the animal back to her room, the debutante assists in preparing an elaborate disguise for the hyena, becoming a willing accomplice in the murder of her maid, Mary. Neatly chewing around the edges of the maid's face, the hyena constructs her mask from human skin before consuming the rest of her body, save for one or two bones she stuffs in a fleur-de-lis bag which she takes with her to the party in case she gets hungry. Thus costumed in all the accoutrements of debutante wear—ball gown, high heels and gloves—the hyena sets out for the ball wearing the face of the reluctant debutante's maid. Meanwhile, the reluctant debutante, "tired by the day's emotions," sits down to read *Gulliver's Travels*. The ruse is unsuccessful, however, because the hyena's overwhelming smell, alluded to throughout the story, attracts the attention of the other guests. The tale ends abruptly when the debutante's mother enters her daughter's bedroom, "pale with rage," and exclaims:

> We'd just sat down at table ... when that thing sitting in your place got up and shouted, "So I smell a bit strong, what? Well I don't eat cakes!" Whereupon it tore off its face and ate it. And with one great bound disappeared through the window. (48)

Shifting in tone between artlessness and canniness, the narrator of the tale recalls Lewis Carroll's Alice narrator, whose own desire for transformation is registered by her favorite parlor game "Let's Pretend ... " and which incites her remark: "Nurse! Do lets pretend that I'm a hungry hyena and you're a bone" (18). The "black humor" in Carrington's narrative is thus established through the literal rendering of Alice's cannibal fantasy and through the dissonant effect of simple declarative sentences narrating a tale of grotesque and absurd violence. When the hyena first mentions her plan of tearing off the maid's face, the reluctant debutante replies with curious but faultless logic: "It's not practical. ... She'll probably die if she hasn't got a face. Somebody will certainly find the corpse, and we'll be put in prison" (47). The narrator's response is reminiscent of Alice's own practical but absurd powers of reasoning in both *Through the Looking Glass* and *Alice's Adventures in Wonderland*. The stark writing practice of the narrative and the intrusion of the banal and the everyday into the fantastic recalls the tension in Carroll's narrative between Alice as innocent unknowing girl and Alice as intrepid explorer, a tension that also illustrates the contradictory performance of caricatured femininity and intellectual competence for the intellectual woman in Riviere's essay. Alice's double persona (as artless and canny) is developed in Carrington's text through the double figure of the reluctant debutante, who withdraws from social action, *and* the hybrid hyena-maid, whose attendance at the ball constitutes a disruptive presence.

Drawn to the rebellious quality of Lewis Carroll's literature, with its satire on Victorian mores and literature as well as its use of the fantastic, many of the Surrealists referenced or illustrated his work. André Breton included him in both *The Anthology of Black Humour* and *The Dictionary of Surrealism,* whilst Ernst and Dali completed illustrations for the Alice series. Dali's illustrations for *Alice in Wonderland* draw on the figure of the *femme-enfant* through their overt display of the eroticism of Alice's child-woman status. The illustrations repeat in emblematic form a blank ink silhouette of

Alice's "womanly" body about to jump through a skipping rope. The prominence of warm hues throughout the illustrations—hot pink, orange, red and yellow seeping into each other, often from black outline or concentrations of black ink—emphasize the libidinal and oneiric quality of Alice's adventures. The art historian Sarah Wilson has noted that Max Ernst's life-long fascination with Carroll intensified during his time with Carrington in Saint-Martin. His paintings *Alice in 1939* and *Alice in 1941* belong to a series of decalcomania portraits of Carrington which extensively explored the theme of "the lost beloved" as the ruin of the world (Wilson 368). Like Dali, Ernst appeals to the incestuous and erotic nature of the *femme-enfant* as an exemplary model for his recreation of Alice and in doing so reminds us of his closing illustration for Carrington's debut publication *The House of Fear*. In this image a horse's head, proud and aloof is contrasted with the adolescent body of a girl (an Alice figure), in modest Edwardian dress, thrown upside down on a rock, her hand clutching her head in a pose that records the consternation of her abandonment and ruin. Wilson, somewhat ironically, comments that this image prophetically encapsulates the effect on Carrington of Ernst's imprisonment as an enemy alien, producing powerful "elisions between pictorial inversion, sexual abandonment and the abandonment of reason" (368).

Like Dali and Ernst, Carrington is interested in the ambiguous status of the child-woman figure. But rather then present her as an icon of erotic transformation, Carrington dwells on the logical contradiction of her status as both child and woman. The space of transition, or if you like, the contradiction of being two things at once, is explored through such hybrid figures as the child-woman (the debutante) and the feral woman. These figures problematize the dichotomous relationships of adulthood and childhood, as well as of nature and culture, in much the same way that Carroll's work destabilized the binary position of logic and nonsense. Moreover, Carrington's satire on English upper-class debutante ritual resembles Carroll's own lampooning of Victorian manners and rituals, such as his satirical exploration of the "madness" of the tea party ceremony. In Carrington's story the cultural and class-bound nature of the debutante ritual—its very "Englishness"— becomes the focus for a satirical reflection on the absurd and violent codes invested in rituals of the proper and the authentic.

The reluctant debutante of the story mirrors Carrington's resistance to her own much discussed 1935 debutante season. Various details of the narrative bear a verisimilitude to Carrington's real life; Mary the maid in the narrative matches Carrington's own working-class Irish nanny, Mary Kavanaugh. The debutante's reluctance in the narrative reflects Carrington's own repeated failure to adopt a conventional mask of appropriate upper class feminine behavior and her increasing rebelliousness within the family home. In an interview with Paul de Angelis, Carrington bluntly sums up the events of her debutante season:

... I was presented at court.... That was the last court of George V. I was on the marriage market ... I went through the season in London, the Royal garden party ... Then you go to Ascot, the races, and you're in the Royal enclosure. And if you please, in those days, if you were a woman, you were not allowed to bet. You weren't even allowed to the paddock where they show the horses. So I took a book. I mean, what would you do? It was Huxley's *Eyeless in Gaza,* which I read all the way through. (4)[11]

Like the fictional heroine in "The Debutante," this autobiographical account places Carrington's resistance to the codes and practices of heterosocial behavior within the conventional trope of the woman reader—a figure whose seduction by the romance plot is seen to circumvent her moral and social responsibilities. But the protagonist in "The Debutante" reads *Gulliver's Travels.* In shifting the scene of rebellion from the contemporary and popular *Eyeless in Gaza,* a romance that warns of the fate of an uppity intellectual woman, to Swift's canonical but iconoclastic *Gulliver's Travels,* Carrington strategically connects her narrative with a tradition of satire and its practice of humorous social critique, rather than the more "feminine" tradition of frustrated romance, represented by *Eyeless in Gaza.* However, the trope of the woman reader, historically theorized as both complicit and resistant, underscores the way in which the narrative action of the story is structured around themes of complicity and resistance or rather rebellious social withdrawal (the reluctant reading debutante) *and* disruptive social participation (the masked hyena).[12] The ambivalence of this strategy highlights the ambivalent position and construction of the woman artist within the male Surrealist aesthetic and erotic imagination as well as the ambivalence registered by the intellectual performance of Riviere's subject whereby adopting the mask of femininity constitutes a strategy that is at once complicit and transgressive.

Carrington's referencing of Swift and her claims to a literary tradition of satire are reinforced by Breton's selection of "The Debutante" for his important Surrealist collection, *The Anthology of Black Humour,* published in 1940 but not distributed until after the war because of its banning by the Vichy Government.[13] Breton's *Anthology* opens with Swift's absurd narrative "Directions to Servants" and concludes (or almost) with "The Debutante." Before each selection in the *Anthology,* Breton formally "introduces" his authors, providing an informal account of their importance within the definitive Surrealist category of "black humor." In these introductory pieces Carrington and Swift are linked via a literary performance of masking. While Swift, "the true initiator" (3) of black humor, is said to carry an impassive glacial mask despite being a man who was constantly outraged, Carrington is described as wearing "the mask that can save her from the hostility of conformism" (335). Breton's description of Carrington's literary style as a kind of masquerading performance immediately registers the hyena's own violent masking in her narrative as well as Carrington's reputation for unconventional and often disruptive social behavior. Breton, in fact, recounts two such episodes in his introduction. The first one involves Carrington's presence at an important dinner during which she lathered her feet with mustard. When asked what she was doing she merely replied that her feet were sore (Breton 335). The second story Breton tells us involves his attendance at a dinner at which Carrington served her guests dishes from a sixteenth century English cookbook, improvising certain ingredients that were unavailable to her. To this episode Breton comments rather wryly: "I will admit that a hare stuffed with oysters, to which she obliged me to do honour for the benefit of all those who had preferred to content themselves with its aroma, induced me to space out those feasts a bit" (335). On another occasion Carrington's surreal recipes included sago dyed with squid ink masquerading as a plate of caviar. Her reputation for eccentric and "surreal" social performances greatly facilitated her reputation within the group since it reinforced the importance of the marvelous within the experience of the everyday. Moreover, Breton's "introduction" plays up the transgressive nature of this performative role, reminding us of his description of Jacqueline Lamba as "scandalously beautiful" at the beginning of *Mad Love*. However, Breton also reduces Carrington's artistic authority to the role of muse, to the "beautiful divine witch," who initiates and performs spectacular rituals for the consumption of the male Surrealist imagination, facilitating the poetic function of woman as transgressive Other:

> Michelet, who so beautifully did justice to the *Witch*, highlights among her gifts two that are invaluable, because granted only to women: "the illuminism of lucid madness" and "the sublime power of *solitary conception*." ... Who today could answer the description better than Leonora Carrington? (335)

In many ways "The Debutante" reminds us that Carrington had already adopted the role of the rebellious and defiant *femme-enfant* long before she met the Surrealists. It also signals her position as "other" in ways apart from her muse-like status. Not only was she English rather than French, but she was also from the upper class whilst many of the Surrealists were from the middle class, hence their anti-bourgeois rhetoric. Moreover, like many of the women that came to Surrealism in the 1930s, she was a generation younger than male peers such as Breton and Ernst.[14] And yet despite Breton's recuperation of Carrington's artistic performance within the traditional surrealist trope of the beautiful, crazy muse, he acknowledges the resistant and ironic capacity of her masking strategy (both within and outside the text) when he concludes: "Over these and many other exploits ... reigns a smooth mocking gaze" (335).

"The Debutante"'s publication history reveals its importance within the defining moment of Breton's transhistorical construction of the Surrealist category of "black humor" as well as within a contemporary feminist revival of modernist women's writing. "The Debutante"'s inclusion in a number of recent feminist anthologies (by Angela Carter, Marina Warner and others) from the 1980s through to the present highlights what Alice Gambrell has outlined as a new interest for contemporary theoretical work in the process of "back-talk." Gambrell situates Carrington's work within an analysis of a cultural history of academic feminism because she finds in the work of a number of interwar women writers and artists—Carrington, H.D., Frida Kahlo and Zora Neale Hurston—an engagement with the issues of alterity and difference in a way that pre-empts contemporary feminist critical practice. She explores

> what it meant, during the 1930's and 1940's, for women to work within the boundaries of schools, movements, or disciplines in which, under more usual circumstances, they would have occupied the position of "Other": the object of investigation, the eroticized source of inspiration, the respondent in—though rarely the initiator of—an interlocutionary exchange. (1)

Calling this kind of engagement "insider-outsider activity" after Teresa de Lauretis's work in the problematizing of identity and practice, theory and experience, Gambrell argues that it forms part of the complex history of modernist women's intellectual modes of interrogation and can hardly be conceived, as it often is, as a newly emergent postmodern concern. She argues that one of the reasons for the "rediscovery" of women such as Carrington, Kahlo, Hurston and H.D. (and here we might add Joan Riviere) in the 1980s and early 1990s is that at about this time feminists began to reconceptualize their own work—literary and cultural—as a complex dynamic of complicity and resistance. Issues of race, class and sexuality were intrinsic to a rethinking of the relationship between theory and praxis. Drawing on Gambrell's important work, I want to illustrate the way in which both Riviere and Carrington, working within and against canonical disciplines used the trope of the mask as a strategy for negotiating and illustrating the embedded dynamic—in any discipline—of complicity and resistance.

In "The Debutante" this is effected through a doubling *and* absenting of the self. Through the narrative events of social withdrawal and disruptive participation, "The Debutante" sets in play a rhetorical turn of ambivalence, which references the historically specific female subject negotiating the conditions of her inscribed image and the wider cultural position of Woman as allegory, as the object and condition of representation (as crazy muse, *femme-enfant* etc.). In the narrative, skin becomes the fetishized site for the enabling strategies of masking and passing, evoking the surface materiality of all forms of feminized display as well as the threshold between an inside marked "natural" and an outside marked "cultural."

The turn of ambivalence that the narrative events play out is symbolically echoed by the hybrid debutante-maid. Unlike canonical Surrealist visual and literary production the hybrid body in this story unfolds a complex narrative of race, class and eugenics within the construction and representation of gender, sexuality and desire: in doing so the story explores issues of power, resistance and complicity with regard to Carrington's own class background and the narratives of gender and sexuality that operated within Surrealist ideology and aesthetic production. The strategies of masking and passing (here and also significantly in the work of Claude Cahun and Frida Kahlo, two other women artists associated with the Surrealist movement) become culturally gendered and racialized responses to the disabling position of women and lower social classes. Through the hyena's performance of passing, the narrative conflates the animal and human body, as well as the social roles of working-class maid and upper-class debutante. Thus the hybrid figure unfolds a series of combinations—hyena-maid, maid-debutante and animal-human—which work against a unified or stable interpretation of this figure. Here hybridity represents the very anxiety of classification, what Homi K. Bhabha calls "that ambivalent turn of the discriminated subject into the terrifying exorbitant object of paranoid classification—a disturbing questioning of the images and presences of authority" (113). Thus the conflation of the animal and human body in the narrative registers a modernist collapse of the reasoned knowing subject while also exploring new kinds of subject positions and ways to represent a more dynamic and complex epistemology of the self. Here Carrington's work acknowledges the importance of destabilizing canonical Surrealist constructions of female "otherness" using a masculinist tradition of satiric critique, a tradition associated with Jonathan Swift and Lewis Carroll, both of whom are obliquely connected to Carrington in Breton's *Anthology of Black Humour.*

As an "object of paranoid classification" the hybrid hyena-debutante in this text (and the many other hybrid identities in Carrington's paintings and stories from this period) evokes the subject's marginalization, alienation and position as grotesque outsider. Echoing Gulliver, the protagonist in the "The Debutante" begins her narration with a confession of misanthropic withdrawal:

> When I was a debutante, I often went to the zoo. I went so often that I knew the animals better than girls of my own age. Indeed it was in order to get away from people that I found myself at the zoo everyday. The animal I got to know best was a young hyena. She knew me too. She was very intelligent. I taught her French and she taught me her language. In this way we passed many pleasant hours. (44)

The debutante's rejection of human social interaction at the beginning of the narrative heralds her ultimate refusal to participate in the formal rite of passage from childhood to adulthood, in much the same way that Gulliver escapes the responsibilities and demands of a wife and children, and Alice resists the formal lessons of instruction by her elder sister. The intellectual exchange between the hyena and the debutante further reminds us of Alice's communicative attempts with the black kitten in *Through the Looking Glass* and Gulliver's own encounters with unfamiliar "beings." In all three texts antisocial behavior leads to an extraordinary journey or event, one that interrogates the given nature of institutional practices and the arbitrary effects of power relationships. Carrington's relationship to both Swift and Carroll is thus carefully orchestrated within Breton's *Anthology*.

The hybrid body of the masked hyena also disrupts the logic of serial reproduction, exemplified by the figure of the conventional debutante, who, as an object of exchange between men is aligned with the serialized body of prostitution and the *faceless* wage labor servant. The removal of the maid's face macabrely registers the impersonal treatment of the working class domestic at the same time that it underscores her indispensable role in holding up the identity—the masquerade—of the upper classes. Furthermore, the narrative mobilizes the trope of hybridity to satirically depict the debutante's increasingly devalued and comic status among the upper and middle classes. The debutante's traditionally symbolic status as "pure" and "noble," color-coded through the fetishization of her "whiteness" and her "blue blood,"[15] had begun to erode by the early decades of this century. Increasingly debutante culture took on the terms and references of commodity culture, signaled by its association with the term "the marriage market" in literature of the period. In her history and analysis of debutante culture, Margaret Pringle has shown how money and not blood became the currency of exchange as this traditionally aristocratic ritual was opened up to more entrepreneurial families. At the same moment that the blood of the aristocracy became "diluted" the debutante ritual was increasingly compared to the "primitive" mating rituals of non western countries. In her examination of this story and its strategic use of the debutante, Alice Gambrell argues that

> with increasing popular awareness of developments within the discipline of anthropology, a series of smugly self-mocking "debutante jokes"—which compared debutante rituals to puberty rites among non-Western peoples—started to emerge from the upper classes. Edith Wharton's *The Age of Innocence* (1920), for example, is filled with jokes of this kind. While these jokes successfully mocked the pretensions of those who presumed that their activities stood for the height of "civilization," they also required a generic (and utterly problematic) hypothesis of a "primitive" cultural "other" to serve as the ultimate butt of the joke. Thus, while Carrington's short story bears some resemblance to this kind of humor, her tone is quite different: she undermines its smugness by foregrounding violence in an extremely disruptive way. (208)

In foregrounding violence in the debutante's masking performance, Carrington's narrative dramatizes the violent cultural shaping of the female body, suggesting that notions of the "primitive" and the "civilized" are themselves caught up in a racial and gendered class narrative of privilege and power. Whilst the narrative dramatizes the cross-class commodification of women's bodies it also self-consciously exposes the human cost of maintaining upper class ritual at the expense of lower social orders; the hyena's attendance at the ball, its very domestication, provokes a blood-lust that evokes the latent violence invested in an aristocratic maintenance of bloodlines.

The figure of the violated maid and the latent "blood-lust" of the masked hyena, who kills in order to attend the ball, recalls the Surrealist fascination with two notorious criminal cases involving young women in Paris in the mid 1930s—that of Violette Nozière and Christine and Léa Papin. Violette Nozière was a teenager when she was accused of poisoning her parents, supposedly because they had refused to allow her to attend a party. The Papin Sisters, both orphans who had been brought up in a convent before they became household domestics, had violently murdered their employer and her daughter. The sensationalist Parisian press had presented these women as "monsters" and "cannibals," unleashing a wave of "anti-woman hysteria" throughout France, despite evidence that the Papin sisters had been strangely mistreated by their employer and Nozière had been repeatedly raped by her father, a prosperous and respected father and husband. According to Penelope Rosemont,[16] the misogyny and hysteria surrounding these cases was evident not only in the popular press but in writers such as Janet Flanner, the Paris correspondent for *The New Yorker*. In her article on Nozière, Flanner writes:

> Violette killed her father like a cannibal, because she wanted to eat and drink up the savings that were his French life and blood.. Violette was, one fears not the last of the faked-silver-foxed, hard-toothed, modern young monsters of mediocre looks and without any sense of the business of life. ... (158-9)

The language and tone of Flanner's piece reflects a modernist cultural anxiety over the corrupting influence of consumer culture on young women as well as an anxiety over women's increasing independence and assertiveness. Violette's greatest crime, according to Flanner, is her wasteful consumption of the nationalist and paternal symbols of French bourgeois culture, her father's hard earned savings, which for Flanner is the unquestioned—here at least—"business of life." Flanner's representation of Violette as a "faked-silver-foxed, hard-toothed, modern young monster" recalls the trope of the modern woman as a voracious cannibalesque consumer, eating away at the traditional moral values of bourgeois culture, leaving out of consideration the violent incestuous relationship that Violette claimed had occurred between her father and herself. The Surrealists, however, championed these women as heroines of a backlash against an increasingly corrupt social order, arguing that their acts of criminal psychosis reflected the prescribed nature of women's lives and the hypocrisy of the bourgeois family. A special book dedicated to Violette Nozière came out in December 1933, with poems and drawings by many prominent Surrealists, including Breton, Péret, and Crével. Magritte also provided an illustration for the book *L'impromptu de Versailles* (1935), which includes an explicit narrative on the Nozière case. That same month Lacan published "Motives of Paranoiac Crime," a case study of the Papin Sisters[17] in the Surrealist journal, *Minotaure*. In his article Lacan describes in graphic detail the events of the crime:

> The sisters each grab an adversary, and tear out her eyes from the socket while she is still alive ... Then using whatever comes to hand—a hammer, a pewter jug, a knife—they fling themselves on the bodies of their victims, smashing in their faces, exposing their genitals, lacerating their thighs and buttocks, and daubing them with each other's blood. They then wash up the instruments they used for their atrocious rites, clean themselves up and go to sleep in the same bed. (Jay 338)

Lacan's explanation of this crime is indebted to the Surrealist obsession with enucleation as a symbol for the crisis of modernist visuality and the fragile nature of the self's boundaries.[18] As well as ripping out the eyes of her victims, Christine, on separation from her sister, had attempted to rip out her own eyes.[19] Lacan's emphasis on the visual nature of paranoid psychosis led to his formulation of the "mirror stage," a stage that Martin Jay suggests reveals "marked similarities to the ... crimes of specular violence committed by the Papin sisters" (341). What is perhaps most significant, however, is Lacan's interest in a Surrealist employment of female criminality as a metaphor for their own project of aesthetic rebellion.

The case of the Papin sisters has continued to captivate the French imagination—with writers such as Flanner, Lacan, de Beauvoir and Genet all providing an extended analysis of the crime and its possible motive. The diverse readings of this crime unfold the problematic way in which femininity, class, trauma, rebellion and psychosis operate in this event. However, the Surrealists' interest in female criminality and their use of these women as emblems of aesthetic and social revolutionary practice seems to gloss over the complicated psychoanalytic, social and political ramifications of these crimes, or the very real sense of trauma and loss of meaning experienced by these women. The visual *frisson* of the famous "before" and "after" photographs of the Papin sisters, published along with Lacan's essay, was used as an image of social and aesthetic revolt. These photographs highlight the way Breton's notion of "convulsive beauty" dichotomized feminine sexuality as either ethereal and transcendent or violently excessive and corporeal. The trope of the "ruined" woman surfaces in the surrealist fantasy of feminine criminality and psychosis as a revolutionary aesthetic and social category, one which many women Surrealists, including Carrington, undoubtedly found particularly disturbing.

Carrington would later ironically exploit the "Before and After" effect for her own political and aesthetic ends. In 1942 she published an account of her psychotic breakdown during the war, in the Surrealist journal *VVV*. This biographical essay, *Down Below*, was accompanied with a photograph of the author "before" the events she describes, dressed as a debutante in the company of her mother. The image presents, like the "before" photograph of the Papin sisters, an image of feminine purity and conformity. Appearing at the conclusion of the essay, however, the image sets up what Alice Gambrell describes as an "interpretive dissonance," contrasting "the essay's many verbal images of degradation and vulnerability with a photographic representation of deliberately constructed purity and protectedness" (83-4). Gambrell further suggests that the photograph "casts a strangely erotic glow around the astonishingly unsexy essay that proceeds it, helping to blunt the effects of 'Down Below' by transforming it, in certain respects, into a kinky story about a debauched aristocrat" (85-6). While I think Gambrell's reading is apt, the photograph's appearance at the end of the narrative actually reverses the "before" and "after" sequencing and thus ironizes the atypical trajectory of the "ruined" woman. Moreover, the essay is explicitly framed as a talking cure, one that attempts to mimetically reproduce the psychotic episode in order to overcome and explore the painful and shocking events of the past. The very real sense of Carrington's pain and confusion in visiting that former period of psychotic breakdown serves to critique the aestheticized and silenced figure of madness in *Nadja* by insisting on the realism of the madwoman as historical subject, but one who is nevertheless very much in control of the possible meanings of her own experience. While the images that accompany *Nadja* destabilize any mimetic reading of Breton's text—providing quite separate narratives of their own through their oblique relationship to them—the photograph in *Down Below* seems to reinsert mimesis to critique Breton's distancing of the madwoman in his narrative. The photographic portrait of Carrington as a debutante insists on the realism of the narrative's embodied subjectivity at the same time that the description (or recreation) of the psychotic subject problematizes any notion of cohesion and stability. Finally, since her narrative of institutional repression within the insane asylum is illustrated with an image of the subject as a debutante with her mother, Carrington seems to be wryly commenting on the ubiquitous powers of social repression and the complicit role of women in this repression.[20]

While "The Debutante" stages the themes of rebellion and criminality through the reluctant debutante's image of unruly adolescence, it complicates a surrealist utopian investment in female rebellion by foregrounding the importance of race and class in the construction and performance of female paranoia. The hyena's working class cockney diction: "So I smell a bit strong, what?," together with its refusal of the class-bound ritual of eating cake, registers the animal's status in a way that collapses the working class body of the maid (the domestic) onto the undomesticated body of the hyena, exposing the female body's abject and liminal status. The hyena's smell and its hairiness ("her hands ... were too hairy to look like mine") thus emerge as a trope for the grotesque leaking body, a body that has escaped the processes of socialization and the successful mask of idealized and commodified femininity. Carrington's narrative reverses the scene of rebellion championed by the Surrealists: while Nozière had murdered in order to attend a party, Carrington's rebellious debutante murders in order to avoid attending one. Moreover, what causes most offence to the other party guests is not the debutante's absence, but the smell of the hyena. The mother's repeated plea that her daughter wash before the party, together with her traumatic outburst over the hyena's presence, suggests the repressed horror of the unclean woman and the violence of propriety itself.

The motif of the feral woman, one who lives on the edges of the civilized world, occurs frequently in Carrington's early fiction where it collapses the boundaries between animal and human as well as nature and culture. In the short story "As They Rode Along the Edge" (1937-40), the Diana-like Virginia Fur enters the narrative shrouded in classificatory ambiguity: "one could not be altogether sure that she was a human being. Her smell alone threw doubt on it—a mixture of spices and game, the stables, fur and grasses" (3). Like the reluctant debutante, Virginia Fur chooses the company of semi-wild animals rather than the pious social world of Saint Alexander and his church. Furthermore, in taking as her lover the beautiful wild boar, Igname, Virginia brings about the jealous retribution of the Saint. Throughout the story these two characters are strongly opposed: unlike the wild but sympathetic terrain that Virginia roams, where "brambles [draw] back their thorns like cats retracting their claws," Saint Alexander cultivates an unforgiving garden of readymades, strange sado-masochistic devices invented for the purpose of atonement:

> chairs made of wire ("I sit on them when they're white hot and stay there till they cool off"), enormous smiling mouths with pointed poisonous teeth; underwear of reinforced concrete full of scorpions and adders; cushions made of millions of black mice biting each other—when the blessed buttocks were elsewhere. (5)

Saint Alexander's garden of "Little Flowers of Mortification" betray an anal-erotic obsession rather than the desired devotional piety. Carrington's satirical lampooning of Saint Alexander and his attempts to tame the flighty

Virginia Fur, recalls her own flight from and rebellion against a Catholic convent upbringing. Unable to tame Virginia, Saint Alexander takes revenge by having Igname killed and served for dinner, an act that highlights a voracious paternal anxiety over miscegenation and female rebellion. Like the feral debutante, Virginia Fur navigates the threshold between the domesticated and the undomesticated where her hybrid status betrays both a cultural anxiety over the feminine and a utopian desire to transcend and alter the prescribed codes of female experience, including the violence of the institutional codes that inform it. Like the exquisite corpse, which is both incidental and intentional, the hybrid female body in Carrington's fiction and painting has a quality of ambivalence that works to alter the authority of prevailing institutional codes and fixed subject positions, at the same time signaling the impossibility of representation within the disciplinary boundaries of Surrealism.

The emblematic incorporation of the hyena into "The Debutante" and into her 1937 "Self-Portrait" is characteristic of Carrington's work. A recurring animal in Carrington's surrealist bestiary, the hyena is symbolic of sexual transgression and hybridity. Once thought to be hermaphroditic, because the male and female genitals are almost identical—the female having both testicles and an enlarged clitoris—the hyena has endured a reputation for profanity and sexual deviancy, including homosexuality. The hyena has also had a maligned reputation within Christianity and folklore. Renowned as a harbinger of death, the hyena is often associated with the devil's dark wisdom, primarily because of its human-like mocking laughter—a characteristic that pays homage to the very notion of "black humor." In medieval mythology it was believed that sorcerers hunted with packs of hyenas and that witches rode upon their backs.[21] Referencing the ambiguity of the hyena's sexual and social status, the hybrid body of the hyena-maid disrupts the static and closed body of bourgeois individualism as well as the sealed and spectral body of commodity culture. Mary Russo argues that the grotesque body functions as a libidinal multiplicity through its refusal of the singular and its embrace of the multiple and the possible: "the grotesque body is the open, protruding, extended, secreting body, the body of becoming, process and change" (62-3). Russo's analysis also reflects a modernist and postmodernist articulation of the hybrid. Within postcolonial theoretical parlance, hybridity also refers to the constructions of race and sexuality at the site of a nineteenth- and twentieth-century discourse on eugenics. In "The Debutante," this eugenicist construction is signaled by debutante culture's fetishization of blood and genealogy within the historically analogous rise of fascism in Europe. During the period in which "The Debutante" was written, Carrington and Ernst had become increasingly preoccupied with the threat of fascism and of Nazi occupation.[22] Eventually fleeing France after Ernst had been interned as an enemy alien, Carrington suffered a serious mental breakdown and was institutionalized in

Santander, Spain. Her account of this period is recorded in her autobiographical narrative *Down Below*. Structured around a series of all-powerful male figures who are all explicitly linked to Hitler, Carrington's account encapsulates
the political and social institutions—fascism and the psychiatric hospital—
underlying her experience of psychosis. Carrington's internal loss of equilib-
rium is repeatedly shadowed by the political and social psychosis of war-torn
Europe and the dehumanizing effects of fascist ideology.

"The Debutante"'s repeated reference to hybridity thus references both
debutante culture's preoccupation with breeding and Nazi culture's obsession
with the contamination of blood lines. Tracing the cultural anxiety about miscegenation within a postcolonial narrative of modernist cultural history,
Homi K. Bhabha writes:

> Hybridity intervenes in the exercise of authority not merely to indicate the
> impossibility of its identity but to represent the unpredictability of its presence.
> ... The display of hybridity—its peculiar "replication"—terrorises authority
> with the ruse of recognition, *its mimicry, its mockery*. (114-15) (emphasis mine)

Reflecting on Bhabha's comments, I would argue that Carrington's use of the
hybrid form is in part a response to the impossibility of the female subject's
identity within the "authoritarian" codes and practices, not only of the bourgeois and upper-class family, but of Surrealism. Within canonical Surrealist
cultural production the grotesque female body is often deployed as a topos
of mutability and instability, one which registers a misogynistic violence as
inherent to its anti-bourgeois political and aesthetic order.[23] One can only
speculate on the uneasiness felt by Carrington and other women Surrealists
in the face of the misogyny and violence of surrealist iconography. While
Carrington may have concurred with the political and aesthetic import of
much surrealist imagery, her work critically reflects on the repeated
dichotomization of female embodiment as both pure and abject. Like Riviere's subject, who moves between caricatured femininity and intellectual
authority as a reflection of the compromised role of the professional woman,
Carrington's use of masking strategies and hybrid configurations together
with the modes of irony and satire betrays the problematic nature of artistic
authority for the Surrealist woman artist or writer as well as a desire to disrupt and mock any such authority. In Carrington's narrative the multiple
ambiguities and possibilities of the hybrid enact both the "nowhere" of
female identity, signaled by the reluctant debutante's social withdrawal into
the utopic textual world of *Gulliver's Travels*, and its "mimicry" and "mock-
ery" of paternal and professional codes of authority, signaled by the masked
hyena's sadistic and disruptive presence at the ball. In critiquing the narratives of authenticity and purity produced within the wider cultural context of
the period, "The Debutante" interrogates the "authority" of Surrealist cultural

production. It also critiques the professional and personal codes of patronage within avant-garde culture by foregrounding the pervasive exchange and manipulation of women's bodies and experiences.

Notes

1. I would like to thank Megan Jones and Kate Lilley for their valuable comments throughout the writing of this piece. My thanks also to Stella Deen for her critical feedback at the final stage of its development.
2. Leonora Carrington, Giselle Prassinos, Jaqueline Lamba, Dora Marr, Frida Kahlo, Léonor Fini, Lee Miller, Meret Oppenheim, Valentine Penrose, Remedios Varo, Nancy Cunard and Claude Cahun were all active as artists, writers and intellectuals within the Surrealist group in the 30s and early 40s. See Whitney Chadwick's *Women Artists and the Surrealist Movement* and Penelope Rosemont's *Surrealist Women: An International Anthology* for more detailed biographical information.
3. For further discussion see Mary Ann Caws, Rudolf Kuenzli, and Gwen Raaberg, eds. *Surrealism and Women.* Cambridge, Massachusetts: MIT Press, 1991.
4   Alice Gambrell shows that during the late Thirties and early Forties, Breton "spent a great deal of time as entrepreneur and patron to a scattered group of younger artists ... [and] began ... quite consciously to seek out and promote work by writers and visual artists, who, for him, embodied and made literal those carefully constructed fictions of difference and alterity" (42).
5. Breton's biographer, Mark Polizzotti writes: "Breton, for his part, was very taken with the stunning Englishwoman, whom he later described as 'superb in her refusals, with a boundless human authenticity'" (448).
6. This narrative was written only months before Ernst was interned as an enemy alien with Hans Bellmer and highlights the personal cost for the Surrealist community of the Nazi juggernaut. His loss and the anxiety of war would eventually lead to Carrington's psychotic breakdown and institutionalization in Santander, Spain in 1940, recorded in her narrative, *Down Below.* In an interview with Paul de Angelis, Carrington speaks of the marvelous period of her travels with Ernst in the South of France, and how the excitement and revelation of this period unfolded against the appalling political undertones of fascism.
7. See Max Ernst's Preface, "Loplop Presents the Bride of the Wind," in Carrington's first Surrealist publication, *The House of Fear,* and André Breton's Introduction of Carrington in his *Anthology of Black Humour.*
8. This includes work by Mary Ann Caws, Susan Rubin Suleiman and Rosalind Krauss. My own work on women Surrealists has been particularly influenced by Suleiman's early use of the Bakhtinian concept of "internal dialogism" to describe Carrington's (and other women Surrealists') relationship to the work of both Breton and Ernst. See Suleiman, *Subversive Intent* 27.
9. Judith Butler adopts a similar strategy to Riviere when she writes: "gender is a kind of imitation for which there is no original." For Butler's own referencing of Riviere in her account of the masquerade and the theory of gender performativity see Chapter Two of *Gender Trouble: Feminism and the Subversion of Identity.*
10. Despite Freud's attempts to deal with the question of feminine identity in his own work, he failed to respond to Riviere's important paper on femininity and the masquerade, as did Jones. The silence of her male colleagues upon the publication of this essay may have inhibited any further work in this area, since Riviere never again returns to the questions

raised in her essay. Similarly, Breton's reputation for his public support of women within the Surrealist movement contrasted to his more traditional and conservative treatment and expectations of the woman he became personally involved with. See Polizzotti, *Revolution of the Mind*.

11. "Huxley, as Jessica Mitford notes in her autobiography *Hons and Rebels,* enjoyed a brief vogue among artistically inclined British debutantes during the 1930's" (Gambrell 78).

12. In the following exchange from *Love in a Cold Climate*, Nancy Mitford provides an example of the increasing resistance to, and parody of, debutante culture by prospective debutantes themselves: "Polly says: 'This coming out seems a great bore—do you enjoy it, Fanny?' to which Fanny replies 'I had never thought ... Girls had to come out, I knew. It is a stage in their existence'" (239).

13. See Mark Polizzotti's "Introduction" to Breton's *Anthology of Black Humour.*

14. Carrington was three years older than Ernst's son, Jimmy Ernst.

15. The cultural historian Angela Lambert suggests that the expression "blue blood" derives from "the sangre azul claimed by certain families of Castile, as being uncontaminated by Moorish, Jewish or other admixture; probably founded on the blueness of the veins of people of fair complexion (Shorter Oxford Dictionary). Thus racism and anti-Semitism are also inherent in the idea of blue-bloodedness" (15).

16. Information about these two cases comes from Rosemont 42-4.

17. As Rosemont notes, surrealist interest in these two criminal cases was later echoed by others: Genet's play *The Maids* was based on The Papin sisters and Claude Chabrol made a film in the 1970s on Nozière, titled *Violette.*

18. Martin Jay comments that in Lacan's analysis of this case he draws on Freud's explanation of paranoia as an unsuccessful defense against repressed homosexual desire, noting that the sisters exhibited an emotional attachment akin to the bonds of identical twins. According to Freud's theory, paranoia results from a narcissistic failure to distinguish self from other; the paranoia turns the repressed desire for the love object into a "delusion of observation" (340).

19. For a fuller account of this see Jay, *Downcast Eyes: The Denigration of Vision in Twentieth-Century Thought.*

20. The mother's presence as a figure of repression in "The Debutante" seems to reinforce this. Moreover, it was Carrington's childhood nanny, Mary Kavanaugh, who was sent to Spain to remove her from the asylum in Santander, only to accompany her to South Africa where she was to be placed in a Sanitarium. See Marina Warner's introduction to *Notes From Down Below.*

21. From "The Bestiary": http://pages.prodigy.com/Christory/hyena.htm.

22. In her interview with Paul de Angelis, Carrington suggests that having met the Surrealists in London, she became aware for the first time of "who Hitler really was" and that later, when she moved to Paris to be with the group, Hitler became the most common topic of conversation.

23. This is perhaps most evident in Hans Bellmer's two series of *Poupées*, which he began in 1934. Bellmer's life-like dolls were composed of various materials and then photographed in a range of poses and settings. In her reading of the dolls, Rosalind Krauss suggests that they invoke a sense of the uncanny in that they stage the adult's repossession of the child's plaything. However, Conley argues that despite Bellmer's revolutionary portrayal of the body as a site of the unconscious, they are nevertheless "based on experiments with the female form just as is in classical art" (84).

184 *Challenging Modernism*

References

Bellmer, Hans. *La Poupée*. 1936/49. Musée National d'Art Moderne, Paris.
Benjamin, Walter. "Surrealism: The Last Snapshot of the European Intelligentsia" in *Reflections*. Edited and Introduced by Peter Demetz. Trans. Edmund Jephcott. New York and London: Harvest-Harcourt Brace Jovanovich, 1978.
"The Bestiary." http://pages.prodigy.com/Christory/hyena.htm.
Bhabha, Homi K. *The Location of Culture*. London and New York: Routledge, 1994.
Breton, André. *Anthology of Black Humour*. 1940. Trans. and Introduction Mark Polizzotti. San Francisco: City Lights Books, 1997.
———. Introduction to "The Debutante," by Carrington. Breton 335-6.
Butler, Judith. *Gender Trouble: Feminism and the Subversion of Identity*. New York and London: Routledge, 1990.
Carrington, Leonora. "As They Rode Along the Edge." Written 1937-40. *The Seventh Horse and Other Stories*. By Carrington. Trans. Katherine Talbot and Anthony Kerrigen. Introduction by Marina Warner. London: Virago, 1989. 3-15.
———. "The Debutante." 1939. Carrington, *The House of Fear* 44-8.
———. *Down Below*. 1944. Carrington, *The House of Fear* 163-214.
———. *The House of Fear: Notes From Down Below*. Introduction Marina Warner. Trans. Katherine Talbot and Marina Warner. London: Virago, 1989.
———. Interview with Paul de Angelis. *El Paseante 17*. Ed. Nadine van Hasselt. Trans. Cecilia Martinez. n.d.
Carroll, Lewis. *Through The Looking Glass*. 1872. London: Penguin, 1994.
Caws, Mary Ann, Rudolf Kuenzli, and Gwen Raaberg, eds. *Surrealism and Women*. Cambridge, Massachusetts: MIT Press, 1991.
Chadwick, Whitney. *Women Artists and the Surrealist Movement*. London: Thames and Hudson, 1985.
Cohen, Margaret. *Profane Illumination: Walter Benjamin and the Paris of Surrealist Revolution*. Berkeley and London: University of California Press, 1993.
Conley, Katharine. *Automatic Woman: The Representation of Woman in Surrealism*. Lincoln and London: University of Nebraska Press, 1996.
Ernst, Max. "Preface, or Loplop Presents the Bride of the Wind." Carrington, *The House of Fear* 25-6.
Flanner, Janet. "Murder Among the Lovebirds." 1936. *Paris Was Yesterday: 1925-1939*. Ed. Irving Drutmen. London: Angus and Robertson, 1973. 157-64.
Gambrell, Alice. *Women Intellectuals, Modernism and Difference: Transatlantic Culture, 1919-1945*. Cambridge: Cambridge University Press, 1997.
Heath, Stephen. "Joan Riviere and the Masquerade." *Formations of Fantasy*. Eds. Victor Burgin, James Donald and Cora Kaplan. London and New York: Methuen, 1986. 45-61.
Huxley, Aldous. *Eyeless in Gaza*. 1936. London: Penguin, 1965.
Jay, Martin. *Downcast Eyes: The Denigration of Vision in the Twentieth Century*. Berkeley and London: University of California Press, 1994.
Krauss, Rosalind. *The Optical Unconscious*. Cambridge, Massachusetts: MIT Press, 1993.
Lambert, Angela. *1939: The Last Season of Peace*. London: Weidenfeld and Nicolson, 1989.
Mitford, Nancy. *Love in a Cold Climate*. 1949. London: Penguin Classics, 1986.
Pellegrini, Ann. "Femmes Futiles: Womanliness, Whiteness, and the Masquerade." *Performance Anxieties: Staging Psychoanalysis, Staging Race*. By Pellegrini. New York and London: Routledge, 1997. 131-47.
Polizzotti, Mark. "Introduction: Laughter in the Dark." Breton, *Anthology* v-xi.
———. *Revolution of the Mind: The Life of André Breton*. New York: De Capo Press, 1997.
Pringle, Margaret. *Dance Little Ladies: The Days of the Debutante*. London: Orbis Books, 1977.

Riviere, Joan. "Womanliness as a Masquerade." 1929. *Formations of Fantasy*. Ed. Victor Burgin, James Donald and Cora Kaplan. London and New York: Methuen, 1986. 35-44.

Rosemont, Penelope, ed. *Surrealist Women: An International Anthology*. Introduction by Penelope Rosemont. Austin: University of Texas Press, 1998.

Russo, Mary. *The Female Grotesque: Risk, Excess and Modernity*. New York and London, Routledge, 1994.

Suleiman, Susan Rubin. *Subversive Intent: Gender, Politics and the Avant-Garde*. Cambridge: Harvard University Press, 1990.

Warner, Marina. Introduction. Carrington, *The House of Fear*. 1-21.

Wilson, Sarah. "Max Ernst and England." *Max Ernst: A Retrospective*. Edited and Introduction by Werner Spies. Munich: Presetel-Verlag, 1991. 363-72. Exhibition, The Tate Gallery, London 13 Feb-21 April, 1991.

9 T.S. Eliot in the "Journalistic Struggle"

Patrick Collier

In May of 1927, T.S. Eliot marked *The Criterion*'s switch from quarterly to monthly publication with a "Commentary" that explicitly defined the literary review's mission in nostalgic terms and in opposition to the popular press. Assuring readers that his *Criterion* would continue to publish lengthy, carefully wrought criticism, Eliot maintained that it would hew to its original mission—to "revive some of the characteristics of the quarterly reviews of a hundred years ago, which had languished in this century of rapid production and consumption" ("Commentary" May 1927, 187). *The Criterion*'s articles, Eliot wrote, were "the work of men who were not hurried, and who could have the incentive of knowing that a part at least of their readers would read their work with corresponding care and leisure" (187). Eliot thus differentiates the writing of *The Criterion* from the majority of contemporary journalism, which, he implies, is both written and read in haste. In a later section of this commentary, subtitled "The Five O'Clock Philosophers," Eliot offers images of such hurried reading and writing, and mulls their effects on readers, journalists, and the journalistic marketplace. He calls daily journalism "rush-hour thought for the City worker" and speaks of the "Tube reader." He wonders whether the popularity of daily and weekly newspapers will erode the audience for publications like *The Criterion*: "It is quite possible that the public of the future will dispense altogether not only with quarterly reviews, but with monthlies and weeklies, and will find all the aliment it requires in its daily and Sunday newspapers. Certainly the daily papers are more and more able to provide mankind with its daily opinions, not only on politics but on everything else" (189). This newspaper-reading may be the lesser among potential evils, Eliot suggests, as it creates interest amongst the mass in something besides "wireless and professional sport." But he finds in these conditions no salutary effect on journalists, who, because of the constant need for quick copy, write about subjects they do not understand. Thus when novelist and critic Arnold Bennett "tells the Tube-reader how poetry should be written, we must protest" (189).

This critique of the popular press shows a familiar side of Eliot, who has long been viewed as a bastion and guardian of "high culture," traditionally defined as a rarefied and culturally powerful sphere distinct from mass culture.[1] The latter is generally identified with the middle- and working-classes and the ephemeral cultural products geared to them. Indeed, Eliot, his contemporaries, and the first generations of critics who studied him helped to establish the high/low culture divide in ways that identified "high culture" with lasting works of art, measurable and answerable only to "objective" and eternal standards, and "mass culture" with escapist entertainment and sensationalism, produced by the new engines of mass-publishing, with unabashedly commercial ends in mind. Eliot's attempt to distinguish *The Criterion* from other publications in a crowded journalistic field can easily be made to fit into this paradigm, as an effort to define and fortify a boundary between the *Criterion* and the literary criticism produced by the more popular daily newspapers, and there can be no doubt that Eliot had such self-definition in mind.[2] But my aim in this paper is to move beyond such "Great Divide" thinking—to use Andreas Huyssen's well-known term—by looking more closely at Eliot's relationship with journalism and uncovering what I consider to be overlooked conflicts in that relationship. In complicating our sense of Eliot's attitude towards the popular press, I hope also to show that his critiques of journalism took part in a widespread, troubled reaction to changes in the press and the publishing world generally—changes which had been arousing anxious commentary since the middle of the previous century.

In reconsidering Eliot's self-positioning through the lens of journalism, I am, in part, mining a vein of Eliot criticism opened by David Chinitz, who argued in his 1995 essay "T.S. Eliot and the Cultural Divide" that Eliot, especially in the 1920s and earlier, had a much more progressive and theoretical view of popular culture than critics generally acknowledge (237). Citing essays such as "Marie Lloyd," which eulogizes the poet's favorite music hall performer, Chinitz argues that Eliot saw a vibrant working-class culture as essential to the British nation's health. Indeed, Eliot saw high culture and working-class culture as symbiotically related: the poet's role was to "refine" the baser materials of working-class culture into something with lasting meaning (238). Working-class culture and high culture figure as allies in opposition to a deadened bourgeois culture in this formulation (239). Eliot consistently treats popular culture in this progressive way in his essays of the 1920s, while his poetry in the same years shows "signs of deep ambivalence" about popular culture, Chinitz argues (241). He cites Eliot's essay on the Edwardian journalist Charles Whibley, with its claim that "the distinction between journalism and literature is quite futile," as another example of the poet's largely-unrecognized respect for popular forms (238).

Eliot's attitudes towards journalism *were* considerably more conflicted, ambivalent, and at times contradictory than a simple high/low cultural divide—or than many of Eliot's best-known remarks about journalism—suggest. But these attitudes do not fit into the "refinement" model as neatly as Chinitz suggests. For while Eliot often praised working-class entertainments in his essays and letters, his public statements about popular journalism are with few exceptions bitterly negative. (As I argue below, his claim to disavow the "distinction between journalism and literature" actually serves, in the context of "Charles Whibley," to fortify the category of "literature" by excluding all but a tiny sample of journalism from it.) Eliot blames the press for a variety of woes, chief among them the breakdown of social consensus and the deterioration of language. His public statements rarely evoke any productive symbiosis between the artist and the press. The irony, as we shall see, is that such a symbiosis—conflicted and uncomfortable as it often was—actually existed in Eliot's career. Eliot used the literary press aggressively to earn money and to build his reputation. He was much more directly engaged in journalism than with any of the "popular arts" he praised in essays and in conversation. Further, Eliot's views of the press and its readership changed markedly as his cultural position varied. His well-known embrace of a small, élite audience was not a stance he maintained consistently; its best-known elucidations came from the position of a mature poet who saw both that a small audience was his fate and that he could enjoy considerable cultural authority in spite of (and partly because of) its size. Eliot wrote in 1943, at the age of 55, that he would suspect the abilities of any poet who enjoyed wide popularity in his own lifetime, "for it leads us to fear that he is not really doing anything new, that he is only giving people what they are already used to. ... But that a poet should have the right, small audience in his own time *is* important" ("Social" 11, emphasis original). A younger Eliot, eager to earn money and build up cultural authority, was less dogmatic and less consistent in his attitudes toward readers. Ten years earlier he had written that "the poet naturally prefers to write for as large and miscellaneous an audience as possible" (*Uses* 146); thirteen years before that, in 1920, he had taken the opposite position, writing to the editor of the avante-garde Ovid Press that "it is just as good at the present time to have an audience of two hundred as two thousand ..." (*L* 383).

But if Eliot's sense of the proper size of his audience wavered, his desire for an authoritative, influential voice remained consistent, and he attempted to achieve both audience and authority through the practice of journalism. His critiques of journalism stem in part from his own experience as a journalist during the years in which he struggled to secure a living and to adjust to the reality that the public sphere—a public sphere so powerfully influenced by journalism—held a diminished place for the literature he considered worthwhile. Eliot lamented the fragmentation and stratification of the public sphere, which he saw as limiting poetry's audience, and thus its potential social impact.[3] His later theories of the social function of poetry, which acknowledge its narrowly circumscribed effect on society, can be seen as an attempt to justify poetry in an age marked by a greatly expanded reading population that is largely indifferent to "literature."

I

Historians of publishing have argued that the British reading public became simultaneously fragmented and stratified between 1870 and 1945. As a means of reaching the new reading public of lower middle- and working-class readers, publishers of books, magazines, and newspapers increasingly tailored their products to distinct segments of the literate population. This move toward specialization in publishing resulted in, among other developments, the creation of papers and magazines geared specifically to young boys and girls, working-class women, middle-class women, and very narrowly defined interest groups such as cyclists and bee-keepers.[4] In book publishing, these years gave birth to the distinction between "literature" and "fiction"—with the former encompassing novels that appeal to the traditional, upper-middle-class audience for books familiar from the nineteenth century and the latter denoting "popular" novels aimed at the new reading public (McAleer 22). This fragmentation and stratification were evident in the London newspaper world as well, where weekly and daily offerings included, to name but a few, the sensationalistic, often lurid *Daily Mail* and *News of the World,* the prestigious, staid *Times,* the socialist weeklies *Clarion* and *New Age,* the liberal *Daily News*, and the Tory *Morning Chronicle* and *Manchester Guardian.* All of these publications contained at least a small amount of literary journalism in the form of book and theater reviews. The period also saw growth in the number of specialized literary publications—and vigorous competition between them. The *Times Literary Supplement,* which would become the most important literary paper in Britain, appeared in 1902. The proliferation of coterie-based "little magazines" has been studied extensively by scholars of modernism,[5] but the period also saw the expansion of more conventional, broadly-based literary weeklies and monthlies, among them the *London Mercury,* the *New English Weekly, Art and Letters* and the *English Review.*[6] These publications, despite their often stridently dogmatic differences about literature, courted similarly educated readers with fiction, poetry, essays and reviews. Meanwhile, popular magazines published reams of "low-brow" fiction.[7]

With the audience so diverse, so fragmented and stratified, we might suspect that literary journalists like Eliot saw themselves as existing on a separate plane and engaged in a totally distinct activity as compared with the purveyors of daily newspapers. But Eliot's commentary introducing the monthly *Criterion* makes it clear that, in 1927, he saw his small-circulation journal as competing to define the direction of national culture against such publications as the daily *Evening Standard,* where one could find Arnold Bennett's musings on fiction and poetry. Thus the need to distinguish the work published in the *Criterion* from the criticism readers could gather, more cheaply, more quickly, and more often, from the daily papers; and thus the fear that the dailies' rapidly written, rapidly consumed criticism would dry up the market for "longer and more considered" reviews ("Commentary" May 1927, 187). One month later, Eliot's "Commentary" claimed that literary monthlies like *Criterion* were better sources of political commentary than daily papers, as well: "only in the literary reviews, which are not the conscientious organs of super-annuated political creeds, are their [sic] any living political ideas" (June 1927, 283). Eliot was not alone in feeling that his small-circulation monthly was threatened by the ubiquity of much larger daily and weekly papers. In 1921 Robert Briffault, writing in the *English Review*, summarized what he called the "laments of the providers of art, of literature":

> The unpopular weeklies with small circulations are doleful with intellectual tears; the popular dailies, with "unexampled circulation" wear the smile of the tiger. ... Public barbarism, the nepotism of the critics, and the price of paper bid fair, the wailing voices lament, to snuff out the light of art and culture from the land of Shakespeare. (512)

That Eliot saw the *Criterion* and the daily papers as competing in the same arena helps explain his constantly shifting usages and definitions of the terms "journalism" and "newspaper." In particular, he would periodically redefine the term "journalism" in a way that justified his own practice of it at any given time. Eliot was also capable, however, of using the terms in vague and generalized ways that can make it seem as though he is attacking the profession even as he practices it. In a characteristic move, Eliot in "Lancelot Andrewes" associated "the newspapers" with the dissolution of the English language, though the essay appeared in the *TLS*, a newspaper in its own right and a family publication of Britain's leading newspaper, the *Times*. Eliot followed common usage in referring to small literary weeklies as "papers" or "newspapers," though he probably (silently) excepted some of them from his generalized critique of the press. As we shall see, such usages forced Eliot, on several key occasions, to re-define terms so as to justify his own, prolific contribution as a literary journalist. Nonetheless it remains clear that Eliot saw the wide universe of British periodicals as competing on the same stage—the stage of a national culture whose health and future increasingly became his primary concerns.[8]

In defining *The Criterion* in opposition to the daily papers, Eliot manipulated the terms and positions of a vigorous contemporary debate about the state of reading in Great Britain and the role popular journalism played in it. Joseph McAleer has identified two sides to this debate, the culturally conservative, "pessimistic" view, which saw popular journalism and popular literature as threats to social order and drains on the national intellect, and the "optimistic" or "improving" position, which held that the working- and lower-middle-class readers could start with newspapers and popular fiction but work their way up, as Randolph Churchill put it, from the pages of the *Daily Mail* to "the pages of the monthly magazines, from those to the quarterlies, and again from those all through to the English classics" (quoted in McAleer 31). While Eliot would clearly fall in the "pessimistic" camp on balance, in the 1927 *Criterion* commentary he makes a concession to the "improving school" by placing daily newspapers higher on an intellectual scale than football games or the radio. But the dominant notes in that essay are its concurrent disdain for daily journalism and concern about its effects—both familiar elements in a pervasive anxiety about the state of British journalism that was a commonplace of public discourse throughout the modernist period. Images of the commuter-reader; jabs at journalists' lack of expertise about their subjects; fear about the effects of journalism on the reader; complaints about the brevity of articles, the haste with which newspaper articles are written and read, the fact that newspapers are written with busy commuters in mind—all of these elements recur often in contemporary writing about the state of British journalism.[9]

This debate dates back at least to Matthew Arnold's late nineteenth-century critiques of journalism, but it sustained a vigorous life in English public discourse through the 1920s and 1930s. Arnold helped set the terms of this debate in a well-known 1887 essay published in the quarterly *Nineteenth Century*, in which he singled out for criticism the work of W.T. Stead, editor of the *Pall Mall Gazette*. There Arnold coined the term "New Journalism," a term which came to describe the rapidly-expanding newspapers characterized by short, briskly written articles expressly geared and marketed to the busy modern reader. Arnold acknowledged the "ability, novelty, variety, sensation, sympathy, [and] generous instincts" of the New Journalism, but concluded that it would take a toll on the quality of public discourse in Britain:

> [I]ts one great fault is that it is *feather-brained*. It throws out assertions at a venture because it wishes them true; does not correct either them or itself, if they are false; and to get at the state of things as they truly are seems to feel no concern whatever. ("Up to Easter" 638)

Shortly after his attack on the New Journalism appeared, Arnold wrote to former *PMG* editor John Morley, "Under your friend Stead, the *PMG*, whatever may be its merits, is fast *ceasing to be literature*" (quoted in Brake 16, emphasis added).

While Laurel Brake has called Arnold's attack the sign of "high culture hegemony now beginning to give way," its greatest insight for my purposes is its reminder that, for much of the history of British print, no distinction between journalism and literature was assumed. In 1887 Matthew Arnold could, without explanation or qualification, assume an identity (or at least a compatibility) between literature and journalism: the best in newspaper and journal prose *is* literature, and it is the *PMG*'s fall from that realm that he asserts in his letter. Indeed Brake argues that in constructing the concept of the New Journalism, Arnold was consciously differentiating it from an implied Old Journalism, which aspires, often successfully, to the distinction of literature (1). While Brake and other historians have challenged the accuracy of the New Journalism as a historical idea, with its claims of a rapid and precisely dateable change for the worse in British journalism, Arnold's explanation retained its currency for Eliot and many of his contemporaries. Following Arnold's model, they continued to look to the early- and mid-nineteenth centuries as a golden age in journalism and publishing, an era when venerable outlets like the *Quarterly Review* and *Edinburgh Review* provided, to use Eliot's terms, "the work of men who were not hurried, and who could have the incentive of knowing that a part at least of their readers would read their work with corresponding care and leisure."

According to this thinking, the prelapsarian world of British Journalism ended with the fall into New Journalism, general education, broadly expanded readerships and publishing, and overtly commercial designs on the part of publishers. Herbert Tracey, a historian and critic who in 1929 compiled the guidebook *British Newspapers: A Survey, a Newspaper Directory, and a Who's Who in Journalism*, illustrates this nostalgic turn in his introduction. He writes that the newspaper public before the 1870 Education Act was a highly-educated, largely homogenous group whose "literary and political interests were characteristic of a well-defined social class"; such readers' "appetite for 'news' was distinctly smaller than its literary and intellectual enjoyments." He suggests that the appearance of *Tit-Bits* in 1881 marked the beginning of the decline of "the literary tradition of British journalism" (28). By contrast, Tracey observes that Victorian editors "were not the kind of men who would accept dictation from an owner, nor would they subordinate the policy of their papers to business considerations" (18). In his own day, he writes, "the Press has become a vast mechanism for making profits, and its 'original design and tendency' has been utterly forgotten by those who control it" (20).

Tracey's analysis speaks to the distinction between art and commerce—another distinction that carried great explanatory and rhetorical value for supporters of "literature" at the time, and one that recent critics have complicated by unearthing the commercial forces and motivations that have been obscured in histories of modernism.[10] The expansion of popular journalism had moved newspapers, as Tracey's essay illustrates, from the "art" to the "commerce" side of this binary in the minds of many educated commentators.[11] Meanwhile, practitioners of "serious" or "high-brow" literature struggled and competed to define their work as non-commercial and thus "artistic." Deploring the developments in popular journalism thus became a ready means for the self-definition of the "serious artist." But at the same time, modern writers recognized the benefits of the traditional symbiotic relationship between literature and the press, whose advertisements and reviews are needed to help writers reach their audiences.[12] As Joyce Piell Wexler has observed, modernist writers were often torn between the contrary drives of self-promotion, which relied to some degree on publicity, and self-definition, which called on them to construct themselves as "artistic" (and thus unpopular) (xii). So Eliot and others can occasionally be seen looking back with nostalgia to a day in which the literary and journalistic élite were one and the same, when it was possible to have a dominant voice in the press *and* a reputation as a serious artist. With the public sphere maddeningly more various than it had been in the heyday of the *Quarterly Review*, and with fear and loathing of the popular press common in intellectual circles, artists like Eliot needed to define a sphere of literary journalism that fell on the proper side of the art/commerce and high/low lines so they could explain and disseminate the principles of modernism. (One of Eliot's first decisions as editor of the *Criterion* was to commission Valery Larbaud's explication of *Ulysses*, which used the Linati schema to puzzle out some of the novel's mysteries.) Eliot's attempts to navigate these difficulties can be tracked through a reexamination of his work as a literary journalist and his polemics against the popular press.

II

In the 1926 essay "Lancelot Andrewes," Eliot surveyed the state of a culture which, he felt, had lost the linguistic ability to appreciate the beauty and brilliance of the best seventeenth-century prose. He wrote:

> To persons whose minds are habituated to feed on the vague jargon of our time, when we have a vocabulary for everything and exact ideas about nothing— when a word half-understood, torn from its place in some alien or half-formed science, as of psychology, conceals from both writer and reader the meaninglessness of a statement, when all dogma is in doubt except the dogmas of sciences of which we have read in the newspapers, when the language of theology itself, under the influence of an undisciplined mysticism of popular philosophy, tends to become a language of tergiversation—Andrewes may seem pedantic and verbal. (305)

Here Eliot blames the press for weakening the sensibilities of the British reader and for disseminating sham science and substandard theology. This quotation strikes one of the most common notes in Eliot's social and literary criticism: the decay of the English language. The 1920 essay "The Perfect Critic" may have marked the first time Eliot assigned journalism a specific role in this process of decay. He opens that essay by assailing the remarks of "a distinguished critic [who] observed recently, in a newspaper article, that 'poetry is the most highly organized form of intellectual activity'":

> ... [W]e were conscious that we were reading neither Coleridge nor Arnold. ... the words "organized" and "activity", occurring together in this phrase, [have] that familiar vague suggestion of the scientific vocabulary which is characteristic of modern writing. ... And if a phrase like "the most organized form of activity" is the highest organization of thought of which contemporary criticism, in a distinguished representative, is capable, then, we conclude, that modern criticism is degenerate. (50)

The pointed reference to a "newspaper article" suggests a divide between the ephemeral work of the newspaper reviewer and the lasting contribution of critics like Coleridge and Arnold. It also represents Eliot's effort to distinguish himself from the mass of critics in a crowded journalistic field. Elsewhere, Eliot argues further that this sort of imprecision in language and the muddled thinking it represents have broader social implications. Such degenerate language is, for one, infectious, and through its spread impoverishes public discourse. (Here we see Eliot picking up the thread of Arnold's critique.) In *Notes Towards a Definition of Culture*—a later work but one which, rather than developing a new idea about the decay of language, works out more thoroughly ideas Eliot first expressed in the 1920s—Eliot wrote that

> The residuum in the public mind is hardly likely to be a distillation of the best and wisest: it is more likely to represent the common prejudices of the majority of editors and reviewers. In this way are formed the *idées reçues*—more precisely the *mots reçues*—which, because of their emotional influence upon that part of the public which is influenced by printed matter, have to be taken into account by the professional politician. ... (88)

Beyond disseminating a degenerate language, the press encourages what Eliot saw as a gathering relativism, which he first perceived as a loss of standards in literature, an undermining of the "objective" qualities that separate the good from the bad. Eliot would argue in the 1933 essay "Religion and Literature" that the flood of new titles and the din of opinions from newspaper and journal critics has left readers with no stable source to look to for guidance on what to read: "There may be too many publishers; there are certainly too many books published; and the journals ever incite the reader to 'keep up' with what is being published" (104). In the 1923 essay "The Function of Criticism," Eliot describes the current state of criticism as "no better than a Sunday park of contending and contentious orators, who have not even arrived at the articulation of their differences" (33). Rather than seeking critical authority outside themselves—in the capital-T Tradition to which he and

Ezra Pound referred themselves—critics and readers rely, Eliot writes, on their personal responses, on what John Middleton Murry approvingly called their "inner voice." Eliot wrote that

> The inner voice, in fact, sounds remarkably like an old principle which has been formulated by an elder critic in the now familiar phrase "doing as one likes." The possessors of the inner voice ride ten in a compartment to a football match at Swansea, listening to the inner voice, which breathes the eternal message of vanity, fear, and lust. (35)

This last quotation, with its class-coded images of moral breakdown, suggests that the fear of a deeper social disorder lies behind Eliot's anxiety about critical relativism. The argument's political connotations become more explicit later in the essay, when Eliot bestows the term "whiggery" on the sort of critical thinking he deplores:

> ... to those who obey the inner voice (perhaps "obey" is not the word) nothing I can say about criticism will have the slightest value. For they will not be interested in the attempt to find any common principles for the pursuit of criticism. Why have principles, when one has the inner voice? If I like a thing, that is all I want; and if enough of us, shouting all together, like it, that should be all that *you* (who don't like it) ought to want. ...
> Thus speaks the Inner Voice. It is a voice to which, for convenience, we may give a name: and the name I suggest is Whiggery. (37)

The press, as Eliot wrote in "Literature and Religion," tends to fortify this anarchic "inner voice" by encouraging people to keep up with contemporary writing rather than subjecting themselves to the discipline of reading great works, a point he clinches by noting, "Individualistic democracy has come to high tide" (104). For Eliot, reading and comparing the impressions created by great works is the only route to "common principles of criticism." The press—figured above as "enough of us, shouting all together"—pushes readers in a contrary direction, thus fostering a breakdown of literary standards which, Eliot felt, betokens a wider social breakdown.[13]

A 1928 *Criterion* essay more transparently links the expanding press to what Eliot viewed as dangerously anarchic, democratic forces: "Our newspapers," Eliot wrote, "pretend that we are competent to make up our minds about foreign policy, though we may not know who is responsible for cleaning the streets of our own borough" ("Fascism" 289). Newspapers have offered more information, and thus invested more authority, in their consumers than they can handle, Eliot suggests (Chace 142). Like many of his contemporaries, Eliot, albeit from an opposite position on the political spectrum, would have agreed with Raymond Williams's claim that the expansion of publishing was an integral part of the democratization of western societies.

Eliot's periodic attacks on the press thus fit in with what Michael North has called Eliotic modernism's "antagonism to the other elements of modernity: rationalism, material progress, liberal democracy" (2).

III

Given Eliot's later disavowal of any interest in commercial success, it is tempting to accept this intermittent polemic against journalism as part and parcel of the art/commerce distinction in which he partook. But to do so would be to accept at face value Eliot's periodic pose as above commerce and disdainful of popularity, and to leave unexplored the degree to which Eliot relied on journalism for income and reputation during the most celebrated years of his career.[14] Publicly, Eliot may have claimed that the *Criterion* existed primarily to rehabilitate the lost, high tradition of British journalism. Privately, Eliot made it clear to his friends and family that he saw journalism as a path to financial independence and personal recognition. His letters reveal the poet as a savvy publicist, both of himself and of other colleagues and literary causes—a skilled and pragmatic viewer and manipulator of the London journalistic scene. They show Eliot knowingly navigating the bitterly competitive world of British literary journalism as he works simultaneously to emphasize his distance from philistine bourgeois culture and to differentiate among the products of the expanding "high-brow" literary press, sniping at competitors, throwing his weight behind some publications, and derogating others.

Eliot began soliciting freelance writing assignments soon after his arrival in London in 1914 and grew increasingly reliant on freelance journalism as a source of income through the 1920s. In November 1922—at a time in which Eliot's financial future was far from assured, and when his day job at Lloyd's bank continued to keep him from getting enough "continuous time" to work on his poetry (*Letters* 451)—Eliot complained to Ezra Pound about his continued need to publish reviews and essays:

> ... I don't want to write articles for the *Times* or for anything else, I don't want to write articles at all, I don't want to write, no sensible man does who wants to write verse. But I don't see how I am supposed to be selfsupporting in five years except by an enormous output of useless articles, literary rubbish etc. instead of the small number of which I have hitherto supplemented my income. It is preferable to run a review and be paid for letting other people write. ... Unless I can edit a paper that pays, or else that is so "important" in some way or other that rich ignoramuses will feel that they MUST subsidize it, I don't see how I can ever earn more than £150 per year maximum. (*Letters* 592-3)

The letter makes a number of important facts plain: first that money at least partially motivated Eliot's journalism from the beginning; and second that he conceived the *Criterion* as a money-making venture. The letter was written while plans for *The Criterion* were coming to a head, and Eliot's language makes it clear that he saw in it a chance to "edit a paper that pays"—not solely an outlet for his literary theories and preferences. We may presume that Eliot was more candid with Pound than he was with critic and *Criterion* contributor Herbert Read, to whom he described the proposed journal as "a more chic and brilliant *Art and Letters*, which might have a fashionable vogue among a wealthy few" (quoted in Margolis 35-6). In spite of the angry and exhausted tone of the letter to Pound, Eliot continued to contribute to journals and to work at the bank. In fact, his journalistic output was just beginning its upward trend at that moment: ten articles of Eliot's appeared in periodicals in England, the United States, and France in 1922—a marked increase in activity from the previous year, according to Donald Gallup's bibliography. His output was to peak in 1927, when he would publish, by Gallup's count, fifty articles.

But the fatigued and cynical Eliot evident in the 1922 letters offers a very partial view of the poet's complicated and constantly shifting relationship with journalism. Earlier letters provide views of another Eliot with a different agenda: Eliot as the young, energetic self-promoter who quickly grasps the realities of the London journalism scene. Eliot aggressively sought out his affiliations with periodicals from about 1915.[15] He wrote to his brother that year, asking him to visit editors to major U.S. periodicals on his behalf. Of the *New Republic*, he wrote, "That pays, and might be persuaded to take criticism, or little articles" (*Letters* 105). His success in gaining assignments and his rapid upward mobility—he steadily wrote for larger and larger outlets—indicate that Eliot had a good grasp of the market for literary essays and a drive to write for continually larger, more prestigious, and better paying periodicals (Ackroyd 97). By 1919, Eliot had worked his way from hopelessly coterie-based publications like *Blast*, to prestigious but esoteric journals like the *International Journal of Ethics*, to the socialist *New Statesman*, then to the more broadly pitched *Athenaeum* and finally to the top of the world of British literary journalism—the *Times Literary Supplement*. While the *TLS* may not have appealed to as broad a public as the million-selling *Daily Mail*, it did have a circulation of more than 20,000—about twenty-five times that of the *Criterion* at its peak (Ackroyd 248). As Michael Kauffman has observed, the *TLS* was "simply put, *the* literary establishment of London"; with a reasonably broad audience guaranteed by its high circulation, writing for the *TLS* meant that one "had to know how to appeal to audiences" (138). Publishing in the *TLS* could thus not be described as the "minority journalism" Eliot would later claim as the reserve of the best critical minds of his age ("Journalists Old and New" 237). And Eliot was anything but embarrassed to hitch his fortunes to the *TLS* in 1919. Literary journalism, he wrote to his mother that year, was preferable to lecturing, which was "more fatiguing"; writing would

> give me notoriety and in the end more money. I enclose a letter which shows that I have been asked to write for the *Times Literary Supplement*—to write the Leading Article from time to time. This is the highest honour possible in the critical world of literature, and we are pleased. (*Letters* 337)

But while he wanted the income and recognition that went with reviewing, Eliot also feared growing too dependent upon it—or too widely identified as a journalist. Earlier that year, he had passed up an offer of an editorship at one of London's top literary papers—John Middleton Murry's *Athenaeum* (*Letters* 283). His explanation to his family shows that the refusal was part of Eliot's careful management of his literary reputation, which he thought could suffer if Eliot the journalist began to overshadow Eliot the poet. The letter, written to his brother Henry in April 1919, also shows that Eliot had a sense of the relative circulations of the literary weeklies. "My reputation," he wrote, "is built on writing very little, but very good, and I should not add to it by this sort of thing. ... I probably have more influence and power and distinction *outside* of the journalistic struggle and having no material stake in it" (*Letters* 283, emphasis original). Making a point more likely to carry weight with his practically-minded brother, Eliot argued that the *Athenaeum* was in danger because of the increased competition in the literary journalism market: "In the prime of the *Athenaeum* there was no competitor; now there is the *Times Supplement* at second. The *Athenaeum* is sixth." Eliot's worries about the paper's future in a saturated market were well-placed: the *Athenaeum* was forced to merge with the more politically oriented *Nation* in 1921, and a number of employees lost their jobs.

Eliot, then, knew enough of the journalism market to foresee the *Athenaeum*'s demise. But if he knew what would fail in that market, he also had strong opinions about what would succeed. His early stewardship of the *Criterion* and his advice to *Dial* editor Schofield Thayer show that Eliot had well-developed ideas about how to reach and appeal to the niche market those publications sought. He suggested advertising the inaugural number of the *Criterion* in ten English newspapers, and provided Richard Cobden-Sanderson, the review's publisher, with an ad he designed and a list of the ten papers "in order of importance." The list shows that Eliot attempted to cast a wide net in attracting readers to *The Criterion*. Rather than advertising strictly in other literary weeklies and monthlies, his list included the major national dailies *The Times*, *The Morning Post* and the *Manchester Guardian* in addition to the *TLS* and several large, provincial dailies. He included the *Morning Post* despite its reputation as the seat of mainstream Tory thought in London—a reputation Ezra Pound referred to in calling it "the real voice of England, and the most concentrated and persistent will toward evil in Europe" (*Letters* 511). Eliot urged Schofield Thayer to do the same for the *Dial*, which he believed was missing out on potential circulation because not enough people knew about it. He wrote Thayer in November, 1922 that

> [t]he *Dial* is gradually establishing itself in London but so far only among the people who make it their business to find out what is good. ... if you could advertise a bit in some of the best English papers ... your circulation would be greatly increased. (*Letters* 602)

Eliot's language here embeds one of the central paradoxes in the early history of modernism: the simultaneous desire of writers to speak to an élite and to reach a wide audience. Eliot flatters Thayer by saying that the *Dial*'s popularity rests with "people who make it their business to find out what is good" but at the same time urges him to take steps to reach beyond that élite audience. The implication is that the *Dial*, despite its target, discriminating audience, should reach out to those who do not seek to "know what is good."

Eliot realized that artists need to engage with literary journalism, much as they may dislike it, in order to make a living and maintain a reputation. Even those who do not work full-time in journalism, it seems, have a "material stake" in the "journalistic struggle." In a 1920 letter to John Quinn, Eliot observes that Ezra Pound is losing readership in London because the literary press is hostile, or at best indifferent, to his work. Part of the problem is that Pound's critical voice—unlike Eliot's—is absent from the literary press. Eliot writes:

> The fact is there is now no organ of any importance in which he can express himself, and he is becoming forgotten. It is not enough for him simply to publish a volume of verse once a year—or no matter how often—for it will simply not be reviewed and will be killed by silence. Here in London a man's first work may always attract attention, because while he is unknown he has no enemies, but later it is essential that he should establish solid connections with at least one important paper. (*Letters* 358)

What emerges in such letters is Eliot's clear understanding that anyone who wanted to become established as a writer needed the help of the press. In the 1920s, modernism had not yet established its important beachheads into the University, which would ultimately, as Gail McDonald and others have shown, become its primary source of cultural authority. Lacking the university as a means of underwriting literary reputations and modernist experimental techniques, writers and critical supporters of modernism had to argue their cases through the press—a condition that produced camps of competing journals—Eliot's modernist *Criterion* and Leavis's *Scrutiny* versus the more conventionally oriented *Mercury* of J.C. Squire, for example. The reality that artists required access to the press—a reality which pushed Pound into a considerably more embittered attitude towards it than Eliot—forced Eliot and many other "high modernist" writers into various unhappy marriages of convenience with the press. Perhaps the greatest natural symbol of these marriages is Eliot's *Criterion* itself, which was initially financed by Lady Rothermere, wife of the publisher of the infamous *Daily Mail*—for years the signifier for the worst excesses of the New Journalism. Eliot's ambivalence about this reliance on journalism suggests that his broad, general critiques of journalism are, psychologically speaking, a form of over-compensation. Between 1916, when Eliot's first book review appeared in the *International Journal of Ethics*, and 1932, when he had established himself as a major force in English poetry and criticism, Eliot published 290 articles, according to the Gallup bibliography. During those years, it did not take an especially attentive reader of the literary papers to see that this sworn foe of the press was curiously reliant on it.

IV

As we have seen, Eliot worked his own particular variation on a cultural discourse that blames the practices of publishers and the press, broadly defined, for the decay of culture. At the same time, within the narrow segment of the press in which he worked, he was a consummate insider, sharp on the latest gossip and savvy in earning himself a niche in that small and highly competitive world. Eliot dealt with this contradiction through periodic commentaries—like the one that inaugurated the monthly *Criterion*—which attempted to define an acceptable sphere of quality journalism and differentiate it from the flood of discourse pouring daily from the expanding British press. Eliot faced this issue most directly in two essays that take up the nature of journalism—"Charles Whibley" of 1931 and the brief "Journalists of Yesterday and Today" of 1940. "Charles Whibley" offers a new definition of journalism that serves to ennoble it by defining it very narrowly and by disavowing "the distinction between literature and journalism"—a distinction which, as we have seen, underlay the tradition of cultural criticism in which Eliot's earlier attacks on journalism took part. "Journalists of Yesterday and Today" abandons this definition in favor of a new distinction between mainstream and "minority" journalism. Close examination shows that both essays re-inscribe the distinction between literature and *most* journalism and set up a separate and superior category for the journalism of Eliot and his contemporaries.

Eliot rehabilitates "journalism" as a term in "Charles Whibley" by redefining it so as to purge the negative connotations that have come to cling to it. (These connotations were so common in the period that, in a 1919 book review, Rebecca West felt compelled to note: "We do not use the term journalist in a disparaging sense, as the aesthetes do.") Eliot constructs his new definition of journalism by writing the daily newspaper out of it entirely, thus separating the journalistic field in which he works—literary journalism—from the rest of the mass of letterpress. (This distinction may seem natural to us, but, as we have seen, it was more common for Eliot to view the literary reviews and the daily papers, however different they may have been, as competing in the same public sphere.) While the 1931 essay purports to dissolve the distinction between literature and journalism, it in fact sets up new categories, making a distinction between "what all would concede to be the *best* in journalism" ("Charles Whibley" 440) and everything else, with the latter a sprawling and ill-defined category represented merely by a dismissive reference to "tonight's evening paper." Not surprisingly, the "journalism" that emerges from this redefinition can be applied to Eliot's social and literary commentary—and the type of journalism found in the *Criterion* generally—just as easily as it can be applied to Whibley's columns. This self-justification is subtle: Eliot merely *hints* at the affinity between his work and Whibley's, noting that he has a "very close sympathy" with the "type of mind" that produces the finest journalism. But the parallels between Eliot's journalism and Whibley's, both of which attain high quality despite their association with deadline writing and the ephemeral context of the monthly review, become more pronounced when one encounters "Charles Whibley" in Eliot's 1932 *Selected Essays*—itself an attempt to elevate periodical writing to a more lasting and dignified position. There the essay was given prominent position, appearing as the final piece, and it appeared second-to-last in subsequent editions. "The best in journalism" serves not only as a laurel for Whibley but, implicitly, as a description of Eliot's journalism and as the final word in a volume that represents Eliot's attempt to rescue his deadline writing from the oblivion for which most journalism is destined.

Eliot acknowledges that Whibley, who had just died at the time of the essay's publication, is in danger of sinking into obscurity because he wrote material "of the kind which will be called ephemeral" (439). In memorializing him, Eliot is forced to defend Whibley's work against the implication that its perishability necessarily reflects some inferiority, either of the work itself or of the metier (journalism) in which it is written. So Eliot argues against the premise that journalism's perishability is one of its defining characteristics—and one that makes it inherently inferior to "literature." This strain of argument leads Eliot to the uncharacteristic position that writing often survives the test of time not because of intrinsic value but because of historical contingencies, the "curious accidents which protect a piece of writing from oblivion" (440). If Whibley's work disappears from view, Eliot argues, it will not be because it is qualitatively different from literature, as

> The distinction between "journalism" and "literature" is quite futile, unless we are drawing such violent contrast as that between Gibbon's *History* and tonight's evening paper; and such a contrast itself is too violent to have meaning. You cannot, that is, draw any useful distinction between journalism and literature merely in a scale of literary values, as a difference between the well-written and the supremely well-written. (439)

A close look at the syntax of that first sentence shows that Eliot is, despite the opening protestation, maintaining a distinction between literature and journalism. If one were to compare the nightly newspaper to Gibbon's *History*, we may infer, the distinction between literature and journalism would not be "futile." Still, as the next clause states, that distinction would be "too violent to have meaning." (Such a comparison, then, we might ask, would be meaningless but not "futile"?) Eliot has here buried the distinction between journalism and literature under a thick cover of subordination and qualification, but he has not extinguished it. But the passage's most telling elements are the antithetical terms Eliot uses to illustrate the futility of the distinction between literature and journalism. The violent contrast lies between Gibbon's *History*—a work of non-fiction which has nonetheless come to be thought of as "literature"—and Gibbon's antithesis: the evening newspaper, non-fiction presumably with no imaginable lasting value. A discernible contrast does exist between these two extremes, Eliot implies: one is literature and one is so clearly not literature as to be laughable, to be easily dismissible. This proviso, which comes in the essay's second paragraph, is its only reference to any kind of journalism besides the kinds of literary and social commentary both Whibley and Eliot wrote. In the definition of journalism Eliot offers in "Charles Whibley," literary journalism and political commentary are the only sorts that qualify. The daily newspaper, by far the largest purveyor of what most people consider "journalism," does not merit consideration.

Eliot's redefinition of "journalism" is necessary, he argues (striking a familiar note), because the word "has deteriorated in the last thirty years; and it is particularly fitting ... to try to recall it to its more permanent sense." Rather than being defined by its ephemeral nature, journalism must be rethought by considering "the type of mind, concerned in writing what all would concede to be the *best* journalism" (440). And Eliot explicitly associates himself with that sort of mind:

> There is a type of mind, and I have a very close sympathy with it, which can only turn to writing, or only produce its best writing, under the pressure of an immediate occasion; and it is this type of mind which I propose to treat as the journalist's. The underlying causes may differ: the cause may be an ardent preoccupation with affairs of the day, or it may be (as with myself) inertia or laziness requiring an immediate stimulus, or a habit formed by early necessity of

204 Challenging Modernism

earning small sums quickly. It is not so much that the journalist works on different material from that of other writers, as that he works from a different, no less and often more honourable, motive. (440)

Eliot's broad generalizations here serve to ennoble journalism. While Eliot does not directly identify himself as a journalist, he does so indirectly, by parenthetically acknowledging—("as with myself")—that "inertia or laziness" have at times prevented him from writing without "the pressure of an immediate occasion."[16] In fact, as we have seen, the need for the "stimulus" of a deadline or an assignment is not the only habit of mind Eliot shares with journalists (as he defines them): to be sure, much of his earliest journalism was motivated by "the early necessity of earning small sums quickly." In Eliot's case, the two motivations may be related. The "early necessity" for money may have created habits that made Eliot into the sort of writer who thrives on the "immediate" stimuli of assignments and deadlines: Eliot kept producing literary journalism after it was no longer an economic necessity, probably because he perceived a symbiosis between his criticism and his poetry. The "immediate stimulus" of his early assignments for the *TLS* and other periodicals provided Eliot with the opportunity to enrich and order his knowledge about previous poets—a knowledge which, as we know, he thought indispensable to the practice of poetry.[17] As McDonald has argued, Eliot's work as an extension lecturer allowed him to study and prepare for his early essays, which he, in turn, used to formulate his model of the literary tradition and prepare a place for himself in it (56). Writing for periodicals and doing extension lectures were both ways of developing the crucial sense of tradition and "earning small sums" at the same time. But perhaps most noteworthy here is the distance Eliot has traveled since 1922: where he once justified his journalism through its similarity with "the work of men who were not hurried," he is here secure enough in his cultural authority to make the self-deprecating suggestion that some of his journalism originated under the "hurrying" influence of deadlines and the need to earn commissions "quickly."

"Charles Whibley," then, shows Eliot taking yet another view of journalism that differs from his positions at other times and in other contexts. The best in literary journalism is here completely distinct from the rest of the "press" (a word that is notably absent from "Charles Whibley"). Literary journalism has also gained considerable dignity now that Eliot does not need it to survive economically. No longer the precinct of "useless articles, literary rubbish etc.," material "for which there is no need and which furthermore is said to damage my brain" (Valerie Eliot 273), "journalism" is now qualitatively equivalent to literature, as noble and worthy of preservation as imaginative literature. The terms of the discussion shift again thirteen years later in "Journalists of Yesterday and Today," which offers Eliot's most insightful commentary on the broad outlines of British journalism. "Charles Whibley" had allowed Eliot to defend the type of journalism he and his closest contemporaries practiced, but at the cost of creating a decidedly narrow and eccentric definition of "journalism" that wrenched the term from its common usage. If the term had become imprecise "over the last 30 years," with negative connotations leaching to it and imperiling the reputation of serious writers who practiced it, Eliot himself could share in the blame. "Journalists of Yesterday and Today," more accurately, acknowledges the existence of journalism that appeals to the broad public and journalism that does not, taking note of the stratification of the reading audience in which *The Criterion* and its competitors took part. In a sense, the essay marks Eliot's withdrawal from competition with the mainstream press, his acknowledgement that quality journalism, by his definition, is bound to a narrower audience and a more limited influence, even in its own time. But Eliot recasts this apparent retreat as a deferred victory by suggesting that the minority journalism of today will get its due far in the future, when the strange gods of a declining culture are forgotten.

In the essay, published in the small circulation *New English Weekly*, Eliot observes that his generation of writers has not produced a "great journalist" of the magnitude of H.G. Wells, George Bernard Shaw, or G.K. Chesterton—three Edwardian lights who were still publishing in 1940. Eliot's contemporaries Wyndham Lewis, John Middleton Murry, and John Macmurray all had "the necessary fluency, earnestness and *desire to influence as large an audience as possible*" that marks a great journalist. "Yet none of them has ever been listened to by more than a minority public" (237, emphasis added). Eliot attributes this generational difference to changes in the audience. Wells was born into a world of "getting on" in which the natural inclination for an aspiring writer was "to make one's living." Eliot's contemporaries, in contrast, have found themselves "in a position where 'getting on' was always out of the question. There was nowhere to get to. That kind of success, for a serious man of letters, is no longer possible" (237). This change in the readership has meant that the "serious journalism of my generation is all minority journalism." While Lewis, Murry and (implicitly) Eliot himself go on writing "for a small number of thinking people prepared for the new 'dogma'" (238), the aging, middlebrow Wells continues to write for the broad public:

> The crowd of season-ticket holders is still there—it is bigger than ever—reading Mr. Wells's latest in the first class as well as the third class compartment: he tells them what they are ready to accept, and part of what he says is true. His great imaginative gifts, and picture-book method, make very real to his public the situation that he describes; and as he does not reason, or draw upon any kind of wisdom inaccessible to the common man, he imposes no great strain upon the minds of his readers. And as his proposals are always in world terms, he does

not ask of his readers individually any great exertion from which they would flinch. (237)

Here we see Eliot re-engaging with the discourse of cultural decay that identifies journalism with the expansion of an unthinking middlebrow that exerts a drag on the culture. But the essay much more clearly and insistently separates out from this mass of letterpress a species of journalism that has lasting value: "Our public is not yet in existence," Eliot writes, placing the journalists of his generation alongside the poets and other artists as the avante-garde of a new dispensation.

> This is not to maintain an attitude of aloofness, but a realistic view of the limits of our possible effectiveness ... we are more disposed to see our hope in modest and local beginnings. ... we must keep alive aspirations which can remain valid throughout the longest and darkest period of universal calamity and degradation. (238)

Huyssen has suggested that the success and popularity of mass culture is always a source of repressed envy on the part of modernist élites (17), and this envy rises close to the surface in "Journalists of Yesterday and Today": despite their "desire to influence as large an audience as possible," Eliot acknowledges, Lewis, Murry, and Macmurray are relegated to a sphere of "minority journalism." Yet he recasts their failure to reach a wide audience as a qualified success—indeed as the only success available to the "serious man of letters." This success lies largely in minority journalism's avoidance of a popular sphere associated with cultural decline and gathering international calamity: to be popular would be to participate in the process of political and cultural decay. The essay's apocalyptic ending posits these minority journalists as guardians of a culture about to descend into "the longest and darkest period of calamity and degradation"—akin (though Eliot does not make the analogy explicitly) to the monks who kept Christianity alive during the dark ages. This ending surely reflects the onset of World War II, which brings out in Eliot a particularly telling—and darkly shaded—version of his belief in the necessity of a cultural élite. And it is unequivocal in expressing Eliot's view of whom we can entrust with the task of carrying on the light: while the aims of Eliot's minority party "are less glittering, they may prove less deceptive: for Mr. Wells, putting all his money on the near future, is walking very near the edge of despair." The familiar terms of the high/low divide come into play: Eliot's brand of journalism has its eye on eternity, while Wells's focuses on the bleak and transient "near future"; Eliot's appeals to a few cognoscenti, while Wells's reaches into "the first class as well as the third class compartments" of the evening train—a common signifier for the mass reading public, with its middlebrow tastes.

"Journalists of Yesterday and Today," then, finds Eliot at a juncture where he can comfortably manipulate the terms of the high/low divide. By 1940, Eliot had long enjoyed a steady income, as well as an insider's advantages, from his position as an editor at Faber and Faber (Sharpe 151). His reputation was secure, and was beginning to pay off in greatly increased press runs and sales. *Collected Poems 1909-1935* had a combined press run, in Britain and the United States, of more than 10,000—a substantial number, considering that *Prufrock and Other Observations* and *The Waste Land* had debuted with press runs of 500 or fewer (Sharpe 156). The months that followed the publication of "Journalists of Yesterday and Today" would see the *New English Weekly* put out a special edition of "East Coker" in response to requests for reprints of the edition in which it first appeared; the book publication of the poem, later that year, would rapidly sell 12,000 copies (Sharpe 159). So it is from a secure place that Eliot inhabits, in "Journalists of Yesterday and Today," the position of defender-of-culture, a position which has become so closely associated with Eliot that it often obscures the much less comfortable, less hegemonic positions he occupied in the course of getting there. Eliot could not always so flatly acknowledge the "minority" status of the sort of journalism he practiced. Nor could he, when neither his livelihood nor his reputation was so assured, survey the overall journalistic landscape with the candid, analytical eye he cast upon it in the 1940 essay. Eliot would continue to publish essays in periodicals through the 1940s, but a large majority of them would deal with larger social, political, and religious concerns: rarely did they deal directly with poetry or literature. Eliot wanted to be heard on matters like the future of English education and the post-war relations among Europe's nations. He needed the press as an outlet, but he truly had ceased to have a "material stake in the journalistic struggle." Or, to use Eliot's own terms, the state of mind that underlay his journalism had switched from the "need to earn small sums quickly" to "an ardent preoccupation with the affairs of the day" ("Charles Whibley" 440).

Notes

1. For an account that views Eliot as such, see Russell Kirk's critical biography *Eliot in His Age*, especially Chapter IV, which argues that *The Criterion* was a "mission to the educated classes" and an attempt to reclaim "the common cultural patrimony of Europe" (97-8). For a further summary of criticism that takes this view of Eliot, see Chinitz 236.

2. Two excellent, relatively recent articles touch on the ways in which Eliot defined himself in relationship to and through the use of the press. Leonard Diepeveen, in "'I Can Have More Than Enough Power to Satisfy Me': T.S. Eliot's Construction of his Audience," argues that Eliot, in his essays, implicitly crafts the appropriate audience for his poetry by opposing it to a (more explicitly defined) "confused," contemptible, average reader—i.e. a reader from the middle class "general reading public." Diepeveen writes that "Eliot's rhetorical strategy divides his readers into two useful groups that serve as

the focus for his discontent: critics and the reading public" (43), and this essay will look at how both of these groups become associated, for Eliot, with the lazy intellectual habits of newspaper writers and readers. In "Does The Waste Land Have a Politics?" Michael Levenson notes, as does my essay, that Eliot felt the need to differentiate himself amidst the journalistic landscape of London in the late teens and early twenties, a landscape he saw as "culturally crowded ... a sharply divided field, where the waves of 'semi-education' overwhelm the apostles of subtlety" (9).

3.   Eliot wrote in 1933, "The most useful poetry, socially, would be one which could cut across all the present stratifications of public taste—stratifications which are perhaps a sign of social disintegration" (*Uses* 246). See Chinitz 238-40, for a discussion of Eliot's vision of cultural disintegration and his resulting "uneasiness with his poetic vocation."

4.   The annual *Writers' and Artists' Year Book*, founded in 1907 and published by A & C Black Ltd., offers a revealing glimpse of the range of publications appearing in Britain during the period. The 1922 edition of the year book, intended as a reference to aspiring freelance writers and artists, lists more than 650 periodicals that accept freelance submissions.

5.   See, for example, Edward Bishop's "Recovering Modernism—Format and Function in the Little Magazines" and Shari and Bernard Benstock's "The Role of Little Magazines in the Emergence of Modernism."

6.   The monthly *London Mercury* ran from 1919-39; the *New English Weekly* from 1932-49, continuing its predecessor the *New Age*; the monthly *English Review* from 1908-37, and the quarterly *Art and Letters* from 1917-20.

7.   For details on the number of magazines publishing fiction, see McAleer 25-7 and *passim*.

8.   A number of fine studies of Eliot's increasing interest in larger cultural and political issues exist. William M. Chace's *The Political Identities of Ezra Pound and T.S. Eliot* traces this development, locating "two Eliots," the first a literary critic concerned about the dwindling sphere of literature and the humanistic tendency for literary criticism to attempt to stand in for religion, the second a self-fashioned cultural critic who "organized his power in such a way that he became more and more interested in the forces, political and religious, that form or malform society as a whole" (135). In *T.S. Eliot and Ideology*, Kenneth Asher builds on Chace's account, arguing that Eliot's literary criticism was, from the beginning, an ideological pursuit, an attempt to "[impose] an ideology on English literature" (46). Both Asher and Chace situate Eliot in relation to late nineteenth- and early twentieth-century critiques of bourgeois liberalism. Michael North's emphasis, in *The Political Aesthetic of Yeats, Eliot, and Pound*, is on the contemporary philosophical (specifically epistemological) crises that underlay Eliot's political positions; he finds that Eliot's emphasis on "local, racial, and temporal particularism"—the disposition that underlay, for example, Eliot's anti-immigration and anti-Semitic pronouncements—was part of a lifelong negotiation of the relationship between general and particular, idea and fact, diversity and unity (83). Michael Tratner, in *Modernism and Mass Politics*, finds Eliot's poetry, like his criticism, concerned with a perceived stratification and decay of culture and invested in a vision of new society in which the "cultural activities" of the élite "become forces for unifying the strata" (167).

9.   The Reverend G.A. Weekes, vice-chancellor of Cambridge University, in 1927 told an audience of booksellers, "When I read in the Press anything about which I consider myself an expert, I generally find that the newspapers have it incorrectly"; Weekes also wondered aloud "what can be the state of mind of a person whose mental pabulum is the daily newspapers" ("The Universities and the Press" 351). Two years later Herbert Tracey, in an introduction to a guide to British newspapers, lamented the developments of the past half-century, rehearsing the common argument that increased literacy had not

had the improving effect hoped for, that "the spread of popular education has diluted the strength and liveliness as much as it has enlarged the volume of the national intelligence." He continued by differentiating modern journalism from Victorian journalism:

> However that may be, it is undeniable that popular journalism, in the importance it attaches to "news" and in the cruder, more sensational, and "snippety" presentation of its product, ministers to a far less cultivated taste and a much more superficial interest (28).

T.H.S. Escott, a late-Victorian journalist who wrote a number of essays and a book-length history of British journalism, wrote in 1927 that "there are to-day whole families innumerable owing all that they think, believe, or say about the topics of the time to the leaderettes and paragraphs with which the halfpenny sheet abounds ... not by any means written by an expert in any of these departments" (366).

10. See, for example, Lawrence Rainey's "The Price of Modernism," which documents the care with which publication of *The Waste Land* was orchestrated to maximize publicity and create notoriety; Joyce Piell Wexler's *Who Paid for Modernism?*, which locates an unacknowledged complicity between the capitalist publishing enterprise and modernism; and Joseph Kelly's *Our Joyce,* a reputation history that carefully studies the marketing of *Dubliners, A Portrait,* and *Ulysses.*

11. See Wexler's introduction for an excellent account of the way the distinction between art and commerce influenced modernist self-fashioning.

12. The editors of the Christian *British Weekly* invoked this symbiosis in taking issue with Reverend Weekes's comments to the booksellers' conference: "What did the Associated Booksellers think of those comments? Do not their sales depend largely on reviews and advertisements in the dailies? Would not every member of the Congress agree with us that the popular demand for cheap editions of the classics has been mainly fostered by the Press?" ("The Universities and the Press" 351).

13. Approaching such statements from a slightly different point of view, Leonard Diepeveen sees Eliot crafting his readership by defining it against other readers with weak and lazy reading habits brought about in part by the influence of bad criticism. Eliot devises "two useful groups that serve as the focus of his discontent: critics and the reading public," Diepeveen writes. "Bad reviewing has bad consequences not so much because it is wrong, but because the reading public accepts what it is told. ... According to Eliot, cultural power proceeds from the top down, and powerful and inept critics stand in the way of the literary paradigm shift that Eliot and others were to effect in the coming years" (43-4).

14. Eliot's critics of the 1960s and 1970s helped to sustain this image of Eliot as unconcerned with material success. See Kirk 7.

15. See Valerie Eliot 104.

16. Eliot's pose of modesty aside, the statement seems an accurate comment on Eliot's composition habits at certain times in his career: his exchange of letters with Pound in late 1921 and early 1922 shows, for example, that he did not finish *The Waste Land* until Pound was negotiating with Thayer and others for its publication: deadline pressure helped him to complete the work he had conceived three years earlier.

17. Eliot wrote, famously, in "Tradition and the Individual Talent," that "Tradition is a matter of much wider significance. It cannot be inherited, and if you want it you must obtain it with great labor. It involves, in the first place, the historical sense; ... the historical sense compels a man to write not merely with his own generation in his bones, but with a feeling that the whole of the literature of Europe ... has a simultaneous existence and composes a simultaneous order" (38).

References

Ackroyd, Peter. *T.S. Eliot*. London: Hamish Hamilton, 1984.

Arnold, Matthew. "Up to Easter." *Nineteenth Century* 22 (1887): 638-9.

Asher, Kenneth. *T.S. Eliot and Ideology*. Cambridge: Cambridge University Press, 1995.

Benstock, Shari and Bernard. "The Role of Little Magazines in the Emergence of Modernism." *Library Chronicle of the University of Texas* 20.4 (1991): 68-87.

Bishop, Edward. "Recovering Modernism—Format and Function in the Little Magazines." *Modernist Writers and the Marketplace*. Ed. Ian Willison *et al*. London: MacMillan, 1996.

Brake, Laurel. "The Old Journalism and the New: Forms of Cultural Production in London in the 1880s." *Papers for the Millions: The New Journalism in Britain, 1850s to 1914*. New York and London: Greenwood Press, 1988.

Briffault, Robert. "The Wail of Grub Street." *English Review* 32 (June 1921): 513-6.

Chace, William. *The Political Identities of Ezra Pound and T.S. Eliot*. Stanford: Stanford University Press, 1973.

Chinitz, David. "T.S. Eliot and the Cultural Divide." *PMLA* 110.2 (March 1995): 236-46.

Diepeveen, Leonard. "I Can Have More Than Enough Power to Satisfy Me": T.S. Eliot's Construction of His Audience." *Marketing Modernisms*. Ed. Kevin Dettmar and Stephen Watt. Ann Arbor: University of Michigan Press, 1996.

Eliot, T.S. "Charles Whibley." *Selected Essays*. New York: Harcourt Brace, 1950. 371-81.

——. "A Commentary." *Criterion* 5.2 (May 1927): 187-90.

——. "A Commentary." *Criterion* 5.3 (June 1927): 283-6.

——. "The Function of Criticism." *Criterion* 2.5 (October 1923): 31-42.

——. "Journalists of Yesterday and Today." *New English Weekly* 16 (8 February 1940): 237-8.

——. "Lancelot Andrewes." *Selected Essays*. New York: Harcourt Brace, 1950. 299-310.

——. "The Literature of Fascism." *Criterion* 8 (December 1928): 288-90.

——. *Notes Towards a Definition of Culture*. New York: Harcourt Brace, 1949.

——. "Religion and Literature." *Selected Prose*. Ed. Frank Kermode. New York: Harcourt Brace, 1975. 97-106.

——. "The Social Function of Poetry." *On Poetry and Poets*. London: Noonday Press, 1961.

——. "Tradition and the Individual Talent." *Selected Prose*. Ed. Frank Kermode. New York: Harcourt Brace, 1975. 37-44.

——. "The Perfect Critic." *Selected Prose*. Ed. Frank Kermode. New York: Harcourt Brace, 1975. 50-8.

——. *The Use of Poetry and the Use of Criticism*. Cambridge: Harvard University Press, 1933.

Eliot, Valerie, ed. *Letters of T.S. Eliot*. Vol 1. London: Faber and Faber, 1988.

Escott, T.H.S. "Old and New in the Daily Press." *Quarterly Review* 227 (1917): 353-68.

Gallup, Donald. *T.S. Eliot: A Bibliography*. London: Faber and Faber, 1952.

Huyssen, Andreas. *After the Great Divide: Modernism, Mass Culture, Postmodernism*. Bloomington: Indiana University Press, 1986.

Kauffman, Michael. "A Modernism of One's Own: Virginia Woolf's *TLS* Reviews and Eliotic Modernism." *Virginia Woolf and the Essay*. New York: St. Martin's, 1998. 137-55.

Kelly, Joseph. *Our Joyce: From Outcast to Icon*. Austin: University of Texas Press, 1998.

Kirk, Russell. *Eliot and his Age: T.S. Eliot's Moral Imagination in the Twentieth Century*. New York: Random House, 1971

Levenson, Michael. "Does The Waste Land Have a Politics?" *Modernism/Modernity* 6.3 (September 1999): 1-13.

Malcolm, D.O. "Charles Whibley." *Dictionary of National Biography*, 1922-30. London:

Oxford University Press, 1931. 905-7.

Margolis, John D. *T.S. Eliot's Intellectual Development*. Chicago and London: University of Chicago Press, 1972.

McAleer, Joseph. *Popular Reading and Publishing in Britain, 1914-1950*. Oxford: Clarendon Press, 1992.

McDonald, Gail. *Learning to be Modern: Pound, Eliot, and the American University*. Oxford: Clarendon Press, 1993.

North, Michael. *The Political Aesthetic of Yeats, Eliot, and Pound*. Cambridge: Cambridge University Press, 1991.

Rainey, Lawrence. "The Price of Modernism: Re-considering the Publication of *The Waste Land*." *Yale Review* 78.2 (Winter 1989): 279-300.

Sharpe, Tony. "T.S. Eliot and Ideas of *Oeuvre*." *Modernist Writers and the Marketplace*. Ed. Ian Willison *et al*. London: MacMillan, 1996.

Tracey, Herbert, ed. *The British Press: A Survey, A Newspaper Directory, and a Who's Who in Journalism*. London: Europa, 1929.

Tratner, Michael. *Modernism and Mass Politics: Joyce, Woolf, Eliot, Yeats*. Stanford: Stanford University Press, 1995.

West, Rebecca. "Towards New Horizons." *Daily News* 21 (March 1919): 4.

Wexler, Joyce Peill. *Who Paid for Modernism?* Fayetteville: University of Arkansas Press, 1997.

Williams, Raymond. *The Politics of Modernism*. London: Verso, 1989.

"The Universities and the Press." *British Weekly* 21 July, 1927: 351.

Index

Abel, Elizabeth 50
abortion
  See sexuality and abortion
Aldington, Richard
  The Colonel's Daughter 104
Anand, Mulk Raj 120
anthropology
  See intellectual movements
anti-Semiticism 44, 128–9, 149, 183, 208
Ardis, Ann 5, 13
Arnold, Matthew 192–3, 195
Asher, Kenneth
  T.S. Eliot and Ideology 208
Auden Generation 7, 117
Auden, W.H. 116
authorship 57

Barnard, Rita 157
Barnes, Djuna 157
Barthes, Roland 26
Beauman, Nicola
  A Very Great Profession 98, 112
Beckett, Samuel 116
Belford, Barbara 55, 70
Bellmer, Hans 182
  Poupées 183
Benjamin, Walter 137–8, 153, 163
Bennett, Arnold 187, 190
Benstock, Shari 4–5, 13
Benstock, Shari and Bernard
  "The Role of Little Magazines in the Emergence of Modernism" 208
Berger, John
  Ways of Seeing 40
Bergonzi, Bernard 4
Berry, Ellen E. 5
Besant, Walter
  East London 18

Bhabha, Homi K. 174, 181
birth control 81, 84, 87–9, 91–2
birth rate 81, 87, 94
Bishop, Edward
  "Recovering Modernism—Format and Function in the Little Magazines" 208
Blair, Sara 138
Blau duPlessis, Rachel 50
Boccaccio, Giovanni
  The Decameron 58
Boer War 35
Booth, Allyson
  Postcards from the Trenches: Negotiating the Space between Modernism and the First World War 157
Bowen, Elizabeth 43, 99, 112, 117
  The Death of the Heart 10, 98–9, 103, 104, 105–8, 110, 111, 113
  The Heat of the Day 36
  "Manners" 107, 113
  "Open to the Public" 105, 106
  "Why Do I Write?" 105, 107
Boyle, Kay 8, 10, 11, 139, 141, 147, 158
  Death of a Man 10, 11, 138–57, 159
    critical reception of 146–7, 151
    experimental representation of reality and dream 140, 142–6
    hallucination of the word 140, 141, 148, 151, 157
    question of sympathy to Nazi movement 146–7, 148–50, 158
    representation of trauma 140–6, 158
    "Revolution of the Word" 139–40
    "The White Horses of Vienna" 146
Brake, Laurel 192–3
Breton, André 165, 168, 177, 182, 183
  Anthology of Black Humour 163, 169, 171, 174, 175
  Dictionary of Surrealism 169

Introduction to "The Debutante" 182
Nadja 163, 178
Briffault, Robert 191
British Empire 42
Brittain, Vera 103
Testament of Youth 49
Brookes, Barbara 89
Browne, Stella 87
Buitenhuis, Peter 74
Burke, Thomas 19–23, 26, 27–33
A Tea-Shop in Limehouse 27
Abduction: A Story of Limehouse 27
City of Encounters 27
Limehouse Nights 27, 30
Living in Bloomsbury 27
London in My Time 27
More Limehouse Nights 27
Nights in Town 27
Twinkletoes, A Tale of Limehouse 27
The Wind and The Rain 27, 28–30
Butler, Judith
Gender Trouble: Feminism and the Subversion of Identity 182

Cahun, Claude 174, 182
canons
See literary canons
Carlston, Erin G. 11, 147–8, 157, 158
Thinking Fascism 138, 157
Carrington, Leonora 11, 12, 163, 164–5, 172, 173, 180–1, 182
"As They Rode Along the Edge" 179
critique of commodification of women 164, 175–6, 180, 182
"The Debutante" 11, 163, 164–5, 168–9, 170–6, 178–9, 183
Down Below 178, 181, 182
"The House of Fear" 165
The House of Fear 170, 182
"Self-Portrait" 180
Carroll, Lewis 174
Alice's Adventures in Wonderland 169–70
Through the Looking Glass 169–70, 175
Carsten, F.L. 140, 158

Carter, Angela 173
Caruth, Cathy 145
Unclaimed Experience: Trauma, Narrative, and History 141–2
Casillo, Robert 157
Castiglia, Chris 158
Caudwell, Christopher 116
Caws, Mary Ann
Surrealism and Women 182
Chabrol, Claude
Violette 183
Chace, William M.
The Political Identities of Ezra Pound and T.S. Eliot 208
Chadwick, Whitney
Women Artists and the Surrealist Movement 182
Chamberlain, Neville 81, 88, 91, 97
Chekhov, Anton 12
Chesterton, G.K. 71, 205
China
1911 revolution 17, 21
Boxer Uprising 21
Second Opium War 21
Chinatown
See London, literary representations of Limehouse district
Chinitz, David
"T.S. Eliot and the Cultural Divide" 188–9, 207, 208
Churchill, Randolph 192
citizenship
Ford Madox Ford's claim to German 56, 59, 65, 69, 70, 71, 75
models of 13, 55, 60, 61, 67–8, 71, 73, 75, 94
Civello, Catherine A. 50
Cixous, Hélène 39
Clark, Suzanne 4, 151, 159
class
and birth rate 87, 88–9, 91–2
concept of 6, 12, 49, 82, 84, 86, 92–3, 94–5, 108
conflict 127
divisions and alliances 128–30
representation of 11, 83

See also middle classes, working class, surrealism

Coates, John 99, 113

Cobden-Sanderson, Richard 199

Cohn, Carol 40

commercial values 108

Common, Jack
  Seven Shifts 121

Compton-Burnett, Ivy 117

Conley, Katharine 183

Connolly, Cyril
  Enemies of Promise 126
  "Ivory Shelter" 126

Conrad, Joseph
  Heart of Darkness 30

consumer culture 108, 132, 176

contraception
  See birth control

Craig, Cairns 157

Crane, Hart 139

Crével, René 177

Croft, Andy 7, 118, 119, 131
  Red Letter Days 117

Crow, Thomas 5

Cultural Studies 5

culture 4–6
  highbrow 5, 7, 12, 112, 187–8, 192, 193, 194, 206
  lowbrow 7, 190, 194
  mass 3, 4, 5, 12, 111, 112, 113, 157, 187–8, 191, 206–7
  middlebrow 7, 67, 116, 206
  working-class 188

Cunard, Nancy 182

Cunningham, Valentine 118, 124, 125
  British Writers of the Thirties 83, 115, 116–17

Cutforth, René 112

Dali, Salvador 169–70

Davis, Phoebe Stein 158

de Angelis, Paul 182, 183

de Beauvoir, Simone 177

de Lauretis, Teresa 51, 173

Deane, Patrick
  History in Our Hands 117

DeKoven, Marianne 137, 138

Depression 3

Diepeveen, Leonard 209
  "'I Can Have More Than Enough Power to Satisfy Me': T.S. Eliot's Construction of his Audience" 207–8

documentary movement 116, 119, 120–2, 126, 127, 130, 131, 132

Dollfuss, Englebert 141, 146

domestic novels 10, 98–9, 103, 111, 112

domesticity 10, 13, 36, 90, 97–101, 102–3, 104, 108, 110–11, 112, 113

Dowson, Jane 97
  Women's Poetry of the 1930s 117

Drabble, Margaret
  Gates of Ivory 37

Eckstein, Barbara 157

Eliot, T.S. 12, 124, 187–92, 193, 194–209
  as journalist 12, 197–201
  attacks on British press 194–7
  attitudes toward audience 189, 200, 205–6, 207–8, 209
  "Charles Whibley" 188, 189, 201–5
  Collected Poems 1909-1935 207
  The Criterion 187–9, 190–2, 197–9, 201, 202, 205, 207
  distinction between literature and popular journalism 12, 187–9, 190–1, 193, 194, 195, 197, 201–3, 204, 206
  "East Coker" 207
  "The Function of Criticism" 195
  ideas about cultural decay 194–7, 201, 206, 208
  "Journalists of Yesterday and Today" 201, 204–7
  "Lancelot Andrewes" 191, 194
  "Literature and Religion" 196
  "Marie Lloyd" 188
  Notes Towards a Definition of Culture 195
  "The Perfect Critic" 194
  Prufrock and Other Observations 207
  "Religion and Literature" 195
  Selected Essays 202

shifting definitions of journalism 201–7
"Tradition and the Individual Talent" 209
The Waste Land 21, 33, 207, 209
Eliot, Valerie 209
Elkins, Marilyn 147, 151
Ellis, Havelock 88
Elshtain, Jean Bethke 37
 Just Warriors and Beautiful Souls 36, 46, 49, 66, 67, 73
Eluard, Nusch 164
Eluard, Paul 164
Englishness 22, 65, 66, 71, 74, 97, 129
Ernst, Marie-Berthe 164
Ernst, Max 163, 165, 169, 180–1, 182
 Alice in 1939 170
 Alice in 1941 170
 "Loplop Presents the Bride of the Wind" 182
Escott, T.H.S. 209
eugenicism 9, 13, 81, 87, 91, 93, 94, 95, 180

family life 10, 98–9, 105, 106, 109, 110, 112
 See also domesticity
fascism 8, 11, 103–4, 128–9, 137–9, 147, 150, 159, 180–1
 and language 151–5, 157
 See also modernism and fascism
Faulkner, William 157
Felski, Rita 4, 7
 "Modernism and Modernity" 13
 The Gender of Modernity 13
female identity 37–8, 39, 40, 88, 89–91, 92–4
 See also war and construction of female identity, gender roles
femininity
 See gender
feminism 4, 61, 101
Filreis, Alan 157
Fini, Léonor 182
Flanner, Janet 176
Foley, Barbara 157

Ford, Ford Madox 9, 55, 59–60, 69, 71, 75
 Between St. Dennis and St. George 72
 The Good Soldier 68
 nationality of
  See citizenship, Ford Madox Ford's claim to German
 "On Heaven" 67
 Parade's End 55–6
 preface to *Their Lives* 69
 relationship with Violet Hunt
  See Hunt, Violet, relationship with Ford Madox Ford
 "The Scaremonger" 70
 The Spirit of the People 74
 wartime political rhetoric of 70
 When Blood Is Their Argument 72
 Zeppelin Nights: A London Entertainment 9, 55, 57–65, 66–8, 69, 71
forgotten writers 7, 97, 98, 116, 130, 131
Formalism 137, 138, 157
Foucault, Michel 8, 62
Freud, Sigmund 102, 141, 166, 167, 168, 182, 183
Fussell, Paul 48, 74
 The Great War and Modern Memory 35
Futurism 137, 154, 159

Gail Braybon
 Women Workers in the First World War 38
Gallagher, Jean
 The World Wars Through the Female Gaze 157–8
Gallup, Donald 198, 201
Gambrell, Alice 173, 178, 182
Gaudier-Brzeska, Henri 62, 75
gender 4, 5, 49, 51, 57
 and war 35
gender roles 3, 9, 85, 173, 180, 181
 See also masking
gendered spaces 51
 See also Spain, Daphne
Genet, Jean 177

The Maids 183
Gilbert, Sandra 70
Gindin, James 83
   British Fiction in the 1930s 117
Glendinning, Victoria 50
Gold, Mike 157
Goldring, Douglas 55, 60–1, 73
Goodman, Celia 120
Goodman, Dena 72
gothic conventions 102–3
Grayzel, Susan R. 73
Great War
   See World War I
Green, Henry 119
Green, Robert 63, 70
Greenwood, James 21
Griffith, D.W.
   Broken Blossoms 30

H.D. 157, 173
Hanley, Lynne 8, 48
Hanson, Clare
   Hysterical Fictions: The "Woman's Novel" in the Twentieth Century 112
Hapke, Laura 157
Hardwick, Joan 70
Harlem Renaissance 157
Harrison, Tom 121
Hartley, Jenny 127
   Millions Like Us: British Women's Fiction of the Second World War 115
Harvey, David 71
Haste, Cate 71, 72
Hatlen, Burton 147, 151
Heath, Stephen 167
Heller, Scott 3
Hewison, Robert 126, 131
Hewitt, Andrew 138, 154, 157, 159
highbrow culture
   See culture, highbrow
Higonnet, Margaret 158
Hitler, Adolf 103–4, 139, 141, 144, 147, 150, 152, 153, 181, 183
Hoffmann, E.T.A.
   The Serapion Brethren 58–9, 63–4
Holden, Inez 3, 10, 115–16, 117, 118–32
   Born Old, Died Young 120
   "Death in High Society" 123, 126
   Death in High Society 123
   It Was Different at the Time 120
   Night Shift 119, 120–3, 126, 131
   Sweet Charlatan 123, 125
   There's No Story There 119, 123, 126, 127–32
Holtby, Winifred 103–4, 117
Hueffer, Elsie 56, 70
Hueffer, Ford Madox
   See Ford, Ford Madox
   See also Hunt, Violet
Hughes, Langston 157
Hunt, Violet 8, 9, 55–69, 71, 74
   The Desirable Alien 56, 62–3, 65, 67, 74
   I Have This to Say 57
   narrative "salon space" in *Zeppelin Nights* 55, 57, 60–2, 64, 68
   relationship with Ford Madox Ford 56, 57, 60, 63, 65, 66, 68–9, 70, 72, 73, 74
   South Lodge social circle 60–2, 72
   Their Lives 69
   Zeppelin Nights: A London Entertainment 9, 55, 57–65, 66–8, 69, 71, 73
Hurston, Zora Neale 173
Huxley, Aldous 119, 183
   Eyeless in Gaza 171
   Point Counter Point 119
Huyssen, Andreas 4, 188, 206
   "Mass Culture as Woman: Modernism's Other" 113
Hynes, Samuel 65, 72
   The Auden Generation 115
   The Edwardian Turn of Mind 73, 112

immigrants 18
   attitudes toward Chinese of Limehouse district 18
   Chinese of Limehouse district 17
imperialism 9, 13, 84, 86, 88, 94
intellectual movements 4, 5
   women's participation in 11

interwar England 98
interwar Europe 3, 4, 6
Isherwood, Christopher 119
   Goodbye to Berlin 122

Jacobs, Deborah 5
James, Henry 60, 62, 125
Jameson, Fredric 157
Jameson, Storm 121, 130
Jay, Martin
   Downcast Eyes: The Denigration of Vision in Twentieth-Century Thought 183
Joad, C.E.M. 112
Joannou, Maroula 97, 111–12
John, Augustus 119, 120
Jolas, Eugene 140
Jones, Ernest 166, 167
journalism, British 191–4, 200–1, 208–9
Joyce, James
   "Araby" 29

Kahlo, Frida 173, 174, 182
Kalaidjian, Walter 157
Kaplan, Alice 137, 152, 153, 158, 159
Kaplan, Sydney Janet
   Feminine Consciousness in the Modern British Novel 83
Kauffman, Michael 198
Kavanaugh, Mary 183
Kehde, Suzanne 74
Kelly, Joseph
   Our Joyce 209
Kent, Susan Kingsley 73
Kineke, Sheila 62
Kipling, Rudyard 25
Kirk, Russell 209
   Eliot in His Age 207
Klein, Melanie 166
Knight, Patricia 89
Krauss, Rosalind 182, 183
Kuenzli, Rudolf
   Surrealism and Women 182

Labor movement 3, 127, 131, 132
Lacan, Jacques 183

"Motives of Paranoiac Crime" 177
Lamba, Jaqueline 182
Lambert, Angela 183
Landes, Joan B. 61, 71, 72, 73
Larbaud, Valery 194
Lassner, Phyllis 99, 113
   British Women Writers of World War II 117
Lawrence, D.H. 60, 64
Leavis, Q.D.
   "Lady Novelists and the Lower Orders" 112
Lee, Hermione 99, 113
Leed, Eric 48, 51
   No Man's Land: Combat and Identity in World War I
leftist literature
   See political dimensions of art
Lehmann, John 127
Lehmann, Rosamond 9, 81–95, 117
   Invitation to the Waltz 85–6
   The Weather in the Streets 9, 10, 81–6, 89–95
Lessing, Doris
   Memoirs of a Survivor 37
LeSueur, Meridel 157
Levenson, Michael
   "Does The Waste Land Have a Politics?" 208
Lewis, Wyndham 60–1, 62, 157, 205, 206
Light, Alison 7, 111
   Forever England: Femininity, Literature and Conservatism Between the Wars 98, 117
Lindsay, Jack 119
   1649 119
Linkon, Sherry Lee
   Radical Revisions: Rereading 1930s Culture 157
literary canons 4, 10, 11, 12, 97, 98, 111, 112, 117, 118, 127, 130, 131, 132
literature
   American poetry 4, 13
   cultural context for 5–7
   literary genres 7
   popular fiction 5, 7, 8, 18, 19, 117–18

socialist 121
See also Thirties' literature, culture, women writers
Little Magazines 4, 190
Loeffelholz, Mary
Experimental Lives 83
London
Limehouse district of 17, 21
literary representations of Limehouse district 8, 19, 22, 23, 25, 26, 27, 29–33
Longenbach, James 72
"Men and Women of 1914" 70
Lucas, E.V.
A Wanderer in London 18
Lyon, Janet 69, 73

Macaulay, Rose 49
Non-Combatants and Others 36
MacDonagh, Michael 71, 72
Mackay, Jane 65, 73
Macmurray, John 205, 206
Malthusian League 87
Man Ray 164
Marcus, Jane 157
Marinetti, Filippo Tommaso 137, 159
Marr, Dora 182
Marwick, Arthur 71, 72
Women at War 38
masculinity
See gender roles
mass culture
See culture, mass
See also literature, popular fiction
Mass-Observation 130
War Factory 121
Masterman, C.F.G. 56, 59, 69, 70, 72
Mayhew, Henry 21
McAleer, Joseph 191, 208
McDonald, Gail 200, 204
McKay, Claude 157
Mellen, Joan 147
middle classes 6, 10, 99, 100, 105, 107–8, 109, 126
middlebrow
See culture

Miller, Lee 164, 182
Mitchell, M.E. 112
Mitchison, Naomi 117
Mitford, Nancy
Love in a Cold Climate 183
Mizener, Authur 70, 72, 73
modernism 3, 4, 5, 10, 11, 12, 61, 72, 73, 83, 97, 113, 125, 139, 140, 157, 194, 197, 200–1, 206
and fascism 138, 157–8
commercial forces behind 12, 193, 209
gender of 138, 157–8
political dimensions of 11, 13, 137, 138–9, 147–8, 151, 157, 159
See also women writers
modernity 107, 111, 197
and femininity 7
and women 111
Montefiore, Janet 97, 111
Men and Women Writers of the 1930s 117
Moore, Marianne 157
Mosley, Sir Oswald 104
Mullen, Bill
Radical Revisions: Rereading 1930s Culture 157
Murry, John Middleton 196, 199, 205, 206

national identity 81, 84
national life 10, 99–100, 103–11
nationalism 56, 57, 68, 74, 84, 94
discourse of 86
Nazi movement 46, 139, 140–1, 150, 152, 156, 158, 159, 180–1, 182
neglected writers
See forgotten writers
Nelson, Cary 4, 157
New Criticism 137, 138, 139
Nicholls, Peter 157
Nicholson, Harold 105
Nicol, Daphne 112
North, Michael 157, 197
The Political Aesthetic of Yeats, Eliot, and Pound 208

Northcliffe Press 4
Nozière, Violette 176–7

O'Brien, Kate 127, 131
Ogden, C.K. 123–4
  Basic English 123–5
  Foreword to *Death in High Society* 124
  "Introduction" to *The System of Basic English* 124
Olsen, Tillie 157
Oppenheim, Meret 182
Orientalism 8, 20, 23, 24, 28–33
  and construction of Western identity 22, 25, 26–7, 29, 31–3
  attitudes toward China 21, 22.
  attitudes toward Chinese 23, 26
  See also China
Orwell, George 116, 118, 119, 120
  "Inside the Whale" 118
the Other 6, 20, 21, 26, 28, 31–2, 46, 128, 163, 173.
  See also Orientalism
Ouditt, Sharon 49, 73

pacifism 13, 36, 138
Pankhurst, Emmeline 61, 73
Papin, Christine 176–178, 183
Papin, Léa 176–178, 183
patriotism 55, 66, 68, 69, 72, 87–8, 106, 129, 132
Pedersen, Susan 74
Peel, C.S. 71, 72
Pellegrini, Ann 167
Penrose, Roland 164
Penrose, Valentine 182
Péret, Benjamin 177
periodization 7, 10, 13, 116, 127, 131
  See also Thirties' literature
personal and political experience, intersection of 155–7
philosophy
  See intellectual movements
physics
  See intellectual movements
Pickering, Jean 74

Piratin, Phil 127
Plain, Gill
  Women's Fiction of the Second World War 117
Plath, Sylvia 148
  "Daddy" 150
Playne, Caroline 58, 73
political dimensions of art 116, 117–18, 119, 124–5, 126–7, 131, 132, 137–8, 141–2, 146, 147–8, 150, 157
Polizzotti, Mark 182
  "Introduction: Laughter in the Dark" 183
population
  See birth rate
Posonby, Arthur 72
postmodernism 5, 13
Pound, Ezra 60, 62, 196, 197–8, 200, 201, 209
Prassinos, Giselle 182
Priestley, J.B. 119
  English Journey 97
Pringle, Margaret 175
Pritchett, V.S. 116
privacy 7, 98, 99–103, 107, 108–9, 110
private vs. public sphere 9, 10, 36, 37, 40, 41–2, 49, 55, 57, 61, 69, 72–3, 99–100, 101–2, 103–5, 106, 107, 111
propaganda
  during World War I 55–6, 68, 72
Prothero, J.K. 71, 75
psychoanalysis 4, 166–8
public vs. private sphere
  See private vs. public sphere
Pykett, Lyn 4, 5, 13

Quinn, John 200
Quinn, Patrick
  Recharting the Thirties 117

Raaberg, Gwen
  Surrealism and Women 182
Rabinowitz, Paula 157
race, concept of 6, 89
  See also surrealism

Radek, Karl 125
Radner, Hilary
  "Extra-Curricular Activities: Women Writers and the Readerly Text" 112
Rado, Lisa 5
  Re-Reading Modernism: New Directions in Feminist Criticism 157
Rainey, Lawrence
  "The Price of Modernism" 209
Read, Herbert 198
reading public, British 191–2, 193
  stratification of 189–90, 208
Reaveley, Constance 115
Redman, Tim 157
reproduction
  See sexuality and reproduction
respectability 60, 61–2, 63, 65, 71, 73, 84, 88, 89, 92–3, 94, 105, 109
Rhys, Jean 62, 117
Richardson, Dorothy 117
Riviere, Joan 173, 181
  "Womanliness as a Masquerade" 165–8
Roberts, Michael
  "Preface" to *New Country* 124
Rohmer, Sax 8, 20, 21, 22, 23, 24, 26, 28, 32–3
  Dope 24
  Fu Manchu thrillers 19, 24, 32
  The Si-Fan Mysteries 24
  Tales of Chinatown 24
  The Trail of Fu Manchu 24
  The Yellow Claw 24
  Yellow Shadows 24
Rose, Jacqueline 148, 150, 159
Rosemont, Penelope 176, 183
  Surrealist Women: An International Anthology 182
Rothermere, Lady 201
Russell, Dora 87
Russo, Mary 180

Said, Edward 22, 23, 24
salons 61–2, 69, 71, 72–3
Samuel, Raphael 74
Saunders, Max 72, 73, 74, 75

Schenck, Celeste M. 5, 13
Schimanski, Stefan and Henry Treece
  Leaves in the Storm 120
Schweik, Susan
  A Gulf So Deeply Cut 157
Scott, Bonnie Kime
  The Gender of Modernism 83
Secor, Marie 62, 70
Secor, Robert 62, 70
Severin, Laura 50
sexology
  See intellectual movements
sexuality 9, 82, 84
  and abortion 9, 81, 82, 84–5, 86–7, 88–9, 90–3, 94
  and reproduction 9, 82, 84–5, 86–9, 91, 94–5
Shaw, George Bernard 205
Simons, Judy 93
  Rosamond Lehmann 83–4
Slater, Humphrey 120
Smith, Stevie 8, 37–8, 120
  The Holiday 49
  Novel on Yellow Paper 37, 39, 49–50
  Over the Frontier 8, 9, 37, 39–51
  critical reception of 49–50
socialism 117, 120, 131
Space Between
  See interwar Europe
Spain, Daphne
  "Gendered spaces" 48
Spanier, Sandra Whipple 147, 151, 159
Spender, Dale 51, 118
Squire, J.C. 201
Stallybrass, Peter 21, 32
  The Politics and Poetics of Transgression 20
Stein, Gertrude 5, 157, 158
Sternlicht, Sanford 50
Stevens, Wallace 157
Stevenson, Randall 112
Stopes, Marie
  Contraception 88–9
  Married Love 88
  Radiant Motherhood 88
Struther, Jan

Mrs. Miniver 104
Suleiman, Susan Rubin 182
  Subversive Intent 182
surrealism 6, 163–5, 168–82
  female practitioners 11, 163, 181, 182
  hybridity 164, 170, 174–6, 179–82
  male practitioners 11
  masking 164, 165–9, 170–2, 173, 176
  representation of race and class in 12, 174, 179
  representation of women in 11, 163, 165, 168, 169, 171, 172, 174, 176–7, 181
Swift, Jonathan 174
  "Directions to Servants" 171
  Gulliver's Travels 171, 174–5
Syrett, Netta 13

Tate, Trudi 55–6
Terkel, Studs 139
Thane, Pat 65, 73
Thayer, Schofield 199, 200, 209
Thirties 97, 98, 103, 116, 118
  treatment of women in 11
  See also periodization
Thirties' literature 7, 97, 98, 104, 111, 112, 115, 116, 117
Tinker, Chauncey Brewster 73
Tomlinson, Nora 70
Tracey, Herbert 208–9
  British Newspapers: A Survey, a Newspaper Directory, and a Who's Who in Journalism 193
Tratner, Michael 157
  Modernism and Mass Politics 208
Trotter, David 5
twentieth-century studies 3, 4, 5
  See also modernism
Tylee, Claire 49, 66, 73, 74

urban exploration 8, 19, 20, 30
urban space
  as site of social struggles 19
  concept of 22, 27–8, 33
  experience of 26

representation in literature of 13, 19, 20
urban spectatorship 20, 22, 27

Van Doren, Mark 146
van Gennep, Arnold 51
Varo, Remedios 182

Waites, Bernard 73
Walkowitz, Judith 19, 20
  City of Dreadful Delight: Narratives of Sexual Danger in Late-Victorian London 19
war 13, 35
  and construction of female identity 37–8, 40–1, 43–51, 55, 61, 66, 70, 74
  See also World War I
Warner, Marina 173, 183
Waugh, Evelyn
  Vile Bodies 119
Weekes, G.A. 208, 209
Wells, H.G. 59, 119, 120, 205, 206
Wesley, Mary 43
  The Camomile Lawn 36
West, Anthony 112
West, Rebecca 60, 103, 202
  Black Lamb and Grey Falcon 103
  The Return of the Soldier 36
Wexler, Joyce Piell 194
  Who Paid for Modernism? 209
White, Allon 21, 32
  The Politics and Poetics of Transgression 20
White, Cynthia 98
Williams, Raymond 196
Williams-Ellis, Amabel
  Women in War Factories 121
Wilson, Sarah 170
Wilson, Trevor 71, 72
woman's novel
  See women writers
women
  and modernist culture 6
  and modernity 3, 73, 82
  and national identity 65–6, 74
  and surrealism 11

exclusion from power structures of war 35–36, 66
intellectuals 166, 167–8, 169, 171, 173
objects of male gaze 40
oppression of 11, 103–4, 178
participation in urban struggles 19
See also sexuality
women writers 6, 7, 9, 10, 13, 112, 116, 117, 121, 127, 131, 138.
and modernism 61–2, 138, 139, 173
and modernity 13
of World War I 55, 74
representation of war 8, 9, 36, 37, 43, 58, 127, 131.
See also war and construction of female identity
romance plot 82
the women's novel 97, 98, 112
See also literature
Women's Social and Political Union 61, 73
Woolf, Virginia 83, 117, 157
Between the Acts 104, 105
A Room of One's Own 109, 158

"The Russian Point of View" 12
Three Guineas 104, 110
working class 6, 10, 115, 118, 119, 132
literary representation of 7, 19, 116, 118–19, 120–3, 125–6, 128–30, 132
participation in urban struggles 19
residence in Limehouse district of London 17
World War I 3, 4, 17, 35, 40, 56, 106, 109
and anti-German feeling 59, 72
and myth 35
women's labor during 38, 73, 111
Zeppelin attacks 71
World War II 10, 36, 206
Blitz 17, 127
literature of 116
women's labor during 131–2
working class and 13

Young, E.H. 111, 112–13
Celia 10, 98, 99–103, 104, 105, 108–10, 111, 112
Chatterton Square 109